Restructure

American University Studies

Series VII
Theology and Religion
Vol. 85

PETER LANG
New York • San Francisco • Bern • Baltimore
Frankfurt am Main • Berlin • Wien • Paris

Anthony L. Dunnavant

Restructure

Four Historical Ideals in
the Campbell–Stone Movement and
the Development of the Polity of
the Christian Church (Disciples of Christ)

PETER LANG
New York • San Francisco • Bern • Baltimore
Frankfurt am Main • Berlin • Wien • Paris

Library of Congress Cataloging-in-Publication Data

Dunnavant, Anthony L.
  Restructure : four historical ideals in the Campbell-Stone movement and the development of the polity of the Christian Church (Disciples of Christ) / Anthony L. Dunnavant.
      p. cm. — (American university studies. Series VII, Theology and religion ; vol. 85)
  Includes bibliographical references.
  1. Christian Church (Disciples of Christ)—Government.   2. Restoration movement (Christianity)—United States.   I. Title.   II. Title: Campbell-Stone movement and the development of the polity of the Christian Church (Disciples of Christ).   III. Series.
BX7326.D85   1993   286.6'3—dc20   90-36892
ISBN 0-8204-1420-4   CIP
ISSN 0740-0446

The paper in this book meets the guidelines for permanence and durability of the Committee on Production Guidelines for Book Longevity of the Council on Library Resources.

© Peter Lang Publishing, Inc., New York 1993

All rights reserved.
Reprint or reproduction, even partially, in all forms such as microfilm, xerography, microfiche, microcard, offset strictly prohibited.

Printed in the United States of America.

for
Edith and Ezra

To Bill and Sally,

with deep appreciation for your gracious friendship and support

Tony

6/25/93

ACKNOWLEDGEMENTS

I am indebted to many people for their help with this work. The basic research drew on the resources of the Divinity Library at Vanderbilt University, the Disciples of Christ Historical Society, and Bosworth Memorial Library at Lexington Theological Seminary. The personnel at each of these facilities were unfailingly helpful. Several teachers and colleagues read the entire manuscript during different stages in its preparation: Michael Downey, H. Jackson Forstman, Dewey Grantham, Dale Johnson, Ruth Kitchen, James Moak, Herman Norton, Ronald Osborn, Albert Pennybacker, James Seale, and Eugene TeSelle. Each reader gave wise counsel and much of it was heeded.

I thank all my colleagues at Lexington Theological Seminary for contributing to continuing reflections on the themes of this work. The administration of the Seminary helped bring this to publication by providing research assistants Karen Leigh Stroup and William Dunning. These two colleagues have been an enormous help. Barbara Miller and Nancy Gragson Dunnavant were of crucial assistance in the preparation of the text.

I am also grateful for permission to reprint material previously published by: Bethany Press (*Declaration and Address, by Thomas Campbell; Last Will and Testament of the Springfield Presbytery, by Barton W. Stone and Others*, 1960; *The Disciples of Christ: A History*, by Winfred E. Garrison and Alfred T. DeGroot, 2nd ed., 1958; *Journey in Faith: A History of the Christian Church [Disciples of Christ]*, by Lester G. McAllister and William E. Tucker, 1975; *Religion Follows the Frontier: A History of the Disciples of Christ*, by Winfred E. Garrison, 1931), Division of Higher Education, Christian Church (Disciples of Christ) (*The Disciples Theological Digest*, 4 [1989]), Council on Christian Unity, Christian Church (Disciples of Christ) (*Mid-Stream: An Ecumenical Journal*, 19 [July 1980]), and Standard Publishing Company (*Christians Only: A History of the Restoration Movement*, by James DeForest Murch, 1962). Finally, my gratitude is extended to two Kentucky Disciples congregations for their support during the preparation of this work: First Christian Church (Disciples of Christ), Guthrie, and Central Christian Church (Disciples of Christ) in Lexington.

TABLE OF CONTENTS

INTRODUCTION 1

CHAPTER I 9
    The Statement of the Ideals of the
    Campbell-Stone Movement by Four Founders

CHAPTER II 37
    The Divergence in the Interpretation of the Ideals
    of the Campbell-Stone Movement in Its Second Generation

CHAPTER III 61
    Twentieth-Century Conflicts in the Campbell-Stone Movement
    and the Prehistory of Restructure

CHAPTER IV 93
    Structure in the Campbell-Stone Movement
    in Its First Generation

CHAPTER V 121
    The Emergence of the Society Concept as the Basis of
    Polity in the Campbell-Stone Movement

CHAPTER VI 153
    The Evolution of Structure beyond the
    Society Concept

CHAPTER VII 183
    An Overview of Restructure

CHAPTER VIII 211
    Four Ideological Options
    in Restructure

CONCLUSION 245

SELECTED BIBLIOGRAPHY 255

INTRODUCTION

In the late nineteen forties and nineteen fifties, leaders in the International Convention of the Christian Churches (Disciples of Christ) were concerned about the Convention's structure. Between 1950 and 1960 representatives of the agencies of the Christian Churches (Disciples) engaged in extensive discussions about their structures and interrelationships. By 1960 the concern and discussions had crystallized into a resolution by the Convention which created a Commission on Brotherhood Restructure.[1] That Commission first met in 1962 and by 1968 it had completed its task of planning, publicizing, writing, and facilitating the adoption of a new "design" for the Christian Churches. "Restructure" (what the total work of the Commission was called) was believed by its proponents to be a way for the Convention and agencies to become more efficient and unified for their constituent congregations' extraparochial efforts in the areas of evangelism, mission, education, stewardship, social action, and benevolence.

Issues beyond organizational efficiency came to the fore in Restructure. The process entailed the argument for important changes in Disciples ecclesiology. One of the most significant of these changes is indicated in the change in the name of the denomination. At the international level (the United States and Canada), what had once been called the International Convention of the Christian Churches (Disciples of Christ) became the General Assembly of the Christian Church (Disciples of Christ). The annual gathering of the Convention, at which members of the Christian Churches "convened," gave way to a biennial assembly of delegates representing congregations which were now defined as "manifestations" of the one Christian Church (Disciples of Christ).

Those who undertook to restructure the Christian Church (Disciples of Christ) in the 1960s were confronted with issues that had long persisted in the tradition of the Campbell-Stone movement. This movement had arisen on the American frontier in the early national period. It was part of the widespread "agitation" for full religious liberty in that period that frequently took the form of "Christian primitivism" movements.[2] The Campbell-Stone tradition subsumed several other rivulets into its stream, but it identifies the ministries of Barton W. Stone in central Kentucky and of Thomas and Alexander Campbell in northwestern Virginia (now West Virginia) and Pennsylvania as its main sources.[3]

Because the Campbell-Stone religious community is rooted in movements that wished to utilize the freedom of the New World to effect a thorough-going religious reformation, it is a community that has been preoccupied with questions of how the Church should be constituted, where the historic churches fit into the Church universal, where the Campbell-Stone community fits into the Church universal, and how the movement relates to the historic churches. These questions have been variously answered in different periods by different groups within the Campbell-Stone tradition. The variety of answers has related to the two major divisions that have occurred in the movement—that creating the Churches of Christ as a separate body and that creating the "Independents" as separate from the "Cooperative" Disciples. These were the kinds of questions that came to the fore in Restructure. It was largely the Campbell-Stone tradition of grappling with these questions that provided the terms in which Restructure was debated. Those who supported Restructure and those who opposed it sought to demonstrate that *they* were embodying the tradition in an authentic way.

What was the tradition that they sought to embody? Part of the tradition consisted of ideals to which the movement was deeply committed. Therefore, Restructure and the development of the polity of the Christian Church (Disciples of Christ) are interwoven with the evolution of a fundamental ideology within the broader Campbell-Stone movement from which the Christian Church (Disciples of Christ) emerged. This study is concerned, then, with both structure and ideology. "Ideology" here "points to the content and way of thinking that characterizes an individual, or a group, or an era."[4]

The secondary historical literature of the Campbell-Stone movement provides clues as to the salient features of its traditional "way of thinking." In 1965 Winfred E. Garrison pointed to an influential convention in the interpretation of Disciples of Christ history when he wrote that:

> There seems to be no superior substitute for the time-honored description of the thought and practice of the Disciples as centering upon two major objectives—the unity of Christians in one church and restoration of all that was designed to be permanent in primitive Christianity. Equally familiar, and equally valid, is the statement that the developments in their thought and practice and the rifts that have appeared in their ranks have been determined by the varying emphases and interpretations that have been placed on these two ideas.[5]

Fourteen years later, Garrison's characterization of Disciples of Christ historiography was underscored by Thomas J. Liggett:

> Our founding fathers stressed two ideas: unity and restoration. Historians are agreed upon this fact. They are not, however, in agreement concerning the chronological priority of each of these ideas in our movement, nor concerning the relationship which existed

Introduction

between the two ideas, and certainly they are not agreed upon the relative value of the concepts. One of the ways to interpret our history and the several movements which emerged from the Campbell-Stone leadership is to analyze the interplay between these two concepts.[6]

There has been, then, a recognized convention among historians to interpret the history of the Campbell-Stone movement in terms of the two specific ideals of unity and restoration. These ideals were present in the Campbell-Stone movement from the beginning.[7] However, the claims for the uniqueness of the position of these two notions in the ideology of the movement may have been exaggerated.

Ronald Osborn's *Experiment in Liberty* (1978) attempts to amend the conventional view of Campbell-Stone ideology:

> It has become conventional to present the movement as concerned with two great emphases, *unity* and *restoration*.
>
> In my view, the effort to understand Disciples in terms of these two principles alone (or of either one of them) oversimplifies the situation. The commitment of heart and mind was not just to unity, not just to restoration of the apostolic order, not just to some dynamic combinations of these two. From the beginning that commitment was given to freedom, unity, and restoration, held together in a varying and sometimes unstable equilibrium. Indeed, one could advance the thesis that freedom has now become the dominant force within the triad.[8]

The idea that liberty should be added to unity and restoration in the list of the most important ideals of the Campbell-Stone movement had been hinted at in works that had stressed the movement's commitment to liberty. What Osborn did was to make explicit the suggestion that freedom may share the importance to the movement's history that the other two ideas have long been believed to possess.

The liberty motif has long been present in the history of the Campbell-Stone movement. For example, W. T. Moore *begins* his 1909 *A Comprehensive History of the Disciples of Christ* with this paragraph:

> The following pages deal with a *movement* rather than a church or churches. The plea of the Disciples of Christ is much more comprehensive than that of any religious denomination that existed

a century ago, or that has existed since that time. The religious awakening, produced by the Campbells and those associated with them, affected more or less the whole of religious society. It was a move on the strongholds of sectarianism, and a high call to liberty of thought, liberty of speech, and the right of individual interpretation. It was, first of all, a protest against the reign of priestcraft and religious despotism.[9]

Alexander Campbell, the most influential of the "founding four" of the Campbell-Stone movement, has been particularly strongly associated with the movement's commitment to freedom. Works that have treated this theme include: *Alexander Campbell and Christian Liberty*, by James Egbert, 1909; *Apostle of Freedom*, by D. Ray Lindley, 1957; and *Creative Freedom in Action: Alexander Campbell on the Structure of the Church*, by Eva Jean Wrather, 1968.[10] Osborn cites several other sources in connection with his thesis as well.[11]

One dimension of the Campbell-Stone commitment to freedom is its relation to "the freedom of the Christian individual to interpret the scriptures according to reason and conscience." This dimension has recently been set forth by Larry Bouchard as the "interpretation principle."[12] A more accurate depiction of the basic ideology of the Campbell-Stone movement would, therefore, seem to require the inclusion of at least the three ideals of unity, restoration, and liberty.

While the inclusion of liberty in the list of the most basic ideals of the movement is undoubtedly a step in the right direction, there is at least one more ideal that belongs on the list. Paul A. Crow commented:

> I'm one of those who believes that the basic ethos of Disciples—Thomas and Alexander Campbell and Barton Stone—was the proclamation of Jesus Christ on the American frontier, the new missionary situation. And that in that proclamation, in the conversion of the world, to use our language, the unity of the Church was the essential message... The experience of those early Disciples leaders was that a divided Church kept people from accepting Christ. Therefore the unity of the Church was an instrument of evangelism and mission.[13]

Martin Bailey Clark had written in 1949 that "missions played a vital part" early in the movement, a fact "many students of the movement's history have overlooked."[14] The strong commitment to evangelism and sense of mission of the Campbell-Stone movement must be included in any description of the

Introduction

group's ideology. The other ideals of the movement have been held in connection to this commitment. Perhaps this fact is too obvious to have been stressed by many of the historians of the movement. However, Clark and David Edwin Harrell, Jr., have given the theme some emphasis.

Harrell points out that one expression of the commitment to evangelism and the sense of mission was "millennialism." In the first volume of his *Social History of the Disciples of Christ*, entitled *Quest for a Christian America: The Disciples of Christ and American Society to 1866* (1966), Harrell writes:

> Prior to 1830 both Alexander Campbell and Barton Stone linked their religious reform efforts with the eventual spiritual and social regeneration of the world. In 1829 Stone wrote that the greatest obstacle in introducing the millennium, when "christ will reign in spirit on earth a thousand years," was the religious degeneration of his day. The following year Campbell summarized his early millennialist view in the prospectus of his new and significantly named journal, the *Millennial Harbinger*.[15]

Millennialism was a part of the movement's sense of mission and commitment to "the conversion of the world."

A number of other historians have recently rediscovered (and joined Harrell and Clark in giving emphasis to) the millennial and missional focus of the Campbell-Stone movement in its founding generations. Differences among the founders on millennialism and mission have been discovered and described.[16] However, for many in the movement the relationship among the ideals is well captured in the statement by Dean E. Walker that "unity and restoration are twin aspects of the mission of the Church" and that these aspects are "secondary . . . to unity unto evangelism."[17] A favorite text of members of the Campbell-Stone movement has been John 17:20-23, which they have interpreted to mean that the unity of the Church (on the basis of the Bible) will persuade the world to believe in Jesus Christ and be transformed by that belief.[18]

This brief "history of interpretation" would suggest that, by tradition, many in the Campbell-Stone community: 1) affirmed the *liberty* they experienced on the American frontier in the early national period; 2) wished to use that liberty to effect a thorough-going reformation in the Church through the *restoration* of the primitive Church's faith and order; 3) believed that the repudiation of Old World "corruptions" of Christianity would allow the Church to emerge in its primitive purity and *unity*; and 4) thought that this primitive purity and unity would prove evangelistically effective; that, in fact, winning the world to

Jesus Christ and, thereby, transforming it was their (for some, millennial) *mission*. This view, associated especially with the Campbells, was near the center of the movement's traditional ideology—its "restoration plea."[19]

Any focus on the Campbell-Stone community's commitment to the ideals of unity, restoration, or liberty in isolation from one another or from a commitment to being part of the mission of God distorts the picture of the early commitments of the movement. A crucial resource, then, for comprehending the contending parties and their divergent commitments in the Restructure process is an understanding of the ways that liberty, restoration, unity, and mission had been interpreted in the century and a half of Disciples history prior to Restructure. This is the focus of the first three chapters of this study.

The fourth through sixth chapters of this history depict the structural evolution of the Campbell-Stone movement. The views of church structure of the founders of the movement, the emergence of the "society" as the basis of extracongregational polity, and the evolution of polity beyond the "society" concept are described.

The Restructure process itself is the focus of the final two chapters of this work. The bodies that undertook this process and the structures they created are detailed. However, the weight of the significance of Restructure comes down on the ideological rather than the formal organizational or structural side. One place this can be seen is in the way that opposition to and support for Restructure were arrayed as ideological alternatives.

During the Restructure process the alternatives were articulated most clearly by four groups: the leaders of Restructure themselves, the Disciples for Mission and Renewal, the Atlanta Declaration Committee, and the Committee for the Preservation of the Brotherhood. The views of these groups will be characterized in terms of the four ideals of the Campbell-Stone movement. It is this ideological account of Restructure that immediately precedes the conclusion of the work.

Though it comes to focus on the development of polity, this study also attempts a revisioning of the history of the Campbell-Stone movement. Often its divisions and its difficulties have been seen as evidence of the failure of a Christian unity movement from one angle of vision, or as the fruits of the apostasy of a Christian primitivism movement from another. Recovering the memory that the movement has been profoundly motivated by a sense of Christian mission is not only more charitable to its past, but also truer to it.

Introduction 7

1. "Brotherhood" was a euphemism that Disciples used in order to avoid acknowledging their identity as a denomination. For more about Disciples' use of this term, see W. Clark Gilpin, "The Integrity of the Church: The Communal Theology of the Disciples of Christ," in *Classic Themes of Disciples Theology: Rethinking the Traditional Affirmations of the Christian Church (Disciples of Christ)*, ed. Kenneth Lawrence (Fort Worth: TCU Press, 1986), 37-42. Sexist language permeates the historical documents quoted in this work. It has been left in the quoted material. The author has attempted to make his own voice in the text more inclusive.

2. For more on this topic, see Nathan O. Hatch, *The Democratization of American Christianity* (New Haven: Yale University Press, 1989); also, Richard T. Hughes and C. Leonard Allen, *Illusions of Innocence: Protestant Primitivism in America, 1630-1875* (Chicago and London: University of Chicago Press, 1988), especially 102-132.

3. For an account of the complex origins of the Campbell-Stone movement, see Alfred T. DeGroot, *The Grounds of Divisions among the Disciples of Christ* (Chicago: By the Author, 1940), 30-31, n. 2.

4. Sidney E. Mead, *History and Identity*, American Academy of Religion Studies in Religion, ed. Conrad Cherry, no. 19 (Missoula, MT: Scholars Press, 1979), 23. "Ideology" is a term that often carries negative connotations related to either falsity or oppressive hegemony. I intend a less pejorative sense of the word--one that denotes an interrelated and influential cluster of ideas.

5. Winfred E. Garrison, "An Overview: The Main Stream of Disciple Thought," *Disciple Thought: A History*, by Alfred T. DeGroot (Fort Worth: By the Author, 1965), 3.

6. Thomas J. Liggett, "Why the Disciples Chose Unity," *Mid-Stream* 19 (April 1980):227-33.

7. For an overview of the Campbell-Stone movement's commitment to Christian unity, see Michael Kurt Kinnamon, "A Special Calling: Christian Unity and the Disciples of Christ," in *Interpreting Disciples: Practical Theology in the Disciples of Christ*, ed. L. Dale Richesin and Larry D. Bouchard (Fort Worth: TCU Press, 1987), 248-73.

8. Ronald E. Osborn, *Experiment in Liberty: The Ideal of Freedom in the Experience of the Disciples of Christ*, The Forrest F. Reed Lectures for 1976 (St. Louis: Bethany Press, 1978), 13.

9. William T. Moore, *A Comprehensive History of the Disciples of Christ* (New York: Fleming H. Revell Co., 1909), v.

10. While Wrather's book is more explicitly concerned with Campbell's ecclesiology, it correctly identifies Campbell's commitment to liberty as pervading his ecclesiology (Eva Jean Wrather, *Creative Freedom in Action: Alexander Campbell on the Structure of the Church* [St. Louis: Bethany Press, 1968]).

11. Osborn, *Experiment in Liberty*, 118-19.

12. Larry D. Bouchard, "The Interpretation Principle: A Foundational Theme of Disciples Theology," in *Interpreting Disciples: Practical Theology in the Disciples of Christ*, 8.

13. Paul A. Crow, Jr., private interview, Indianapolis, Indiana, 13 July 1982.

14. Martin Bailey Clark, "The Missionary Position of the Movement of Disciples of Christ in the Early Years of the Nineteenth Century Reformation" (B.D. thesis, Butler University, 1949), 1.

15. David Edwin Harrell, Jr., *A Social History of the Disciples of Christ*, vol. 1: *Quest for a Christian America: The Disciples of Christ and American Society to 1866* (Nashville: Disciples of Christ Historical Society, 1966); vol 2: *The Social Sources of Division in the Disciples of Christ, 1865 to 1900* (Atlanta: Publishing Systems, 1973): 2 vols., 1:41-42.

16. See, for example, Hughes and Allen, *Illusions of Innocence*, 108-112, 121-23, 130-31, 171-77, 181-87; Stephen V. Sprinkle, "Alexander Campbell and the Doctrine of the Church," *Discipliana* 48 (2: Summer 1988):22-24; Hiram J. Lester, "Alexander Campbell's Millennial Program," *Discipliana* 48 (3: Fall 1988):35-39; Richard T. Hughes highlights the differences between Barton Stone and Alexander Campbell and the consequences of those differences in "The Apocalyptic Origins of Churches of Christ and the Triumph of Modernism," *Religion and American Culture: A Journal of Interpretation* 2 (2: Summer 1992):181-214.

17. Dean E. Walker, "Restoration? . . . Unity? . . . Mission!" *Fellowship* 1 (March 1974):13-14.

18. Anthony L. Dunnavant, "United Christians, Converted World: John 17:20-23 and the Interrelation of Themes in the Campbell-Stone Movement," *Discipliana* 46 (3: Fall 1986):44-46.

19. The four-part ideological framework I am suggesting here is very much in line with what Ronald Osborn has called the "four emphases" of the Campbell-Stone heritage: "unity, integrity, invitation, and discipleship." The differences are that "invitation" and "discipleship" in Osborn's language are both closely related to what I am calling evangelistic mission and that freedom is not identified in Osborn's later scheme as one of the emphases (Ronald Osborn, "Epilogue: A Future for Disciples of Christ," in *Classic Themes of Disciples Theology*, 131-52).

CHAPTER I

THE STATEMENT OF THE IDEALS OF THE CAMPBELL-STONE MOVEMENT BY FOUR FOUNDERS

The Campbell-Stone movement's basic ideals—unity, restoration, liberty, and mission—were not new. Each was part of a larger Christian history of ideas. "The unity of all Christians is an idea which exists from the time of Jesus until the present."[1] Similarly, the restoration idea has a history that may be traced through the Ante-Nicene, Reformation, and modern periods of church history, as in Alfred T. DeGroot's 1960 book, *The Restoration Principle*.[2] The ideal of liberty, too, has a long history in the Church universal, with such prominent expressions as the letter of Paul to the Galatians and Martin Luther's 1520 treatise on *Christian Liberty*.[3] The idea of mission is at least as old as the "Great Commission" of Matthew 28:19-20.

In some cases, these ideals were nurtured by more immediate contexts as well. With respect to liberty, the Campbell-Stone movement was deeply affected by the democratic ethos of the place and time from which it sprang—the United States in the early nineteenth century.[4] The movement's ideal of mission, too, was nurtured by its contemporary context. As the movement emerged, it took its place among "the English-speaking evangelical denominations . . . which believed themselves to be especially charged with making America a Christian nation."[5] Although the movement long maintained an exclusivist understanding which placed itself at the center of this mission, it nonetheless partook of the missional and frequently millennial hopes that were widely current in early nineteenth century American Protestantism.[6]

The Campbell-Stone movement may be said to have its deepest roots in the long history of the universal Church, because the basic ideals of the movement are as old as the New Testament. But those deep roots are entangled with others closer to the surface: in the Reformed tradition, British independency and dissent, and in the cultural milieu of eighteenth-century North America, which had included a number of primitive Christianity movements. The roots and background of the movement may be separated from the movement itself which emerged as two religious communities: one in Kentucky whose primary leader was Barton W. Stone, the other in western Pennsylvania and (now West) Virginia whose primary leaders were Thomas Campbell, Alexander Campbell, and Walter Scott. It is because of the merger of much of these two communities in 1832 that the term "Campbell-Stone movement" is used to describe the whole body, and that Stone, the Campbells, and Scott are regarded as the four founders of that movement.

Of the four men recognized as founders of the Campbell-Stone movement, Barton W. Stone stands apart from the others in several ways. First, Stone was, until 1832, the leader of a religious community different from that of the Campbells and Scott. Second, Stone was the only one of the four born and educated in the United States. It is an often-overlooked fact that three of the four founders of what W. E. Garrison called "an American religious movement" were first-generation European immigrants.[7] Though tensions and differences in ideology and emphasis existed among all of the four founders, Stone's thinking probably remained the most distinctive.

Barton Warren Stone was born in Maryland in 1772 and reared principally in Virginia. He was educated at the Academy of Dr. David Caldwell in Guilford, North Carolina. During a revival at the school brought on by the preaching of James McGready, Stone became impressed with the Calvinistic understanding of the state of the human being and with the state of his own soul. Significantly, however, Stone's conversion came when he heard William Hodge preach on the theme "God is love." Hodge came to Stone's rescue again when, having decided to seek a license to preach, and having been assigned a paper on the Trinity, Stone became troubled and confused. Hodge provided Stone with a copy of Isaac Watts's *Glories of Christ*. Stone was licensed by his presbytery to preach. After a period of teaching and itinerant ministry, Stone looked to the prospect of ordination and a permanent pulpit. His preparation for ordination required the study of Presbyterian doctrine and his misgivings about the Trinity resurfaced. Consequently, he hedged on his response to his examination on the Confession of Faith, accepting it only "as far as I see it consistent with the Word of God."[8] Thus, even at this early stage in Stone's career, a biblicism is clear in his perspective. He later articulated this biblicism in terms that were long characteristic of the Campbell-Stone movement:

> But what is truth? The Bible, and the Bible alone—not opinions, which men have formed of the Bible, whether comprised in a confession of faith, or in a christian system, or in thirty-nine articles, or in a discipline.[9]

What was not characteristic of Stone's biblicism, in terms of the later movement, was that it was not linked to a fullblown restoration ideology. Shortly before the Campbell and Stone movements united, Alexander Campbell and Barton Stone engaged in an editorial exchange in which Campbell pointed out,

Statement of Ideals 11

not without bias but nonetheless accurately, that Stone's emphasis lacked the explicit restoration element:

> I trust our brother Editor will not think that we are merely disputing his claims to priority, as it is not assumed by us that he has set up such a claim; but only that in appearance it squints that way: but that he will consider us as endeavoring to prevent the confounding of the *ancient gospel* and *ancient order of things* with the anti-creed, or anti-council, or anti-sectarian cause.[10]

Campbell's assertion that Stone's ministry lacked the restoration element is confirmed by an examination of *The Last Will and Testament of the Springfield Presbytery*.[11] This 1804 document has been called one of the "two basic documents of the Disciples of Christ."[12] The precise authorship of the document is unknown, since it was signed by Barton W. Stone and five others. However, it may be assumed that its content reflected Stone's convictions, since he signed it. The "Witnesses' Address," which accompanies *The Last Will and Testament*, explains the circumstances of its composition:

> ... With deep concern they viewed the divisions and the party spirit among the professing Christians, principally owing to the adoption of human creeds and forms of government. While they were united under the name of a Presbytery, they endeavored to cultivate a spirit of love and unity with all Christians; but found it extremely difficult to suppress the idea that they themselves were a party separate from others. ... At their last meeting they undertook to prepare for the press a piece entitled Observations on Church Government, in which the world will see the beautiful simplicity of Christian church government, stript of human inventions and lordly traditions. As they proceeded in the investigation of that subject, they soon found that there was neither precept nor example in the New Testament for such confederacies as modern Church Sessions, Presbyteries, Synods, General Assemblies, etc.[13]

It was the discovery that their Presbytery was a body without New Testament foundation that led the members to will its death. The basic character of the document is that of a plea to eliminate the divisive "human creeds and forms of government" from the Church universal so that "the universal spread of the gospel, and the unity of the church" would result. This character is sensed in the *Will*'s famous "Imprimis":

> We *will*, that this body die, be dissolved, and sink into union with the Body of Christ at large; for there is but one Body, and one Spirit, even as we are called in one hope of our calling.[14]

This sentence does not deny, but rather asserts, the existence of a Body of Christ beyond the boundaries of the witnesses' own fellowship. Further, it asserts that there is already a oneness in that Body. The conviction of Stone and the other witnesses was that an already existent unity would emerge if the "human" structures obscuring it were removed. The significant difference between this and a restoration emphasis is that the basic continuity of the Church through history and the fundamentally Christian character of its historic expressions is not denied.

The Last Will and Testament of the Springfield Presbytery devotes its body to advocating the elimination of the Presbytery's "name of distinction, with its *Reverend* title," and "power of making laws for the government of the church, and executing them by delegated authority." It also emphasizes the right of individual Christians to study the Bible, the right of individual preachers to preach if licensed by God, the right of individual congregations to choose, send, and support their own preachers, and the need for both preachers and the people to "pray more and dispute less." Another clear emphasis in the *Will* is the Holy Spirit as the constitutive element of the Church. This is mentioned in connection with the oneness of the Church, the government of the Church, and the preaching of the Church's gospel.[15] The Spirit remained a central element in the ecclesiology of Barton W. Stone.[16] He wrote:

> The great secret of church government and organization has been almost overlooked. It is the indwelling of the Holy Spirit in each believer, and member of the church. . . . Let us be filled with the Spirit and walk in the Spirit, and the simple government of Christ will be all sufficient.[17]

Stone, then, was not a restorationist in quite the way that Alexander Campbell was, or the way second-generation members of the Campbell-Stone movement were. Stone was a biblicist, a Christian primitivist, a strong unionist, a libertarian, and a committed evangelist. Stone's libertarian emphasis can be seen clearly in *The Last Will and Testament*. In fact, the *Will* has been called "one of the first statements of religious freedom ever proclaimed in the Western Hemisphere."[18] However, Stone's commitment to liberty is a commitment to liberty under the absolute monarchy of Jesus Christ.[19]

Stone's commitment to Christian unity and his missional concern are closely linked. He identified the particular missionary situation of the Church in his times in these terms: "About the close of the 18th century, Christianity had nearly lost its form and spirit in its professed advocates—a few only remained, who wept over the desolations of Zion, and prayed for her prosperity."[20] It was into this perceived situation that the Great Revival in the West came. Stone became especially involved in the revival at Cane Ridge, Kentucky, in 1801. Although some of the violent physical manifestations, the "exercises," disturbed Stone, he nonetheless concluded that the revival was the work of God. Even though the occasion for the revival had been a Presbyterian communion (a sacramental meeting), it was significant to Stone that Baptist, Methodist, and Presbyterian preachers had worked side by side during this revival.[21] The notion of a unified Christian effort made to confront an especially urgent missionary situation was thus planted early in Stone's mind by his own experience. Stone watched with sadness this spirit of cooperation disappear among some of his peers.[22] But he continued to embody it.

Part of the motivation for Stone's continued emphasis upon Christian unity was his own apocalyptic and millennial worldview.[23] But perhaps the clearest example of the depth of his commitment to unity was his conduct in the union of his followers with those of the Campbells. Stone commented once upon the personal cost of this union:

> ... I feel myself a citizen of the world, and would never be confined to the interests of a party exclusively. For this spirit, and for endeavoring to act it out, I have been the foot-ball of the illnatured world of religionists. My own children and brethren in the Lord, whom I have nourished with care, have forsaken me, & have joined the sectaries in their opposition against me. And why, you may ask, do they thus act? Because acting up to the principles of the gospel, I will have fellowship with christians—but with christians, whom they call Campbellites, and whom they denounce, because of some peculiarities of opinion. Many of the latter people also are in doubts of me, because I am suspected of leaning too far towards my old brethren, the Christians—they too have forsaken me. I pity the ignorance, and narrow spirit manifested by both parties. I envy not their sectarian partialities, nor will I countenance them.[24]

Christian union has been sometimes depicted as the principal ideal of Barton W. Stone. However, his commitment to this ideal was inextricably linked with a millennialist's sense of the urgency of the Church's missionary situation. Similarly, Stone's commitment to Christian liberty cannot be separated from his conviction that all Christians are subject to the absolute monarchy of Christ. While Stone stopped short of explicating an ancient gospel or ancient order of things, he shared the biblistic and primitivistic premises upon which others would build. Finally, however, in Stone these values were all tempered by a profound sense that the Spirit is the central ingredient in Christian life.[25]

Thomas Campbell not only is the next chronologically of the four founders of the Campbell-Stone movement (in terms of ministry in the United States) but also is a transitional figure between Stone and the younger two in that he has been linked with Barton W. Stone. One link that has been identified is the similarly "irenic" spirit of the two older men.[26] This is frequently seen in terms of the contrast between Thomas's temperament and that of his son Alexander, who "was to give evidence of an aggressive and disputatious nature in contrast to the indecisiveness and avoidance of conflict so apparent in the father."[27] Another commonality between Stone and Thomas Campbell is their conviction of the dire straits of the Church on the American frontier. The most famous instance in which Thomas acted on this conviction involved a communion service:

> As a communion season approached, Mr. Campbell's sympathies were aroused by the spiritually destitute condition of some in the vicinity of his labors who belonged to other branches of the Presbyterian family, and who had not for a long time enjoyed an opportunity of partaking of the Lord's Supper, so that he felt it to be his duty, in his preparation sermon, to lament the existing divisions, and to suggest that all his pious hearers who felt disposed and duly prepared, should without reference to denominational differences, enjoy the approaching communion. This furnished a basis for formal charges against Thomas Campbell before the Presbytery of which he was a member.[28]

Since B. B. Tyler wrote that account in 1894, the notion that Thomas Campbell was ousted by the Presbyterians for acting on his sympathy for his "spiritually destitute" frontier congregants has found a lasting place in Campbell-Stone folklore. While it is true that Thomas Campbell was an individual of sympathetic temperament, and that he was impressed by the uniqueness of the missionary situation of the American frontier, his parting of the ways from the Presbyterians reaches far back into his career.

Thomas Campbell, in contrast to Stone, was an immigrant. He was born in Ulster, Ireland, in 1763. Thomas's father had been a Roman Catholic, but later joined the (Anglican) Church of Ireland. Thomas, however, sought fellowship with the Presbyterians. His theology was, and remained, Calvinistic.[29] He therefore sought, and after some struggle received, an experience of assurance that he was among the elect. With the receipt of this assurance came Thomas's commitment to the ministry.[30]

Thomas's father had already equipped his son with "an excellent English education" at a military school not far from the family home.[31] After teaching for a time, which Thomas Campbell was destined to do intermittently throughout his active life, he entered the University of Glasgow. He completed the university course with honors and entered the theological school of the Anti-Burgher Seceder Presbyterians. The seminary course consisted of five eight-week-long annual sessions, which Thomas completed.[32]

Thomas had become a minister in an obviously much-divided church. The Seceders were a group whose separate existence was rooted in their insistence that the congregation had the right to choose its own ministers. "The Anti-Burghers opposed the requirement that the burgesses of the Scottish cities swear to support the established church."[33] The last issue was hardly relevant to the Presbyterians in Ireland and Thomas Campbell at one point participated in an unsuccessful attempt to heal that breach in his own land. By 1806 his brethren had divided again and he became an *Old Light* Anti-Burgher Seceder Presbyterian.[34]

Thomas Campbell's restiveness in a divided Presbyterian church was no doubt fed by his contact with a nearby congregation of independents through whom he came in contact with the primitive Christianity movement of James and Robert Haldane.[35] Furthermore, Campbell was both a subscriber and committee member of the Evangelical Society of Ulster. This involvement is significant for at least three reasons: it shows Campbell to have been committed to evangelistic work on a interdenominational basis, it was an occasion for some conflict with Presbyterian authorities before he emigrated, and it provided the direct model for the later Christian Association of Washington, Pennsylvania.[36]

Thomas Campbell's principal biographer has demonstrated that Thomas's eventual ouster by his presbytery was quite even-handed. By the time that event occurred, Thomas had departed the Presbyterian faith in matters of ecclesiology. He had been received into full fellowship upon arrival in Pennsylvania in 1807; but by early 1808 he was teaching a view of faith as the response of reason to testimony, a form of anticreedalism, and a blurring of the distinction between clergy and laity.[37]

In 1809 Thomas Campbell produced what has been the most influential primary document in the history of the Campbell-Stone movement—the *Declaration and Address of the Christian Association of Washington, Pennsylvania*.[38] The core of the document is thirteen propositions which Louis and Bess White Cochran have summarized as follows:

> 1. The church of Christ is essentially, intentionally and constitutionally one.
> 2. Congregations, locally separate, ought to be in fellowship with one another.
> 3. Nothing ought to be an article of faith, or a rule, for the constitution and management of the church except what is expressly taught by Christ and His apostles.
> 4. The New Testament is as perfect a constitution for the worship, discipline, and government of the New Testament church and as perfect a rule for the duties of its members, as the Old Testament was ... for ... the Old Testament church.
> 5. The Association will support only such ministers as conform to "the original standard."
> 6. The church can give no new commandments where the Scriptures are silent.
> 7. Creeds may be useful for instruction, but must not be used as tests of fitness for membership in the church.
> 8. Full knowledge of all revealed truth is not necessary to entitle persons to membership; neither should they for this purpose be required to make a profession more extensive than their knowledge. Realization of their need of salvation, faith in Christ as Savior, and obedience to Him, are all that is necessary.
> 9. All who are thus qualified should love each other as brothers, and be united as one.
> 10. Division among Christians is a horrid evil.
> 11. Divisions have been caused in some cases by neglect of the expressly revealed Will of God; in others, by assuming authority to make human opinions the test of fellowship, or to introduce human inventions into the faith and practice of the church.
> 12. All that is needed for the purity and perfection of the church is that it receive those, and only those, who profess faith in Christ,

and obey Him according to the Scriptures; that it retain them only as long as their conduct is in accord with their professions; that ministers teach only what is expressly revealed, and that all Divine Ordinances be observed as the New Testament [church] observed them.

13. When the church adopts "necessary expedients" they should be recognized for what they are, and should not be confused with divine commands, so that they will give no occasion for dissension or division.[39]

These propositions demonstrate that Thomas Campbell is a pivotal figure in the development of Campbell-Stone movement's tradition. The commitment to Christian unity is present, as it was in Stone's thought. Similarly, a biblicism and primitivism are present. But unlike Stone's, Campbell's biblistic and primitivistic emphasis takes the form of restorationism. That is, it is not the spirit which is regarded as constitutive of the Church, but rather the express letter of the New Testament. Thomas Campbell later wrote:

> As to the nature and object of the proposed reformation, it is clearly and definitively expressed in the following proposition, viz.—"The restoration of primitive apostolic christianity in letter and spirit—in principle and practice;"—and has been so stated from our commencement.[40]

It is significant that Thomas Campbell's *Declaration* was issued by a "Christian Association," a body which he did not conceive of as a rival to the churches. Thomas's assumption was that authentic Christians existed in all churches.[41] The harshness of the restorationist position with respect to the historic churches was mitigated by Thomas's personality, and when it emerged unbuffered in the hands of others, Thomas was disturbed:

> In the absence of the Editor [Alexander Campbell], we feel induced, by the above communications, to express feeling of deep regret, that a *reformation*, which we humbly suggested, and *respectfully submitted* to the consideration of the friends and lovers of the truth and peace *throughout all the churches*, more than twenty-five years ago, for the express purpose of putting an end to religious controversy among Christians, should appear to take the unhappy turn, to which with

painful anxiety, we have seen it verging for the last ten years.[42] (Italics mine.)

Nonetheless, the restoration route to Christian union was the only route that Thomas Campbell could support.[43] What made this "unhappy turn" difficult for Thomas to live with was the other fundamental conviction about Christianity which he held:

> Christianity is emphatically, supereminently—yea, transcendentally, the religion of love: that is, of affectionate attachment, benevolence, and beneficence; for its Divine author, subject matter, and effects are all love in the highest possible degree.[44]

In addition to his interlocking commitment to unity and restoration, Thomas Campbell had a commitment to liberty and a sense of the unique mission of the Church on the frontier of the Untied States. In short, he viewed the religious liberty of the United States as a unique opportunity for the Church and gave it great significance:

> The favorable opportunity which Divine Providence has put into your hands, in this happy country, for the accomplishment of so great a good, is, in itself, a consideration of no small encouragement. A country happily exempted from the baneful influence of a civil establishment of any peculiar form of Christianity; from under the direct influence of the anti-christian hierarchy, ... Still more happy will it be for us if we duly esteem and improve those great advantages, for the high and valuable ends for which they are manifestly given, and sure where much is given, much also will be required.[45]

The founders of the Campbell-Stone movement were uniform in their commitment to civil disestablishment.[46] They were also uniform in their anti-Roman Catholicism.[47] But each of these must be understood as part of their fundamental value-commitment. Roman Catholicism represented the "apostasy"—the falling away of the Church from its pristine primitive state—and a hierarchical, nondemocratic structure that flew in the face of the ethos of the young nation which had been sought out by three of the four founders of the Campbell-Stone movement. In sum, while Stone failed to articulate specifically the restoration element of Campbell-Stone tradition, Thomas Campbell sought to soften that element because of his irenic temperament. Both Stone and Thomas Campbell emphasized, in their own fashion, liberty and the mission of the Church.

In Alexander Campbell were combined a commitment to the notion of restoration and the confidence to *specify* the content of "the ancient gospel and ancient order." He was born in Ireland in 1788. His education was principally conducted by his father, Thomas, and his paternal uncles. Like his father, he taught for a time. At the age of nineteen, when Thomas emigrated, Alexander was left in charge of an academy. When Thomas sent word for his family to join him in America, Alexander and the others embarked. However, on their first attempt to make the voyage they were shipwrecked. It was during that experience that Alexander made his commitment to the ministry, though panic seems not to have been part of that decision.[48]

The most important fact about that shipwreck was that it provided the occasion for Alexander to spend a year at the University of Glasgow. There he had the opportunity to "widen his acquaintance with the main currents of British thought and culture," and to come into contact with Greville Ewing. Ewing was in charge of the training school for lay preachers associated with the primitive Christianity movement of Robert and James Alexander Haldane. Ewing became "Alexander's closest and most helpful friend during that year at Glasgow." Alexander Campbell encountered the Haldane movement at a time when it was "turning more definitely toward the restoration of the exact practices of the primitive church, rather than the general evangelism with which it had been chiefly concerned a few years earlier."[49]

Alexander Campbell's arrival in the United States was almost simultaneous with his father's publication of the *Declaration and Address*. His year at Glasgow had led him to discomfort in the Seceder Presbyterian Church, and he had broken with it symbolically at the last semiannual communion service he had attended before leaving for America.[50] When he reported this and his decision for the Christian ministry to his father, the elder Campbell again became the tutor of the younger. Thomas insisted that Alexander devote six months to disciplined study of the scriptures.[51]

Meanwhile, the strategy of reformation which lay behind the *Declaration and Address* did not seem to be working. That essential unity of the Church which Thomas regarded as a "given" was not emerging from the various denominations.[52] Much to Thomas Campbell's chagrin, other Christian associations were not being formed. Instead, the Christian Association of Washington, Pennsylvania was beginning to take on the characteristics of a church. To avoid being responsible for the creation of still another "sect," Thomas applied, on behalf of the Association, for membership in a Presbyterian synod as a

Presbyterian congregation. This application was denied. In 1811 the Association constituted itself a church and adopted a congregational form of government.[53] This step, being a clear departure from the type of reformation urged in the *Declaration and Address*, is a good symbol of the transition of primacy in leadership of the Campbell movement from Thomas to Alexander. Thomas had sought to enable the unity of the Church to emerge. Alexander would seek to build the "restored" Church from the ground up.

The first tangible evidence of Alexander's dominance in the fledgling movement came in connection with the issue of baptism. Barton W. Stone had long held that the mode of baptism was a matter of forbearance.[54] This, too, was the opinion of Thomas Campbell at the time that Alexander arrived from America. However, the younger Campbell came to believe that only baptism by immersion of believers was acceptable and, eventually, that baptism was for the remission of sins. In what turned out to be the establishment of the Campbell-Stone movement's normative understanding of baptism, it is significant that Alexander led and Thomas followed. Alexander convinced his father, on the basis of biblical evidence, that only immersion was acceptable.[55]

Once the Campbell movement began to practice baptism by immersion, fellowship with the Baptists became a possibility. In the years between the formation of the Campbells' church in 1811 and 1815 this possibility was explored. In 1815 it became a reality when the Campbells' Brush Run Church joined the Redstone Baptist Association. Interestingly, Thomas seemed more anxious to preserve this new relationship than did his volatile son. When the Redstone Baptist Association met in 1816, Thomas read a document on the Trinity which, though it did not contain the word "Trinity," was accepted without amendment by the Association. In contrast, Alexander preached a "Sermon on the Law" which, in its sharp distinction between the Old and New Testaments, was highly offensive to Baptists.[56] Although the Campbells and their followers would remain nominally Baptist until 1830, it became clear long before that date that Alexander Campbell had his own agenda for those he influenced.[57]

Alexander Campbell's specification of the program of restoration which his father had suggested in principle came in the form of a thirty-part series of articles published between 1824 and 1829 on "A Restoration of the Ancient Order of Things," and a ten-part series of articles published between 1828 and 1829 on the "Ancient Gospel." Both series appeared in the *Christian Baptist*, of which Alexander was the editor. In the initial entry in the first of these series, he wrote:

Statement of Ideals

> Celebrated as the *era of Reformation* is, we doubt not but that the *era of Restoration* will as far transcend it in importance and fame, through the long and blissful Millennium as the New Testament transcends in simplicity, beauty, excellency, and majesty, the dogmas and notions of the creed of Westminster and the canons of the Assembly's Digest.[58]

Alexander Campbell viewed restoration as a task of cosmic significance, tied to the coming of the expected millennium.[59]

By 1835, Campbell had written enough on the particulars of the restoration in his periodicals, the *Christian Baptist* and its successor the *Millennial Harbinger*, that he felt compelled to pull together his principal thoughts in a book. The short title that appears on the binding of the 1835 edition is *Christianity Restored*. However, the short title of the better known 1839 edition is *The Christian System*. The book's full title forms a good summation of Alexander Campbell's fundamental ideology: *A Connected View of the Principles and Rules by which the Living Oracles May Be Intelligibly and Certainly Interpreted; of the Foundation on which All Christians May Form One Communion and of the Capital Positions Sustained in the Attempt to Restore the Original Gospel and Order of Things; Containing the Principal Extras of the "Millennial Harbinger," Revised and Corrected*. In this title may be observed: 1) the assumption that the Bible may be interpreted with clarity and certainty; 2) a commitment to the union of all Christians (not all churches) in one body; and 3) a commitment to restoration of a primitive gospel and Church order. These points were also tied in Campbell's mind to the mission of the Church—the conversion of the world. "Until . . . a union, a communion and co-operation amongst christians actually appear as in good faith existing, all efforts to convert the world to Jesus Christ must be abortive."[60]

Even though Alexander Campbell's series on "The Restoration of the Ancient Order of Things," "set forth in great detail the nature and work of the church of the New Testament,"[61] the author was willing to summarize the "three capital points" of his restoration agenda:

I. The Christian Scriptures, the only rule and measure of Christian faith and learning.
II. The Christian Confession, the foundation of Christian union and communion.
III. The Christian ordinances—baptism, the Lord's day, and the Lord's supper, as taught and observed by the Apostles.[62]

In most of his writings these points appear inseparable. For example, Alexander Campbell wrote quite cordially about various efforts at Christian union such as the Evangelical Alliance.[63] However, he basically understood Christian union as being that which is "legitimately founded upon one Lord, one faith, *one immersion*, one God and Father of all, one body, one Spirit and one hope."[64] (Italics mine). Alexander Campbell's other most typical depiction of the basis of Christian union is exemplified in this statement:

> Hence it is that nothing is proposed as a bond of peace on earth other than the bond of peace in heaven, which is all comprehended in the cardinal and sublime proposition—JESUS THE NAZARENE IS THE MESSIAH, THE SON OF GOD.[65]

These two ingredients, baptism by immersion for the remission of sins and the Petrine confession, became distinguishing characteristics of the Campbell-Stone movement. Alexander bluntly summarized his view of the constitutive elements of Christian faith and churchly life when he brought these ingredients together:

> THE BELIEF OF ONE FACT, *and that upon the best evidence in the world, is all that is requisite, as far as faith goes, to salvation. The belief on this*, ONE FACT, *and submission to* ONE INSTITUTION *expressive of it, is all that is required of Heaven to admission into the church.* . . . The one fact is expressed in a single proposition—*that Jesus the Nazarene is the Messiah* . . . The *one institution* is baptism into the name of the Father, and of the Son and of the Holy Spirit.[66]

Alexander Campbell believed that the scripture contains unambiguous facts, the principal fact being the Messiahship of Jesus of Nazareth. Therefore, Christianity consisted primarily of the rational acceptance of that fact, repentance, and the willingness to *"reform and be immersed for the remission of sins."*[67] Because Campbell regarded this view as scriptural, he thought it also catholic (i.e., worthy of universal acceptance). Thus, Alexander Campbell could appear to be very committed to Christian union. However, this appearance should not conceal the fact that Campbell envisioned no surrender, change, or compromise of his position as being profitable to Christian union. For example, he wrote:

> I will . . . propose,—1st. That a congress of all Protestant parties (and if any one choose to add the Greek and Roman sects, I will vote for

Statement of Ideals

> it) be convened according to appointment, *the rule of union* shall be, that, whatever in *faith*, in *piety*, and *morality* is catholic, or universally admitted by all parties, shall be adopted as the basis of union; and whatever is not by all parties admitted as of divine authority, shall be rejected as schismatical and human.[68]

Campbell clearly believed that such a process would yield a basis for union precisely as he had already proposed. After all, his was no "human" program but the self-evident, divine, catholic, scriptural basis of Christian union. This has been the characteristic irony of the whole history of the Campbell-Stone movement. The first generation leaders of the movement cherished a naive belief that their "plea" would have immediate and universal acceptance and that their movement was somehow exempted from taking on the characteristics of another "sect." This naive belief was aptly stated by Thomas Campbell, when he said he "once thought the thing so plain, and so important, that no serious professor of any sect could refrain from embracing it, as soon as it was fairly proposed."[69]

In terms of the four characteristic values of the Campbell-Stone movement, Alexander Campbell demonstrably was committed to an integrated ideology. In his mind, biblistic restorationism was the basis for Christian union, a union which would further the mission of the Church (the conversion of the world and amelioration of society). Alexander Campbell was also committed to liberty in at least two important ways. First, he was committed to a liberty of opinion which would extend up to the point of "self-evident" scripture. In this connection, Campbell printed the following quotation on the title pages of his volumes of the *Christian Baptist*:

> What a glorious freedom of thought do the Apostles recommend! And how contemptible in their account is a blind and implicit faith! May all Christians use this liberty of judging for themselves in matters of Religion, and allow it to one another, and to all mankind.[70]

Second, Campbell was a strong advocate of the civil disestablishment of religion:

> I am a cordial friend to the sanctification of the Lord's day in a christian manner, but to sanctify it by law at the solicitation of the priesthood, would be at best, a solemn mockery—and a precedent of fatal omen to the civil as well as the religious liberties of this happiest of lands.[71]

Campbell regarded the existence of ecclesiastical establishments as worthy of condemnation, and this was understood in connection with his understanding of Christian union:

> I have no idea of seeing, nor one wish to see the sects unite in one grand army. *This would be dangerous to our liberties and laws.* ... Let them unite who love the Lord, and then we shall soon see the hierling [sic] priesthood *and their worldly establishments prostrate in the dust.*[72] (Italics mine.)

In Alexander Campbell's ideology, then, liberty was linked to restoration, union, and mission. Liberation from "human creeds" and "worldly establishments" was part of the restoration which would bring about union and fulfill the Church's world-converting mission.

The youngest of the four founders of the Campbell-Stone movement was Walter Scott. Scott's background was similar in several ways to that of the Campbells. He was born in Scotland in 1796. His mother was a deeply religious and firmly committed member of the Presbyterian Church of Scotland, and his father was a music teacher. His parents hoped that Walter would enter the Presbyterian ministry, and arranged for him to enter the University of Edinburgh. Scott did not enter the ministry at that time, "not from lack of religious inclinations but because he never grasped the whole matter of church and Scripture with one clear, luminous insight."[73] After he completed his education at Edinburgh, Scott was given an opportunity to emigrate to America. After a brief stay on Long Island, he made his way on foot to Pittsburgh where he found employment as assistant to George Forrester, who had an academy there.[74]

Though a Scot, Forrester did not practice the conventional Presbyterianism of the Church of Scotland. Rather, he participated in a congregation that seems to have been influenced by the Haldanes.[75] Forrester's congregation was engaged in the quest of the "doctrine and practice of the apostolic church."[76] "The members of the congregation greeted one another with a 'holy kiss'"; they washed one another's feet; they practiced weekly communion; they recited no creeds; they worshipped simply and with scriptural language; they baptized confessing adults by immersion and not infants; and each congregation was an independent unit, over which no authoritative body held sway. Scott began to participate in Forrester's congregation and to study the New Testament. Before long, Scott asked Forrester to immerse him. He then turned his attention to the problem of conversion.

Statement of Ideals

The mystery of conversion, upon a fresh study of the Acts of the Apostles, was found to be no mystery at all. It was not, as his Calvinistic training had led him to expect, a matter of long and agonizing "seekings," or of strange signs and mystical feelings induced by the Holy Spirit, selecting some and rejecting others. A converted person was one who heard, believed, and obeyed! It was that simple.[77]

According to Dwight Stevenson, the next important ingredient in the formation of what Scott was to call the "gospel restored" was a new understanding of the meaning of baptism.[78] In 1821 a pamphlet produced by a "Haldane congregation" in New York City came into Scott's possession. He came to agree with its position "that it was 'in baptism that men professed, by deed, as they had already done by word, to have the remission of sins through the death of Jesus Christ.'"[79] Still wanting in Scott's mind, however, was a concept of the central teaching of the gospel. The discovery of such a teaching was the next development in his thinking. He came to believe that *"it was possible to sum up the whole Christian life as the law of faith in Christ!"* To Scott, this was the "'Golden Oracle' . . . the creed of the Christian, the bond of Christian union, and the way of salvation."[80] Once the "Golden Oracle," which Scott understood fundamentally as the Petrine confession's expression of the Messiahship of Jesus,[81] was placed alongside Scott's understanding of baptism, his summary of the gospel looked remarkably like Alexander Campbell's.

Alexander Campbell and Walter Scott had been acquainted for some five years when, in 1827, Scott was made the itinerant evangelist for the nominally Baptist Mahoning Association, which was actually dominated by the Campbell movement. It was in his work as an evangelist that it became clear that Walter Scott was willing to identify vigorously his understanding of Christian faith as the restored gospel. Scott pinpointed the "True Gospel" as having been restored in November of 1827[82] when he baptized "the first person in modern times who received the ordinance of baptism in perfect accordance with apostolic teaching and usage."[83] This propensity of Scott's to pinpoint the restoration and speak of it as a *fait accompli* annoyed Alexander Campbell, who wrote, "I cannot regard anything done by him in 1827, or myself in 1823, as a restoration of the Gospel of Christ either to the church or to the world."[84]

Scott was both the most effective early evangelist of the movement and the founder most closely linked to restorationism. Alexander Campbell said of Scott:

> Brother Walter Scott . . . in the fall of 1827, arranged the several items of faith, repentance, baptism, remission of sins, the Holy Spirit and eternal life, restored them in this order to the Church under the title of the *Ancient Gospel*, and successfully preached it for the conversion of the world.[85]

This was the famous "five-finger exercise." Scott preached that if one would *believe* (give rational assent) that Jesus is the Messiah, *repent*, and *be baptized by immersion*, then God would *remit sins*, bestow the *Holy Spirit*, and grant *eternal life*. He would place these points, collapsing the last two, before his audience as the five fingers of the hand.[86] When the Mahoning Association met in 1828:

> *Over 1,000 additions* for the year were reported. Walter Scott was thought to have recovered the "divinely appointed" and "effectual means" necessary to restore the purity of the church and ultimately the union of all Christians, *if only they would listen and obey the simple commands of the Scriptures* . . . Such was the progress of evangelism in Ohio under Scott's leadership that, when the Mahoning Association met at Sharon, Pennsylvania, in the latter part of August, 1829, the messengers learned that *another thousand* converts had been added to the congregations.
>
> The force and freshness of Scott's evangelistic appeal, the exciting sense of rediscovery of a long-lost truth, the sense of witnessing the beginning of a new period in Christian history, all gave Scott's revival an extraordinary character. . . . With Scott there was no frenzy of emotion, but a blending of rationality and authority, an appeal to common sense and to Scriptures suited to the temper of the frontier. *Other preachers in the association caught the new note and began to sound it. Hundreds were converted.* New congregations were organized. The Campbell followers (and later the Stone and Campbell movements combined) had no difficulty in accepting Scott's evangelistic method. *It became the standard emphasis* for many years afterward.[87] (Italics mine.)

With Walter Scott the Campbell-Stone movement had a leader who created a simplistic, forthright, and popular version of their ideology, the development of which prepared the way for the hardening of that ideology into the "legalistic

Statement of Ideals

restorationism" of the movement's second generation.[88] This second generation has been characterized as the period of "Disciples scholasticism."[89]

In Scott's version, the commitment to the ideals of unity, restoration, liberty, and the mission of the Church showed a clear interrelation. He wrote:

> In relation to the Unity of the Saints, I here most solemnly profess, that at the Restoration of the true gospel of Jesus Christ, in 1827, nothing except the conversion of the world was more before my mind than the union of Christians; and I absolutely thought then, as I think now, that the unity of the body of Jesus Christ would be effected by the diffusion of those principles and privileges which are inculcated and bestowed in the true gospel.[90]

The "true gospel" that Scott refers to is that which he had "restored" in 1827. Both Christian union and the mission of the church to convert the world are to be accomplished, in Scott's view, by the promotion of his restored gospel. That this was his view was reiterated when he wrote: "The opponent objects again, 'Your scheme will only create another sect.' Grant it. But then it will be a sect which, in its progress will consume all others."[91]

As in the case of the Campbells, Walter Scott saw the liberty characteristic of American society as a great good. "In the United States the two forms of liberty, the political and the religious, are, it is confessed, well-defined, and, as we trust, permanently established."[92] However, Scott held a view of ecclesiastical liberty that was destined to place him at cross-purposes with Alexander Campbell.

In August 1830 the Baptist Mahoning Association met as usual.

> Then, abruptly, the character of the assembly changed when a reform preacher arose to move that the association "as an advisory council, or an ecclesiastical tribunal, should cease to exist."
>
> Alexander Campbell, struck with amazement and consternation, started to his feet to protest. But his friend Walter Scott was at his side, urging him back to his seat with the admonition: the majority of the messengers had made their decision, and by opposition now Campbell could only weaken his influence for the future.

This is Eva Jean Wrather's understanding of Scott's role in what she calls "the pivotal event" in the "history of the Campbell reform movement."[93] Others have suggested that it was something far different from concern over Campbell's future influence that compelled Scott to dissuade him from vocal opposition to the dissolution of the association. Dwight Stevenson suggests that Scott was "alarmed at the tyranny of . . . Baptist associations, and also convinced that they were without scriptural sanction," and that it was Scott who "had determined to end the Mahoning organization."[94] James DeForest Murch concurs with Stevenson that the action was taken "perhaps at Scott's instigation."[95] This view is made plausible by Walter Scott's own statement, made some thirteen years later, relative to extralocal church cooperation:

> The truth is that church cooperation is alike unscriptural and unphilosophical. It is a mere expedient of no permanence; and survives the first experiment only when confined to a very limited number of churches. . . .
> But the cooperation of the scriptures is not sectarian but corporate. It is not the cooperation of churches as a sect but of individuals as a church; and each church is "God's Co-operation" for all ecclesiastical purposes in its respective locality. Every other cooperation except for purposes incidental, is unauthorized. It is human and will in most, if not in all instances interfere with the cooperation of God and come to naught at last.[96]

This would lend credibility to the view that Scott concurred philosophically with the dissolution of the Mahoning Association.[97]

Alexander Campbell realized that this action, which he so regretted, was partially a result of his own iconoclastic blasts as editor of the *Christian Baptist*.[98] He later wrote, "I confess I was alarmed at the impassioned and hasty manner in which the Association was, in a few minutes, dissolved . . . Reformation and annihilation are not with me now as formerly, convertible or identical terms."[99] This may be taken as an admission on Campbell's part that his utterances, reflecting changing views, had not been consistent.

"Church Organization" became a major topic in Campbell's *Millennial Harbinger* during the 1840s.[100] By the end of that decade Campbell had concluded that in

> matters of prudential arrangement for the evangelizing of the world, for the better application of our means and resources, according to the exigencies of society and the ever varying complexion of things around us, [we] are left without a single law, statute, ordinance, or enactment in all the new Testament.[101]

It is clear that during the nearly two decades of seeking an organizational pattern for his movement, from 1830 to 1849, Campbell became increasingly committed to extracongregational structures arranged according to expediency.

There is, then, a definite tension between the early Alexander Campbell and the later one. Differences were also visible among the founding four. In addition to the differences in the approaches of Alexander Campbell and his father, the disputed claims of "priority" between Barton W. Stone and Alexander Campbell, similarly disputed claims of having "restored" the gospel between Walter Scott and Alexander Campbell, and the different organizational philosophies that may have existed between Walter Scott and Alexander Campbell, must be placed tensions in the movement resulting from the merger of the Campbell and Stone forces. It is perhaps not surprising that the national solidarity of the movement was wrenched in the years after the Civil War and the death of Alexander Campbell. It was a precarious solidarity weakened by these inherited fissures and having very little organizational expression. In the second generation these cracks in the movement's internal unity would make their contribution to a widening divergence in the interpretation of its basic ideals.

---

1. Liggett, "Why the Disciples Chose Unity," 227.

2. Alfred T. DeGroot, *The Restoration Principle* (St. Louis: Bethany Press, 1960).

3. The idea of liberty has had many different nuances in its long history in the Church universal. However, the fact that it was important in the thought of the Church's first influential writer (Paul, see Galatians 5:1) and that of the most famous of the reformers, is a testimony to the depth of its rootage in the Christian tradition. See Martin Luther, *Christian Liberty*, trans. by W. A. Lambert, ed. by Harold J. Grimm (Philadelphia: Fortress Press, 1957).

4. George G. Beazley, Jr., "Who Are the Disciples?" in *The Christian Church (Disciples of Christ): An Interpretative Examination in the Cultural Context*, ed. George G. Beazley, Jr. (St. Louis: Bethany Press, 1973), 6; also, Mark G. Toulouse, *Joined in Discipleship: the Maturing of An American Religious Movement* (St. Louis: Chalice Press, 1992), 17-22.

5. Robert T. Handy, *A Christian America: Protestant Hopes and Historical Realities* (New York: Oxford University Press, 1971), vii.

6. Harrell, *Social History*, 1:41-53.

7. Winfred E. Garrison writes, "The movement is distinctively American," in his Preface to *An American Religious Movement: A Brief History of the Disciples of Christ* (St. Louis: Bethany Press, 1946), 5-6.

8. Lester G. McAllister and William E. Tucker, *Journey in Faith: A History of the Christian Church (Disciples of Christ)* (St. Louis: Bethany Press, 1975), 62-68.

9. B[arton] W[arren]S[tone], "A Letter to the Church of Christ Scattered Abroad Throughout the United States of America," *Christian Messenger* 14 (August 1844):117.

10. Editor [Alexander Campbell], "Reply on Union, Communion and the Name Christian," *Millennial Harbinger* 2 (September 1831):391.

11. *Declaration and Address, by Thomas Campbell; Last Will and Testament of the Springfield Presbytery, by Barton W. Stone and Others*, with an Introduction by F. D. Kershner (St. Louis: Bethany Press, 1960). No copy of the first edition of *The Last Will and Testament* is known to exist. It first appeared "as a small pamphlet, probably at Lexington, Ky." (111). (For further information see the Appendix in this 1960 edition.)

12. Ibid., in the Preface, 7.

13. Ibid., 20-21.

14. Ibid., 17-18.

15. Ibid., 18-19.

16. See Allen Van Dozier Eikner, "The Nature of the Church among the Disciples of Christ" (Ph.D. dissertation, Vanderbilt University, 1962), 148.

17. Stone, "Letter to the Church of Christ," 119.

18. Preface to *Declaration and Address; Last Will and Testament*, 7; David Roos argues strongly that "Stone's primary category by which he interpreted ethical questions was freedom of the individual Christian from ecclesiastical tyranny" (David C. Roos, "The Social Thought of Barton Warren Stone and Its Significance Today for the Disciples of Christ in Western Kentucky" [D.Div. dissertation, Vanderbilt University, 1973], 34).

19. B[arton] W[arren] S[tone], "Reflections of Old Age," *Christian Messenger* 13 (August 1843):124.

20. B[arton] W[arren] S[tone], "A Synopsis of the Reformation of the 19th Century," *Christian Messenger* 13 (September 1843):161.

21. Barton Warren Stone, "A Short History of the Life of Barton W. Stone," in *The Cane Ridge Meeting House*, by James R. Rogers (Cincinnati: Standard Publishing, 1910), 167.

22. Of his fellow Presbyterians, Stone wrote: "At first they were pleased to see the Methodists and Baptists so cordially uniting with us in worship, no doubt hoping they would become Presbyterians. But as soon as they saw these sects drawing away disciples after them, they raised the tocsin of alarm—the Confession is in danger!—the church is in danger!—O Israel, to your tents!"

Statement of Ideals 31

And, according to Stone, the other denominations were soon to follow suit: "The sects were roused. The Methodists and Baptists, who had so long lived in peace and harmony with the Presbyterians, and with each other, now girded on their armour, and marched into the deathly field of controversy and war." Ibid., 166-67.

23. Stone, "Reflections of Old Age," 126; Hughes, "Apocalyptic Origins of Churches of Christ," 189-90.

24. Editor [Barton Warren Stone], *Christian Messenger* 9 (June 1835):128.

25. Hughes, in "Apocalyptic Origins of Churches of Christ," contrasts the "rational, progressive primitivism" of Alexander Campbell with the "apocalyptic primitivism" of Barton Stone and points out that Stone's primitivism had more to do with "lives of simple holiness" than with the programmatic specifics of the ancient faith and ancient order (191, 189).

26. Frederick D. Kershner, Introduction to *Declaration and Address, by Thomas Campbell; Last Will and Testament of the Springfield Presbytery, by Barton W. Stone and Others*, 15.

27. Lester G. McAllister, *Thomas Campbell: Man of the Book* (St. Louis: Bethany Press, 1954), 147.

28. Benjamin B. Tyler, *A History of the Disciples of Christ* (New York: Christian Literature Co., 1894), 44.

29. So Robert Richardson quotes Thomas Campbell in connection with the controversy over the ministerial standing of the Universalists Aylett Raines: "Brother Raines . . . has been with me during the last several months, and we have freely unbosomed ourselves to each other. He is philosophically a Restorationist [Universalist] and I am a Calvinist, but notwithstanding the difference of opinion between us, I would put my right hand into the fire and have it burnt off before I would hold up my hands against him" (Robert Richardson, *Memoirs of Alexander Campbell*, vol. 1 [St. Louis: John Burns, 1868]: vol. 2 [Cincinnati: Standard Publishing, 1890]: 2 vols., 2:245).

30. Ibid., 1:23.

31. Ibid., 1:21.

32. McAllister, *Thomas Campbell*, 29-30.

33. McAllister and Tucker, *Journey in Faith*, 97.

34. McAllister, *Thomas Campbell*, 44-56.

35. McAllister and Tucker, *Journey in Faith*, 99-101.

36. David M. Thompson, "The Irish Background to Thomas Campbell's *Declaration and Address*," *Discipliana* 46 (2:Summer 1986):23-27.

37. McAllister, *Thomas Campbell*, 78-83.

38. This judgment is based upon the fact that the *Declaration and Address*

is regarded as important by writers in all three of the major contemporary religious communities that trace their origins to the Campbell-Stone movement. In contrast, the *Last Will and Testament of the Springfield Presbytery* is somewhat played down in the work of James DeForest Murch, who represents the undenominational fellowship of Christian Churches and Churches of Christ. See James DeForest Murch, *Christians Only: A History of the Restoration Movement* (Cincinnati: Standard Publishing, 1962), 35-52 and 87-90, for his differing treatment and emphasis with regard to these documents.

39. Bess White Cochran and Louis Cochran, *Captives of the Word* (Garden City, New Jersey: Doubleday & Co., 1969), 6.

40. Thomas Campbell, "To the Editor of the *Millennial Harbinger,*" *Millennial Harbinger* 7 (May 1836):214.

41. *Declaration and Address; Last Will and Testament*, 27.

42. T[homas] C[ampbell], in *Millennial Harbinger* 6 (June 1835):272.

43. Thomas Campbell, "Christian Union," *Millennial Harbinger*, n.s., 3 (April 1839):164.

44. Thomas Campbell, "Christianity," *Millennial Harbinger*, ser. 3, 1 (November 1844):481.

45. *Declaration and Address; Last Will and Testament*, 30.

46. Ibid.; Editor [Barton Warren Stone], "Sundays and Sunday Mails," *Christian Messenger* 4 (May 1830):140-41; Ed. C. B. [Alexander Campbell], "Hear the Priestly Hierarchs!," *Christian Baptist* 7 (June 1830):279-80; and Osborn's citation of Walter Scott in *Experiment in Liberty*, 29.

47. Osborn quotes both Thomas and Alexander Campbell in this connection (*Experiment in Liberty*, 24). See also Stone, "Reflections of Old Age," 125, for an example of the Campbell-Stone movement's tendency to denounce both "papists and Protestants" for their polities. Alexander Campbell's anti-Catholicism is given a similar context in A[lexander] C[ampbell], "The Seven Ecclesiastic Isms: Patriarchism, Papalism, Protestantism, Episcopalianism, Presbyterianism, Congregationalism, Methodism," *Millennial Harbinger*, ser. 4, 5 (July 1855):361-63. However, Alexander Campbell's understanding of history was much more sympathetic to Protestantism. See his Preface to *A Connected View of the Principles and Rules by which the Living Oracles May Be Intelligibly and Certainly Interpreted; of the Foundation on which All Christians May Form One Communion and of the Capital Positions Sustained in the Attempt to Restore the Original Gospel and Order of Things; Containing the Principal Extras of the "Millennial Harbinger," Revised and Corrected* (Bethany, [West] Virginia: M'Vay & Ewing, 1835), 3-4. Walter Scott shared this view of history and referred to it in a way that hinted at its wide currency: "The history of Christianity, from Christ to

the Millennium, may be divided into three parts, *Primitive Christianity*, the *Apostasy*, and the *Reformation*" ("The Reformation," *Evangelist* 1 [January 1832]:19).

48. Alfred T. DeGroot and Winfred E. Garrison, *The Disciples of Christ: A History*, 2nd ed. (St. Louis: Bethany Press, 1958), 141.

49. Ibid., 142.

50. Ibid., 143-44.

51. McAllister and Tucker, *Journey in Faith*, 116.

52. Ibid. For a discussion of the idea of "unity as given" in the Campbell-Stone movement, see Ronald E. Osborn, "One Holy Catholic and Apostolic Church: The Continuing Witness of Disciples of Christ," in W. B. Blakemore, gen. ed., *The Renewal of Church: The Panel of Scholars Reports*, vol. 1: *The Reformation of Tradition*, ed. Ronald E. Osborn; vol. 2: *The Restructure of Theology*, ed. Ralph G. Wilburn: vol. 3 : *The Revival of the Churches*, ed. W. B. Blakemore, 3 vols. (St. Louis: Bethany Press, 1963) (hereafter cited as Blakemore, gen. ed., *Panel of Scholars Reports*), 1:306.

53. McAllister and Tucker, *Journey in Faith*, 116-17.

54. "The Biography of Eld. Barton Warren Stone, Written By Himself: With Additions and Reflections. By Elder John Rogers" (Cincinnati: Published for the Author by J. A. & U. P. James, 1847), in *The Cane Ridge Reader*, ed. Hoke S. Dickinson (Cane Ridge, Ky.: n.p., [ca. 1972]), 60.

55. McAllister, *Thomas Campbell*, 156.

56. McAllister and Tucker, *Journey in Faith*, 119-22.

57. In the years between the beginning of Alexander Campbell's periodical the *Christian Baptist* (1823) and 1830, it became increasingly clear that the Campbells' association with the Baptists was mutually unsatisfactory. The "Campbellites" ceased to be even nominal Baptists with the dissolution of the Mahoning Baptist Association in 1830. Alexander also dropped the "Baptist" from his editorial identity with the launching of the *Millennial Harbinger* in 1830. See McAllister and Tucker, *Journey in Faith*, 135-45.

58. Editor [Alexander Campbell], "A Restoration of the Ancient Order of Things, No. 1," *Christian Baptist* 2 (February 1825; reprint ed.; Nashville: Gospel Advocate Co., 1955-56):136 (page references are to the reprint edition).

59. Richard T. Hughes has written succinctly that Alexander Campbell's restorationism was, ultimately, forward-looking. Campbell believed that "a complete restoration of the apostolic institutions would transform human society and launch the millennial dawn" ("Apocalyptic Origins of Churches of Christ," 186). Hiram Lester has also sketched Campbell's millennialist philosophy of

history and pointed out its transformative focus on "social amelioration" ("Alexander Campbell's Millennial Program," 38).

60. Editor [Alexander Campbell], "To Elder William Jones, of London; Letter VIII," *Millennial Harbinger* 7 (January 1836):27.

61. Murch, *Christians Only*, 71.

62. A[lexander] C[ampbell], "Necessity of Evangelical Reformation, and the Character of It," *Millennial Harbinger*, ser. 3, 4 (September 1847):487.

63. See the *Millennial Harbinger*, ser. 3, 4 (1847):31, 78, 165, 217, 253.

64. Alexander Campbell, "Seven Ecclesiastic Isms," 363.

65. Alexander Campbell, "To Elder William Jones," 29.

66. Alexander Campbell, *A Connected View*, 118-19.

67. Ibid., 199.

68. A[lexander] C[ampbell], "Union of Christians," *Millennial Harbinger*, n.s., 3 (May 1839):212.

69. Thomas Campbell, "To the Editor," 215.

70. "Benson," quoted by Alexander Campbell on the title pages of the seven bound volumes of the *Christian Baptist*.

71. Alexander Campbell, "Hear the Priestly Hierarchs," 280.

72. Editor [Alexander Campbell], "A Restoration of the Ancient Order of Things, No. II," *Christian Baptist* 2 (April 1825; reprint ed.):173.

73. Dwight E. Stevenson, *Walter Scott: Voice of the Golden Oracle—A Biography* (St. Louis: Christian Board of Publication, 1946), 18-23.

74. Murch, *Christians Only*, 97.

75. Stevenson, in *Walter Scott* says, "It was a 'Haldane' church" (24). However, McAllister and Tucker say in *Journey in Faith* that "Forrester was ... the leader of a small congregation of 'primitive Christians' similar to those of the Haldanes in Scotland" (130). Scott's most recent biographer agrees with Stevenson that it was a "Haldanean congregation" (William A. Gerrard, III, *A Biographical Study of Walter Scott: American Frontier Evangelist* [Joplin, MO: College Press, 1992], 21).

76. Murch, *Christians Only*, 98.

77. Stevenson, *Walter Scott*, 24, 26-27.

78. Ibid., 26-27.

79. Ibid., 28. Stevenson quotes the pamphlet, which he calls *On Baptism* from William Baxter, *Life of Elder Walter Scott* (Cincinnati: Bosworth, Chase & Hall, 1874), 52. Baxter quotes the pamphlet at length without identifying the author or clearly indicating the title of the work. He does state that it was published by a Scotch Baptist congregation in New York in 1820 (46). DeGroot quotes from the same pamphlet in *Disciple Thought*, citing it as Henry Errett,

An Essay on the Order and Discipline of the Apostolic Churches (New York: 1811). See DeGroot, *Disciple Thought*, 106, n. 9. Gerrard confirms the Errett authorship (Gerrard, *Walter Scott: American Frontier Evangelist*, 22).

80. Ibid., 36.

81. Murch, *Christians Only*, 99.

82. Walter Scott, *The Gospel Restored* (Cincinnati: O. H. Donogh, 1836), in the Preface, quoted in DeGroot, *Restoration Principle*, 143.

83. Baxter, *Walter Scott*, 108, quoted in DeGroot, *Restoration Principle*, 143.

84. A[lexander] Campbell, "Letters from Brother Campbell and Brother Scott," *Evangelist* 7 (November 1839):259.

85. Editor [Alexander Campbell], in *Millennial Harbinger* 2 (October 1831):480.

86. Stevenson, *Walter Scott*, 74.

87. McAllister and Tucker, *Journey in Faith*, 133-34.

88. Eikner used the phrase "legalistic restorationism" to describe the attitude of one group of second-generation leaders in the Campbell-Stone movement ("Nature of the Church," 182-220). The role of Walter Scott in preparing a constituency for the legalistic leaders was suggested to me, in part, by Paul A. Crow, Jr., in the interview cited above.

89. Beazley, "Who Are the Disciples," 27-39.

90. W[alter] S[cott], in *Evangelist* 6 (April 1838):90.

91. Walter Scott, *To Themilion: The Union of Christians on Christian Principles* (Cincinnati: C. A. Morgan & Co., 1850), 46.

92. Walter Scott, *The Messiahship, or Great Demonstration, Written for the Union of Christians, on Christian Principles, as Plead for in the Current Reformation* ([Cincinnati: H. S. Bosworth, 1859] facsimile ed., Kansas City, Mo.: Old Paths Book Club, n.d.), 321, quoted in Osborn, *Experiment in Liberty*, 29.

93. Wrather, *Creative Freedom in Action*, 9.

94. Stevenson, *Walter Scott*, 116.

95. Murch, *Christians Only*, 104.

96. Walter Scott, "Organization and Co-operation," *Carthage Evangelist* 11 (July 1843):54, quoted in John Watson Neth, *Walter Scott Speaks: A Handbook of Doctrine* (Milligan College, TN: Emmanuel School of Religion, 1967), 93-94.

97. Walter Scott did not maintain a consistent opposition to extracongregational cooperation, however. See for example, Walter Scott, "The American Christian Missionary Society: Address," *Millennial Harbinger*, ser. 4, 5 (February 1855):76-90.

98. Wrather, *Creative Freedom in Action*, 10.

99. A[lexander] C[ampbell], "Church Organization, No. IV," *Millennial Harbinger*, ser. 3, 6 (May 1849):272, quoted in Stevenson, *Walter Scott*, 117.

100. McAllister and Tucker, *Journey in Faith*, 170.

101. A[lexander] C[ampbell], "Church Organization—No. III," *Millennial Harbinger*, ser. 3, 6 (May 1849):270.

CHAPTER II

THE DIVERGENCE IN THE INTERPRETATION OF THE IDEALS OF THE CAMPBELL-STONE MOVEMENT IN ITS SECOND GENERATION

If the years preceding the death of Alexander Campbell may be regarded as the "founding" or first generation of the Campbell-Stone movement, then the second generation may be said to have begun with his death in 1866. Between 1866 and the "official" recognition in 1906 of the existence of two separate bodies which had emerged from the Campbell-Stone community, there were many important leaders who were active in the movement. As historians have noted, the principal leaders were editors. Four of these important editors represent well the developing divergent ideologies among second-generation followers of the Campbells and Stone. Two of these men, James Harvey Garrison and Isaac Errett, have come to be regarded as the principal leaders, in their generation, of what came to be the Christian Church (Disciples of Christ). Significantly, Errett is also a hero to writers in the undenominational fellowship of Christian Churches and Churches of Christ, and represents the last national leader of the Campbell-Stone movement to be relatively untouched by the second major schism within it. The third, David Lipscomb, is viewed as the leading figure of the second generation by the Churches of Christ. And the fourth, J. W. McGarvey, is held in especially high regard by the undenominational fellowship of Christian Churches and Churches of Christ, and embodies many of the issues involved in the second schism.[1] An examination of the views of these four individuals on the basic values of the Campbell-Stone movement—unity, restoration, liberty, and mission—will illustrate the ideological development of the movement in its middle period, show the basis for the schism that came to full blossom in the second generation, and begin to identify the issues which underlay the second schism.

In the dates of his birth and death, Isaac Errett preceded the other three leaders; he was born in 1820 and died in 1888.[2] In *The Disciples of Christ: A History*, Alfred T. DeGroot and W. E. Garrison gave what became the best-known assessment of Errett's significance from the point of view of the Christian Church(es) (Disciples of Christ): "More than to any other journal and person, it was to the *Christian Standard* and Isaac Errett that the Disciples were indebted for being saved from becoming a fissiparous sect of jangling legalists."[3] James DeForest Murch, an historian of the undenominational fellowship of Christian

Churches and Churches of Christ, is even more laudatory. Murch writes of Errett:

> A figure now arose who was in many respects as significant to the Restoration movement as Alexander Campbell in his day. In the midst of controversy and confusion, a leader of understanding, insight, and broad vision was essential to preserve and perpetuate the original purposes of the movement. Isaac Errett possessed all these qualities and more.[4]

It was not immediately apparent that Isaac Errett would rise to journalistic prominence in the post-Civil War era. Until his death in 1866, Alexander Campbell was doubtless the most influential editor in the Campbell-Stone movement. In the years immediately following Campbell's death, the most influential periodical in the movement was Benjamin Franklin's Cincinnati-based *American Christian Review*.[5] Franklin's enduring significance as an editor was diminished by the fact that Nashville (where David Lipscomb and the *Gospel Advocate* were headquartered) was on the ascendancy as the center of the point of view that Franklin championed, while the future of Cincinnati, and the Northern membership in general, lay with Isaac Errett and his *Christian Standard*.[6]

David Edwin Harrell, Jr., writes that "Isaac Errett's influence was unequaled in the church in the 1880's and the *Christian Standard* shared in this personal prestige." Churches of Christ historian Earl I. West dissents on the issue of this "prestige."[7] But Harrell finds an Isaac Errett that lies somewhere between the "savior" of DeGroot and Garrison's famous view and West's "prophet of digression." Harrell calls Errett a "moderate" and "well versed in the literalistic nuances of the Disciples tradition."[8] Errett's own pen lends support to Harrell's view. The classic elements of Campbell-Stone tradition come forward through Errett as an interwoven pattern of commitments to unity, restoration, liberty, and mission.

Errett's commitment to restoration is evidenced in the motto that appeared on the front page of the *Christian Standard*: "Devoted to the Restoration of Primitive Christianity—Its Doctrine, Its Ordinances and Its Fruits."[9] Errett expected one of the principal "fruits" of the restoration to be the unity of Christians. Christians primitivism was, in Errett's mind, the only means to Christian union. In light of the subsequent history of the Campbell-Stone movement, it is significant that, like the early Alexander Campbell, Isaac Errett identified individuals rather than communities as the appropriate unit of union. Errett had an often controversial penchant for writing as if a spokesperson of

Divergence in Interpretation

the entire Campbell-Stone movement.[10] However, when he wrote of "Our Work" in an 1875 editorial, his description of the historic plea of his movement was such that few in it could dissent.

> We plead then for Christian union—not a fraternization of sects and parties, but a union of individuals to Christ himself. We urge the primitive faith and the primitive method of confessing that faith. We propose to all the simple yet significant institutions of the gospel—the primitive methods of discipleship—the original foundation of Christianity as the only true and trustworthy means of terminating religious division, and enabling all true believers to maintain the unity of the Spirit in the bond of peace.[11]

Errett elsewhere clarifies his reservations (those characteristic of the movement, in his view) about other Protestant communities and in so doing discloses his own understanding of the necessity of both ecclesiological (church structural) and, to a degree, theological (in the realm of religious "opinion") liberty. Like writers in the first generation of the Campbell-Stone movement, Errett finds the Roman Catholic Church to be the perfect foil against which to state his community's commitments. Again, though Errett and others of his faith might not have been completely untainted by anti-Catholic bigotry, his statements relative to Catholicism and to the "Protestant sects" (which, in Errett's view, had been unsuccessful because they had not moved far enough away from Catholicism) are best understood as an expression in negative terms of a commitment to Christian primitivism with its attendant union, mission, and *liberty*.

> They [members of the Campbell-Stone movement] regard the Protestant sects as the product of partially successful efforts to *recover from the spiritual thraldom* and corruption of the Roman Catholic Church—the great apostasy. But they regard them as failing to reach Jerusalem, and some of them as scarcely beyond the walls of Babylon. Their substitution of sects for the one Church of Christ, of human creeds for the Word of God, of *powerful ecclesiastical organizations for the simple individual church organization of the Scriptures*, of philosophical speculations and *theological dogmas* for the simple faith of Christ, which the Scriptures teach, and the corrupt superstitions of Rome, which yet cling to them, as in their *hierarchical authorities*, their infant sprinkling, etc.: all these they regard as standing in the

way of that complete *restoration* of the simple, spiritual religion of apostolic times, and especially of that *union* without which the *mission* of the Church cannot be fulfilled. Therefore, while rejoicing in all that has been accomplished for reformation, they lift a cry for a further movement, having for its goal the complete restoration of the religion of the New Testament.[12] (Italics mine.)

In addition to a clear commitment to liberty (liberation from "thraldom"), the linkage among all four of the movement's characteristic values is evidenced: liberty enables restoration (by eliminating the "thraldom" of "dogmas" and "hierarchial authorities" that stand in the way); restoration, in turn, creates union; and union makes possible the fulfillment of the Church's mission.

Further evidence that Roman Catholicism was principally understood by Errett as a symbol of opposition to freedom is found in this explicit statement:

Look at Roman Catholicism, with its shameless avowal of the despotic spirit and doctrines of the darkest ages, and its impious claim to papal infallibility; its open hostility to freedom of conscience, freedom of speech, free schools and State education.[13]

Against the "despotic spirit" and "impious claim to papal infallibility" of Catholicism, Errett proposed what he regarded as the freer spirit and the pious claim of biblical infallibility. He advocated "the alone-sufficiency and all-sufficiency of the Bible, as a revelation of the divine character and will, and of the gospel of grace by which we are saved; and as a rule of faith and practice."[14] But this biblicism was intended to be liberating. Errett insisted upon "the largest liberty to explore the realms of revelation and learn more and more of the will of God."[15] He thus asserted simultaneously a biblistic restorationism—Christian primitivism—*and* a commitment to ecclesiological and theological liberty.

Although the Roman Catholic Church and its "despotic spirit" was perhaps Errett's favorite object for condemnation, he would condemn those even in his own movement who wished to "compel uniformity." When the *Apostolic Times*, a periodical launched to advocate "the primitive faith, and the primitive practice, without enlargement or diminution, without innovation or modification,"[16] claimed that the Campbell-Stone movement was tending toward apostasy, Errett replied:

Any attempt to compel uniformity in thinking or in practice, where the Apostles have left us free, is virtual apostasy. . . .

Divergence in Interpretation

> Two things it strikes us, must be carefully kept in mind, if we would legitimately work out the spiritual emancipation contemplated in the reformation which we plead.
>
> 1. The necessity for free and unembarrassed research with a view to grow in grace and in knowledge. . . . Grant that errors may sometimes be thrust upon us. Free and kind discussion will soon correct them. . . . Murderous stifling of free thought and free speech . . . not only *renders union worthless by the sacrifice of liberty*, but will defeat its own purpose and compel, in time, new revolutionary movements.
>
> 2. The absence of all right to control our brethren where Christ has left them free. Such freedom may sometimes alarm us. Creedbound communities may lift their hands in holy horror at the "latitudinarianism" that we allow. But it is not worthwhile to accept principles unless we are willing to follow them to their legitimate results; and we insist that Romans xiv. allows a *very large liberty* which we have no right to trench on except with the plea of the demands of Christian love.[17] (Italics mine.)

Errett not only insists upon a kind of liberty that the historic churches ("creedbound communities") might label "latitudinarianism," but even alleges that the cherished value of union would be "worthless" without liberty. And this insistence is not in the face of the challenge of Roman Catholicism or of the "Protestant sects," but rather a response to the accusations of conservatives of his own movement.

Isaac Errett's statement on the dependency of the fulfillment of the Church's mission upon the achievement of union was noted earlier. Like the leaders of the first generation of the Campbell-Stone movement, Errett looked to the prayer of Jesus as written in the seventeenth chapter of John's gospel for the integration of union and evangelistic mission. The following excerpt from an 1868 editorial not only shows *this* integration, but, again, echoes Errett's understanding of the extent and grounds of Christian liberty.

> Let the bond of union among the baptized be *Christian character* in place of *orthodoxy*—right doing in place of *exact thinking*; and outside of plain precepts, let all acknowledge the liberty of all, nor seek to impose limitations on their brethren, other than those of the law of love.

> A union of Christians thus effected would have all the grandeur of a miracle in its superhuman triumph over the narrowness and bitterness of sect. . . . Infidelity, stripped of its supplies, would grow pale and die; Romanism would yield before the enthusiasm and power of God's united freemen. . . . Sweetly would the words of prayer that came from the agonized heart of the sufferer on the brink of Gethsemane's strife, echo along the hill-sides, and through the valleys and over the seas, until every heart would drink in their matchless inspiration: "Father, I pray for all who shall believe on me through their word— THAT THEY MAY ALL BE ONE; as thou, Father art in me, and I in thee, that they may be one in us; *that the world may believe that thou hast sent me.*"[18]

Since Errett so clearly advocated the four-part ideology of the Campbell-Stone movement that had come forward from that movement's first generation, it may not be immediately clear what the grounds for controversy were between Errett and those of similar views and others in the movement. Disagreement arose not on the *validity* of these basic values but on their definition and application. Additionally, the divergence of definition and application of these principles was, as historians have noted, compounded by social, regional, and economic issues. This is best illustrated by turning to the editor who best represents the side opposite from Errett in each of these social, regional, and economic issues that skewed the interpretation of the movement's basic ideals—David Lipscomb.

David Edwin Harrell, Jr., reminds his readers that "increasingly the center of conservatism in the church became the South, and the most powerful of the conservative papers by the 1880's was the *Gospel Advocate*, published in Nashville." David Lipscomb and Tolbert Fanning edited the *Advocate* at the time of its rebirth in 1866. However, Fanning resigned shortly thereafter and Lipscomb's coeditor for the next generation was Elisha J. Sewell. "Stubborn, caustic, and plodding, the editors of the *Advocate* virtually defined conservative Disciples orthodoxy. The *Gospel Advocate* was the nucleus which the Churches of Christ gathered around."[19]

The *Gospel Advocate*'s editors declared their view of the Bible and its place as the supreme religious authority as well as their view of the Church[20] in the periodical's prospectus:

> Our purpose is to maintain the right of Jesus Christ to rule the world, the supremacy of the Sacred Scriptures in matters spiritual,

and to encourage an investigation of every subject connected with the church of Christ, which we may consider of practical interest. "The Kingdom of God" was a real, permanent institution, "the pillar and support of the truth," upon a proper appreciation of which the welfare of the world and the happiness of man depend; her origin, organization, history, labor, mission; her relation to worldly powers, civil, military and religious, and her final triumph, will occupy much of our attention.[21]

A strain of biblicism is evident in this prospectus. The restorationist's understanding of the Church is also implied here. As will later become clear, "the Kingdom of God," in Lipscomb's understanding, consisted only of his own religious community; the historic churches fell into the category of "worldly powers . . . religious."

If a commitment to biblistic restorationism is clear in Lipscomb, what is less clear is a commitment to the historically related Campbell-Stone ideal of Christian union. Here Lipscomb sounded a more uncertain tone. He did suggest that the divisive ingredient in the practice of Christians was their insistence upon practices not authorized by the Bible:

Let each man appeal to the Bible only. . . . Opinion then will give place to Christian faith, convenience, and preference, and expediency to divine authority. How common it is for Christians to retain their distinct peculiarities, because they *are not forbidden by the word of God*. This is a dangerous principle. It is one of the rocks on which sects split.[22]

Clearly, in Lipscomb's mind the union of Christians was dependent upon a particular brand of biblistic restorationism—a doctrine of *sola scriptura* which constituted an absolute distinction between revealed truth and human opinion. Further, the Church was to make not a single "innovation" in its practices.

Although union is desirable in Lipscomb's view, "innovation" makes division inevitable:

We have not doubted, for years, that if the course of adding innovation to innovation, pursued by many, is persisted in, that division and separation will come. Nay, it ought to come. God will cause it to come. . . . If a separation will, and ought to come, it may be asked, how will it be brought about? All the true disciple has to do, is to firmly stand for the truth, and to be true to it. God in His providence will then bring it.[23]

With these words Lipscomb distances himself and those with his point of view from the responsibility for division. Rather, it is the responsibility of God and those who have added "innovation to innovation." This shows a reluctance on Lipscomb's part to abandon a nominal commitment to the ideal of union. Elsewhere he made this reluctance even more explicit:

> No sin is more severely condemned, no sin is denounced as having more fatal and ruinous tendency, and Christians are entreated, admonished, besought to avoid no sin more earnestly or frequently than the sin of division among the members of the church of God. . . .
>
> The integrity, union and harmony of the church of God are dear to the Savior. To destroy these is the greatest of sins before God. We have never seen a circumstance arise in which we were willing to advise division . . . in a church of Christ. Our friends have frequently, when evils have entered a church, blamed us for not advising division, withdrawal from a church, etc. They have chided us with cowardice in action—we plead this. We are too cowardly to advise a step in religion never advised by the Spirit of God. The Spirit of God, so far as we have learned, never saw a church of God so corrupted as to advise withdrawal from it.[24]

Lipscomb's references to union in the Church, however, had little, if any, application beyond the narrow confines of the Campbell-Stone movement. The historic churches, "the sects" in Lipscomb's terminology, were to be denounced. Equally worthy of condemnation was any rapprochement between the Campbell-Stone movement and other denominations. "To join a sect or party in religion is a crime against God."[25] Lipscomb wrote these words in 1878. Later, when some of the "progressives" in the movement began to express sympathy for some kind of federation among Protestants, Lipscomb labeled the suggestion "federated rebellion against God."[26] Lipscomb demonstrated the difference between his own view of the historic churches and that of others in the Campbell-Stone community with his accusation that: "The leading advocates of the [Missionary] Society within my knowledge all look with approval upon the recognition of the sects as Christian bodies, and close affiliation with them."[27]

Ultimately any inclusive understanding of Christian union in Lipscomb was negated by his commitment to an understanding of Church which extended only to his own community:

> One cannot be immersed by a Church of Christ preacher and remain a Presbyterian—all must be done to obey God. For a person to be baptized to join a church other than God's church is to take the pledge of fidelity to God in order to dishonor him.[28]

The clear implication is that Lipscomb's church is God's Church. By 1905, Lipscomb was identifying exclusivity as a virtue characteristic of God himself and challenging the Church to embody it as well:

> But until the Christian Church takes this high and holy ground, until she becomes exclusive, until she learns fully to appreciate her peculiar privileges and glorious prerogatives and to guard them with a jealous eye, even as God is a jealous God, the cause of true Christianity will continue to pine and languish.[29]

Lipscomb represents an early articulation of the characteristic pattern of the Churches of Christ in emphasizing the value of (biblistic) restorationism to the point that the ideal of union is jettisoned or given a severely circumscribed interpretation. This process is repeated with respect to mission and liberty as well.

In relation to the mission of the Church to evangelize the world, Lipscomb's restorationism limited the means by which this goal could be pursued. Specifically he opposed the creation of missionary organizations or societies: "A chief objection we make to your societies is, that they ignore the overruling and guiding hand of God, and organize a human association to do that which God has reserved for himself."[30] That this conflict was between the restoration and mission values is evident in the reproach placed upon "human" organizations—that they were "unscriptural." Lipscomb opposed both the American Christian Missionary Society and the Louisville Plan (a plan for creating a delegate convention for the churches of the Campbell-Stone movement) on the grounds that they were "alike unknown to the scriptures."[31] Here it becomes evident, too, that Lipscomb's view of the Campbell-Stone value of liberty is circumscribed by his commitment to restorationism. Clearly, he did not think, as Alexander Campbell apparently had, that the churches of his movement were free to organize for mission.

One of the characteristic expressions of the Campbell-Stone commitment to liberty had been the insistence upon liberty of individual opinion. This was another form of liberty about which David Lipscomb stated his reservations:

> For a man to make an opinion a principle of action, where others must act with him, is to force them to conform to his opinion, or to withdraw from his association. When a man has an opinion that an organ is admissible in the church service, and forces it in, he compels every man to accede to his opinion, or to withdraw from the church. When a man holds the opinion that sprinkling is baptism, and insists upon acting upon that opinion, he forces everyone in the church to accede to his opinion, or to withdraw from the church. This is making an opinion the test of fellowship; making others accept and act on our opinion, or withdraw from the fellowship of the church.[32]

Thus Lipscomb supported the notion that one could *hold* an opinion freely in private. However, in matters such as instrumental music and baptism, the freedom to *act* upon an opinion was, again, severely circumscribed by the restoration ideal. Lipscomb himself recognized the conflict between restoration and liberty, but he saw it in terms of "legalism" versus "license."

> We have been pained for some time to see reproach cast upon those who insist upon faithful obedience to the law of God, as the condition of his blessing, as *legalists*, and the principle that required the submission as *legalism*. . . . Some of our progressive brethren have even gone so far as to deny there is any law in the New Testament as there was in the Old. . . .
> The tendency of our brethren's speculative distinctions on these subjects is to weaken the sense of obligation to comply with the full requirements of God's will, and to give people license to follow some impulse, passion or prejudice which they may conceive to be the suggestion of faith within, that becomes law to itself.[33]

Having seen that the ideals of Christian union, liberty (to organize or to act upon opinion), and mission were at the very least severely circumscribed by Lipscomb's understanding of the restoration ideal, we recall that Lipscomb's *ideological* development is inseparable from the divergent *sociological* development of the North and South in the post-Civil War period. That the direction of David Lipscomb's thought somehow expressed the perspective as well as helped shape the thought of Southerners within the Campbell-Stone community is suggested by Lipscomb's own sectional views.

> The tendency of Northern thought infecting all the religious bodies has been towards rationalism and unbelief. There are many individual exceptions, but this is the manifest tendency in all the churches...
>
> This tendency to rationalism—to the exaltation of human reason at the expense of divine authority—is as marked among the Disciples as among others. Hence all the innovations upon apostolic precept and practice have come from the North.[34]

Lipscomb saw the opposite tendency in the South:

> Our Southern people while not zealous and earnest in their religious service as they should be, kept themselves free from the infidel influences that so largely prevail in the North. Respect for religion, and at least a passive recognition of the truth of the Bible ... are much more common among all classes in the South than in the North.[35]

David Lipscomb represents the emergent view of the predominantly Southern Churches of Christ. His is a sectionally influenced[36] version of the classic Campbell-Stone ideology which collapses or severely limits the ideals of union, mission, and liberty into a particularly legalistic and biblistic restorationism.

The third of the four journalists who represent the diverging interpretations of the ideology of the Campbell-Stone movement as it experienced its second generation is James H. Garrison. In the Preface to his biography of Garrison, William E. Tucker writes:

> Since the middle period of Disciples history was one of theological reconstruction and rapid institutional growth, it is doubly important that the central figures in that era receive adequate treatment.
>
> Certainly one of the two or three most significant leaders in this transitional middle period was James Harvey Garrison (1842-1931). ... For over sixty years (1869-1931) he edited or contributed regularly to the *Christian-Evangelist* (and its predecessors), the journal which in 1912 became the "official" weekly periodical of the brotherhood.[37]

Tucker traces the career of Garrison through several of the major controversies of the Campbell-Stone movement's second generation. Among these were controversies over the understanding of baptism and of the status of unimmersed persons in the Church, a series of issues related to the historical-critical approach to the Bible, the changing interpretation of the restoration or "Christian primitivism" ideal of the movement, the Christian union ideal (particularly as it related to federation), and the conflicts among rival publishers in the Campbell-Stone movement.[38]

Garrison's long career makes him an individual who spans the distance between the first generation of the Campbell-Stone movement and the emergence of the issues that made an impact on that movement in the twentieth century. With Garrison the issues emerge which were destined to create the *second* major schism in the Campbell-Stone movement.

The Garrison of the 1880's and earlier would articulate the ideology of the Campbell-Stone movement in the familiar terms of "union through restoration":

> A Body of religious people, convinced of the evil of division, resolve to seek a remedy for the state of things in a complete return to the faith, the doctrine, the ordinances and the life of the New Testament Church. To realize this high aim they have rejected all human formulations of doctrines as wanting in divine authority, and have committed themselves, unreservedly, to the sole guidance of the Holy Scriptures, by whose teachings they have been led to discard infant baptism, sprinkling or pouring, and all party names, and to restore the "one baptism" of the New Testament with the primitive confession of faith which preceded it. Thus, having for their guide a common Book—the Bible—and for their creed the original and divinely revealed confession of faith, and the "one baptism" recognized by all as genuine, and wearing names which are common to all Christ's followers, with Christian character as the only test of fellowship, the Disciples claim to have made some progress toward a true Catholicity, and in the interest of Christian union.[39]

The Christian primitivism, the biblicism, the insistence upon restoration as the means to Christian union is undoubtedly present. However, the authentic Campbellism of the Lunenburg Letter is present, too.[40] Freedom of opinion is upheld in the identification of "Christian character as the only test of fellowship."

Divergence in Interpretation

Having upheld union, restoration, and liberty, Garrison immediately completes the quartet with special emphasis: "But there is another department of Christian work not less important than the union of Christians, and to which, indeed, such union looks as its chief end, namely, the conversion of the world to Christ."[41] This statement is significant because it implies a distinction among the values of the movement. The "missional" value is the *ultimate* value to which the union value is instrumental.[42] This does not demean, however, the union ideal. Relatively early in Garrison's journalistic career, he expressed his high devotion to the idea of Christian union:

> If the religious movement known as "the reformation of the nineteenth century" had produced no other effect than to infuse the desire for union among the religious parties of the day, it would have been worth infinitely more than all the prayers, tears, toils, sacrifices and precious lives it has cost.[43]

Garrison also displayed, in 1870, the typical early Disciples view of Roman Catholicism, which may be understood as both a motivating factor behind Protestant unionism and as an expression of the Campbell-Stone commitment to ecclesiastical liberty. "Shall we sit in cool deliberation on the propriety of uniting our scattered forces, while the legions of the pope and the cohorts of infidelity—the two co-operating wings of Satan's army—are moving in solid phalanx upon our broken columns and divided ranks! God forbid!"[44]

A more positive expression of Garrison's understanding of liberty in religious organization is his approving description of the polity of the Campbell-Stone movement in his day.

> As to form of church government among the Disciples, it is congregational, very similar to that among Baptists. Our State and National organizations are missionary societies for co-operative work in spreading the gospel at home and abroad, and have no legislative or judicial function in reference to matters of faith and practice.[45]

Obviously, in contrast to the views of David Lipscomb and his Southern brothers and sisters, Garrison supported the notion that Christians were free to organize for mission.

Another expression of Garrison's understanding of the liberty ideal came in the traditional arena of individual liberty of opinion. A case in point is his support of the liberty of the individual to determine his/her own fitness to partake of the Lord's Supper:

> The vexed question of "open" or "close" communion cuts no figure whatever, as a disturbing issue in our American churches. . . . We neither "invite" nor "debar." We believe that the Lord's supper is for the Lord's people, and that He has issued his own invitation. We spread the table, repeat his invitation, but institute no inquisition to find out if any of the proposed communicants be unimmersed, relying on the faithful preaching of the word and self-examination as the best preventatives against unauthorized participation in this memorial feast.[46]

Admittedly, this is a cautious expression of the ideal of freedom. However, Garrison increasingly evolved in the direction of a freer and more inclusive interpretation of the Campbell-Stone ideology.

The factor which apparently pushed J. H. Garrison in the direction of "increased tolerance and charity" was his conviction of the primacy of mission among the ideals of his movement. This is clear in his 1893 discussion of "The Parliament of Religions":

> With increased tolerance and charity, a better understanding between Christianity and other religions, a higher appreciation of Christ among Christians, resulting from a study of comparative religions, increased activity in missionary work, and a closer union of the followers of Christ, Christianity would move forward with quickened pace in its world-conquering mission.[47]

A decade later, in the midst of the storm of controversy over the idea of federation, it was again the missionary task of the Church which lay at the base of Garrison's inclusive view of Christianity:

> . . . When I contemplate the appalling darkness that yet lies on pagan lands, and see the wretched condition of millions of our population in this, our own beloved land . . . [I] realize the truth that only a united effort on the part of all who call Jesus Lord . . . can cope successfully with these powers of darkness. I would not, for my life, assume the responsibility of placing the slightest obstacle in the way of a closer co-operation.[48]

Divergence in Interpretation 51

There is, clearly, evidence in Garrison that not all of the four ideals of the Campbell-Stone movement are held equally. In contrast, again, to Lipscomb, for whom the biblistic understanding of restorationism was preeminent and the other values defined and limited in terms of it, Garrison held the value of the Church's missionary task as ultimate. Even the liberty of the Church (as represented by a strictly congregational polity) was not to be allowed to interfere with the accomplishment of the Church's mission:

> One of the lessons which we have learned from the experience of the past is that the theory of church independency which prevents co-operation between churches and individuals, in an orderly and systematic way, for the spread of the gospel, and for doing anything that can be accomplished only by united effort, is a foe to religious progress, an apology for doing nothing, and a hindrance to the evangelization of the world.[49]

The last of the four representative figures from the second generation of the Campbell-Stone movement is J. W. McGarvey.[50] McGarvey was born on 3 March 1829, in Hopkinsville, Kentucky. He entered Bethany College in 1847 and was graduated with honors in 1850. After a short time teaching in an academy he was ordained in 1851 and finally became pastor of a congregation in Lexington, Kentucky, in 1862. In that same year he published his *Commentary on Acts*. Three years later he assumed a professor's chair at the College of the Bible in Lexington.[51] "For nearly half a century, from 1865 to 1911, the name of The College of the Bible was all but synonymous with that of John W. McGarvey."[52] McGarvey conducted the "Biblical Criticism" column of the *Christian Standard* from January 1893 to October 1911.[53] It was from his chair at the College of the Bible and from his column in the *Christian Standard* that "McGarvey labored indefatigably to keep his students and Disciples everywhere from adopting the approach and findings of biblical critics."[54]

In terms of the basic ideals of the Campbell-Stone movement, McGarvey emphasized restorationism—biblicism and Christian primitivism—in a way that severely limited his commitment to Christian union and liberty. However, McGarvey was committed to the missionary ideal of the evangelization of the world *and* he supported missionary societies to undertake the task.[55] The case of McGarvey supports the notion that Southern opposition to the American Christian Missionary Society was largely a sectionally motivated rather than a biblically motivated phenomenon. A staunch biblicism permeates McGarvey's utterances, yet he found no basis in the Bible for opposition to the Society.

The centrality of the Bible, and especially the New Testament, to McGarvey's understanding of the Church and Christian faith is clearly seen in his article, "The Exclusiveness of Our Creed."

> A great deal has been written of late years in our periodicals to show how broad a basis of fellowship is furnished by the simple creed of the New Testament, and this subject has been so emphasized to make the impression on some that in this direction it has no limit. ... We have long emphasized the *in*clusiveness of our Creed; let us now for a time emphasize its *ex*clusiveness....
>
> The Creed, in its narrowest form, as the confession of faith required of candidates for baptism, is the well-known confession first expressed in full by Peter: "Thou art the Christ, the Son of the Living God." ... In the broader sense ... the Creed embraces the whole of the New Testament; and *the man who denies the truth or the authority of any part of the New Testament,* ascertained interpolations excepted, *has denied to that extent the faith which he had previously confessed.*[56] (Italics mine.)

The implications for Christian union are clear. Since the "Creed" of the New Testament Church is an "exclusive" one, the only method of achieving Christian union is through restoration of that "Creed." Thus, to McGarvey, the historic churches ("denominations" or "sects" in a pejorative sense) as well as any Campbell-Stone congregations who recognized them as legitimate were outside of the "exclusive" Christian community.

McGarvey's understanding of the limitation of Christian liberty relative to methods of seeking Christian union is shown in his comment upon a congregation's resolution to admit to fellowship persons from nonimmersionist churches:

> This is a deliberate departure from New Testament order and authority; for, according to the latter, men were baptized into Christ, baptized into the one body of which he is the Head. There is one body and one baptism; but this church proposes to receive men into the one body without baptism; that is, if it claims, as it does, to be a part of the body of Christ. Its act implies that it is a different body—a sect. The procedure cuts it off from the churches of the New Testament order....

Divergence in Interpretation 53

> Strange to say, this divisive resolution is adopted "to illustrate in our practice a method of Christian union." ... If it were adopted generally as a method of union, it would be a union of sects instead of a union of Christians.[57]

McGarvey specifically repudiated the notion earlier asserted by James H. Garrison that Christian character is the only test of fellowship beyond which liberty must be respected:

> It is constantly reiterated by this class of opinionists that so long as they have faith in Jesus Christ, and manifest it by a life in accordance with his teaching, they must be left free to form and announce their own opinions; but this plea, specious as it is, can not be accepted of opinions which contradict express assertions of Christ or his apostles.[58]

Freedom of opinion, the freedom to accept the unimmersed as Christians, and the freedom to "deny the truth or authority of any part of the New Testament" (synonymous to McGarvey with "contradicting the express assertions of Christ or his apostles" and "adopting the approach and findings of biblical critics") were clearly identified by McGarvey as "misapplications" of Christian liberty. Another "misapplication" of the ideals of Christian union and Christian liberty was the federation movement.

McGarvey ridiculed the Council of the Federation of American Churches' consideration of comity in a predictable way:

> The Council . . . recently held a meeting in Louisville, Ky. The *Western Recorder*, published there, says of it editorially: "Dr. E. B. Sanford, the corresponding secretary, said: 'When a community is over-churched, it means giving up the surplus church or churches. Where a church is needed, it means friendly agreement on the church to be placed there.'"
>
> The *Recorder* adds: "According to this, the Federal Council would have a perfect right to close out and put out of business a Methodist, Presbyterian or Baptist church whenever, in its lordly judgment, it should be deemed wise." And I may add that it also means to "close and put out of business" any church of the disciples which might exist in the overchurched community; for it is well known that all the other churches would heartily agree that this would, in every instance, be

the surplus church. "Will you walk into my parlor? said the spider to the fly." And when another church was needed, it would never be a Christian Church.[59]

The churches of the Campbell-Stone movement could not, in McGarvey's view, legitimately involve themselves with federation.

There is much similarity between the views of John W. McGarvey and David Lipscomb. Their unbending anti-historical-critical view of the Bible is similar. Their exclusivist understanding of the Church as coterminous with their own religious community is similar. The dramatic difference between McGarvey and Lipscomb was McGarvey's support of the American Christian Missionary Society. In 1897 McGarvey wrote of the missionary hopes of his movement:

> Fortunately there is no difference of opinion among us as to the wisdom of sending the gospel into those portions of our own country where congregations devoted to the restoration of primitive Christianity are few and feeble.... We know that if we take time by the forelock and plant churches in all these regions they will leaven with the truth the vast masses of human beings soon to be collected there, and that thus we shall be laying a solid foundation for the subsequent evangelization of the whole world.[60]

McGarvey not only expressed his support of the missionary ideal and his hopes for the evangelization of the world, but also exhorted his readers to become supporters of cooperative missionary work:

> My word of exhortation is, that we shall all push forward our work of missions with all our might, doing our very utmost to enlist in the work every disciple of the Lord. Let us stimulate to far greater liberality those who are cooperating with us; and let us enlist others as fast as possible. As yet there is but an infinitesimal number of our brethren who are doing anything at all for the evangelization of the world beyond the bounds of their own congregations; and there is a very small minority of our churches engaged in any kind of cooperation for this divinely appointed work. Let us not rest day or night until every church, and every individual of every church, is doing something. When once they are enlisted in the work, it will be an easy task to induce them to give more liberally.[61]

Divergence in Interpretation

McGarvey's interpretation of the quartet of Campbell-Stone ideals stressed primarily a biblistic restorationism. This emphasis, like Lipscomb's, led to a severe delimitation of the union and liberty ideals. Unlike Lipscomb, McGarvey did support the freedom of Christians to organize cooperatively beyond the congregation for the purpose of evangelism. But, unlike Garrison, McGarvey's zeal for mission did not extend to the point of cooperation with or even recognition of the historic churches as authentically Christian.

The Campbell-Stone movement's ideological divergence in the second generation is revealed in the utterances of the four representative leaders here considered. Although each of them was nominally committed to the interrelated ideals of restoration, union, liberty, and mission, different emphases are clear.

Isaac Errett placed a high value upon liberty, both ecclesiastical and intellectual. He understood restoration as a *means* to Christian union, which was itself a necessary prerequisite for the fulfillment of the Church's evangelistic mission. Also, Errett was a Northerner whose ongoing relationship with the American Christian Missionary Society and Union soldiers like James Garfield fueled the Southern perception that his paper, the *Christian Standard*, was sectionally motivated.[62]

To David Lipscomb, it was a particularly biblistic version of the restoration ideal which was paramount and which defined the other values. Thus, he saw liberty as tending to license, and Christian union as excluding the historic churches. The evangelistic mission of the church could neither be pursued in missionary societies, which were unscriptural, nor in federation efforts involving the historic churches, which were "sects" in the restorationist view. Lipscomb also saw the North as the breeding ground of unbelief.

J. H. Garrison regarded evangelistic mission as the ultimate end of his movement, as Errett had. This was the goal which interpreted the others. Since Garrison saw Christian union as a prerequisite to successful evangelism, in his thought a union-and-mission axis of values comes to the fore and both restoration and liberty, conceived as strict congregationalism, recede.

Finally, the emphases of J. W. McGarvey are virtually indistinguishable from those of Lipscomb, with the sole exception that McGarvey supported the Missionary Society. This difference was soon negated by McGarvey's emerging community, the constituency of the *Christian Standard* after 1900.

---

1. McAllister and Tucker, *Journey in Faith*, 219-21; Earl I. West, *The Search for the Ancient Order: A History of the Restoration Movement*, vol. 2: *1866-1906*

(Indianapolis: Religious Book Service, 1950), 6; Murch, *Christians Only*, 165, 203.

    2. McAllister and Tucker, *Journey in Faith*, 496.

    3. DeGroot and Garrison, *The Disciples of Christ*, 358.

    4. Murch, *Christians Only*, 165; Henry Webb, in the successor volume to Murch's, is slightly more circumspect in his assessment of Errett and even quotes W. E. Garrison (Henry Webb, *In Search of Christian Unity: A History of the Restoration Movement* [Cincinnati: Standard Publishing, 1990], 208-209).

    5. Harrell, *Social History*, 2:17.

    6. Ibid., 18.

    7. West devotes a chapter of his book to refuting the heroic proportions given to Errett by historians of the Campbell-Stone movement from outside the Churches of Christ. West debunks Errett's alleged "qualities" and presents a picture of a "prophet of digression" from the ancient faith and order (*Search for the Ancient Order*, 2:23).

    8. Harrell, *Social History* 2:19, 18.

    9. E.g., *Christian Standard* 6 (7 January 1871).

    10. See McAllister and Tucker's *Journey in Faith* for a brief discussion of one instance in which Errett's attempt to describe the "faith and practice" of his movement proved controversial (244). Murch cites another example—the tract *Our Position*—in which Errett summarized his view of the characteristic beliefs and practices of his community (Murch, *Christians Only*, 172).

    11. [Isaac Errett], "Our Work," *Christian Standard* 10 (29 May 1875):172.

    12. Isaac Errett, "Historico-Doctrinal Sketch of the Disciples, Number Three—Continued," *Christian Standard* 6 (22 April 1871):121.

    13. Isaac Errett, "Opportunity and Opposition: or Seasons of Advantage Also Seasons of Peril: An Address Delivered before the Ohio Christian Missionary Society, at Dayton, O., May 23, 1871," *Christian Standard* 6 (10 June 1871):177.

    14. Isaac Errett, *Our Position: A Brief Statement of the Distinctive Features of the Plea for Reformation Urged by the People Known as Disciples of Christ* (Cincinnati: Standard Publishing Co., 1873), 3.

    15. Isaac Errett, "Historico-Doctrinal Sketch of the Disciples, Number Four," *Christian Standard* 6 (13 May 1871):145.

    16. Moses E. Lard et al., "Prospectus of the *Apostolic Times*," *Christian Standard* 4 (9 January 1869):16, quoted in Murch, *Christians Only*, 170.

    17. [Isaac Errett], "Apostasy" editorial, *Christian Standard* 4 (14 and 21 August 1869):260, 268, quoted in Murch, *Christians Only*, 171.

    18. [Isaac Errett], "The True Basis of Union," *Christian Standard* 3 (20 June 1868):196.

Divergence in Interpretation 57

19. Harrell, *Social History*, 2:20-21.

20. The use of "Church" (capitalized) here does not conform to Lipscomb's own usage, but refers to the Church universal which Lipscomb believed his own religious community to be.

21. T[olbert] Fanning and D[avid] Lipscomb, "Prospectus of Volume VIII of the *Gospel Advocate*," *Gospel Advocate* 8 (9 January 1866):32, quoted in West, *Search for the Ancient Order*, 2:14.

22. D[avid] L[ipscomb], "How Shall Christian Union Be Maintained," *Gospel Advocate* 12 (28 July 1870):697-98, quoted in Eikner, "Nature of the Church," 205-206.

23. David Lipscomb, "Union and Schism," *Gospel Advocate* 25 (26 December 1883):822, quoted in West, *Search for the Ancient Order*, 2:223.

24. David Lipscomb, "The Sin of Dividing the Church of God," *Gospel Advocate* 24 (26 January 1882):46, quoted in Arthur Van Murrell, "The Effects of Exclusivism in the Separation of the Churches of Christ from the Christian Church" (Ph.D. dissertation, Vanderbilt University), 167-68.

25. David Lipscomb, "Can a Person Serve God in a Sect?," *Gospel Advocate* 20 (31 October 1878):680, quoted in Murrell, "Effects of Exclusivism," 110.

26. David Lipscomb, "Concerning the Federation," *Gospel Advocate* 35 (13 April 1893):225, quoted in Murrell, "Effects of Exclusivism," 112.

27. David Lipscomb, "False to Christ," *Gospel Advocate* 26 (20 August 1884):534, quoted in Murrell, "Effects of Exclusivism," 109.

28. Lipscomb, "Can a Person Serve God in a Sect," 680, quoted in Murrell, "Effects of Exclusivism," 183.

29. David Lipscomb, "The Cause of Christian Lifelessness," *Gospel Advocate* 47 (8 June 1905):360, quoted in Murrell, "Effects of Exclusivism," 199-200.

30. David Lipscomb, "Discussion—Missionary Societies," *Gospel Advocate* 9 (14 March 1867):208, quoted in West, *Search for the Ancient Order*, 2:59-60.

31. West, *Search for the Ancient Order*, 2:105-106.

32. David Lipscomb, "Strange Developments," *Gospel Advocate* 26 (12 March 1884):166, quoted in West, *Search for the Ancient Order*, 2:242-43.

33. David Lipscomb, "Legalism and Obedience," *Gospel Advocate* 13 (27 April 1871):389-90, quoted in West, *Search for the Ancient Order*, 2:144.

34. David Lipscomb, "Religious Tendencies North and South," *Gospel Advocate* 25 (11 April 1883):226, quoted in Murrell, "Effects of Exclusivism," 192.

35. [David Lipscomb], "A Visit to Chattanooga," *Gospel Advocate* 21 (3 April 1889):214, quoted in Harrell, *Social History*, 2:331.

36. To say that Lipscomb is "sectionally influenced" is not to deny the possibility that the early Stoneite movement in Kentucky and Tennessee provided the roots the Churches of Christ before the Civil War (See Hughes, "Apocalyptic Origins of Churches of Christ," 182-85).

37. William E. Tucker, *J. H. Garrison and Disciples of Christ* (St. Louis: Bethany Press, 1964), 18-19.

38. Ibid., 22-23.

39. J[ames] H. Garrison, "The Religious Movement Urged by the Disciples—Its Origin and Aim, III," *Christian Evangelist* 23 (25 March 1886):180.

40. Both Alexander and Thomas Campbell stated publicly that Christian character was the true basis of the Christian fellowship. Thomas so stated in the most famous proposition of his *Declaration and Address*: "PROP. I. That the Church of Christ upon earth is essentially, intentionally, and constitutionally one; consisting of all those in every place that profess their faith in Christ and obedience to him in all things according to the Scriptures, *and that manifest the same by their tempers and conduct, and of none else; as none else can be truly and properly called Christians*" (44). (Italics mine.)

A famous articulation of the same idea from Alexander Campbell has come to be called the "Lunenburg Letter": "Should I find a Pedobaptist more intelligent in the Christian Scriptures, more spiritually-minded and more devoted to the Lord than . . . one immersed on a profession of the ancient faith, I could not hesitate a moment in giving the preference of my heart to him that loveth most. Did I act otherwise, I would be a pure sectarian" ("Any Christians among Protestant Parties," *Millennial Harbinger*, n.s., 1 [September 1837]:412, quoted in McAllister and Tucker, *Journey in Faith*, 157).

41. J. H. Garrison, "Religious Movement," 180.

42. Don Herbert Yoder briefly identifies "the conversion of the world" as the "ultimate principle" in the Disciples' "Plea," in "Christian Unity in Nineteenth-Century America," in *A History of the Ecumenical Movement:1517-1948*, 2nd ed., edited by Ruth Rouse and Stephen C. Neill (London: SPCK, 1967), 238.

43. J[ames] H. G[arrison], "The Common Basis," *Gospel Echo* 8 (October 1870):462.

44. Ibid., 464.

45. J. H. Garrison, "Religious Movement," 180.

46. Ibid., 181.

47. J[ames] H. Garrison, "The Parliament of Religions—Its Character and Ultimate Effect," *Christian-Evangelist* 30 (9 November 1893):710.

48. J[ames] H. Garrison, "Church Federation: What Is It and What Should Be Our Attitude Toward It? III," *Christian-Evangelist* 40 (4 June 1903):449-50.

49. J[ames] H. Garrison, "Lessons from Our Past Experience; Or, Helps and Hindrances," in *The Old Faith Restated: Being a Restatement, by Representative Men, of the Fundamental Truths and Essential Doctrines of Christianity, as Held and Advocated by the Disciples of Christ, in Light of Experience and of Biblical Research*, ed. J[ames] H. Garrison (St. Louis: Christian Publishing Co., 1891), 446.

50. McGarvey's importance in the middle period of the history of the Campbell-Stone movement has led to a recent assessment of his work by M. Eugene Boring, "The Disciples and Higher Criticism: The Crucial Third Generation," in *A Case Study of Mainstream Protestantism: The Disciples' Relation to American Culture, 1880-1989*, ed. D. Newell Williams (Grand Rapids and St. Louis: William B. Eerdmans Publishing Company and Chalice Press, 1991), 29-70.

51. J. H. Garrison, *Old Faith Restated*, 9.

52. Dwight E. Stevenson, *Lexington Theological Seminary, 1865-1965* (St. Louis: Bethany Press, 1964), 11.

53. *"Christian Standard" Index 1866-1966*, vol. 4 (Nashville: Disciples of Christ Historical Society, 1972), 2045-2056.

54. McAllister and Tucker, *Journey in Faith*, 232.

55. Earl I. West, *The Search for the Ancient Order: A History of the Restoration Movement, 1849-1906*, vol. 1: *1849-1865* (Nashville: Gospel Advocate Co., 1949), 305.

56. J. W. McGarvey, "The Exclusiveness of Our Creed," *Christian Standard* 25 (22 February 1890):124.

57. J. W. McGarvey, "Biblical Criticism: Schism for the Sake of Union," *Christian Standard* 42 (19 January 1907):96.

58. J. W. McGarvey, "Biblical Criticism: Freedom of Opinion," *Christian Standard* 45 (27 February 1909):377.

59. J. W. McGarvey, "Biblical Criticism: The Federal Council," *Christian Standard* 46 (15 January 1910):95.

60. J. W. McGarvey, "Where We All Agree," *Christian Standard* 33 (17 April 1897):492.

61. J. W. McGarvey, "Heed the Exhortation," *Christian Standard* 30 (11 August 1894):792.

62. West, *Search for the Ancient Order*, 2:31.

CHAPTER III

TWENTIETH-CENTURY CONFLICTS IN THE CAMPBELL-STONE MOVEMENT AND THE PREHISTORY OF RESTRUCTURE

The divergence in the interpretation of the basic ideals of the Campbell-Stone heritage seen in the writings of Errett, Lipscomb, Garrison, and McGarvey was one factor underlying both the first and second major schisms. Both splits were gradual and slow to be fully acknowledged. In the case of the first schism, which produced the Churches of Christ as a separate body, tensions had been present in the movement's first generation and exacerbated by the death of Alexander Campbell and the emergence of a "truly sectional" journalism in 1866. However, forty years elapsed before the "official" recognition of this split (in 1906).[1] In the second case, more than sixty years elapsed between the emergence around 1900 of the *Christian Standard* as the center of criticism of and opposition to aspects of the cooperative (extralocal) life of the Campbell-Stone movement (without the Southern conservatives now) and the "official" recognition of the second division during Restructure.[2]

In actuality the two schisms are closely related ideologically. The first division "left in a large constituency of those who still believed that there was a pattern laid down in the New Testament for the church, and that Disciples, historically, *had* followed, and *should continue to* follow it."[3] Eventually a second conservative restorationist body–the undenominational fellowship of Christian Churches and Churches of Christ–came into being. A. T. DeGroot has dubbed this second group, "Church of Christ Number Two"[4] and his designation makes sense in terms of basic commitments. The "Church of Christ Number Two" is very like the Churches of Christ *theologically* without the Southern *sectional* characteristic. The common name for the second emergent restorationist community is "Independents." This term distinguishes them from those who were "Cooperatives" with regard to the extralocal structures of what became the International Convention of Christian Churches (Disciples of Christ).

One relatively early treatment of the division between the Cooperatives and Independents is contained in Alfred T. DeGroot's *Grounds of Divisions Among the Disciples of Christ*. Writing in 1940, he was not able to see that the division would prove to be a permanent one and has difficulty in judging whether and when a division had taken place. His statements that "schism was averted" and "practical division" had been "resolved in part" underscore his reluctance to recognize the split between Independents and Cooperatives.

DeGroot placed open membership (recognizing the validity of the baptism of the unimmersed) at the center of the "practical division."[5] However, he also listed other issues which had "disturbed the Disciples." Among these were "higher criticism, federation connections with other Christian bodies, . . . a delegate convention, and the unification of missionary and other co-operative activities." He also stressed the role of periodicals in advocating divergent points of view on these issues.[6]

The role of periodicals is also emphasized in what may be the most complete history of the emergence of division between Cooperatives and Independents: Stephen J. Corey's *Fifty Years of Attack and Controversy: The Consequences Among Disciples of Christ*. Corey describes and documents fifty years of "attack" by the *Christian Standard*. The fifty years are, roughly, 1900 to 1950. The targets of the "attack" are federation, the Campbell Institute, the Rockefeller gift, Archibald McLean, Nanking University, the Pittsburgh program, Guy W. Sarvis, the International Convention of the Disciples of Christ, Transylvania College and The College of the Bible at Lexington, the Christian Woman's Board of Missions, and especially, the United Christian Missionary Society (UCMS).[7] The limitations of Corey's work as a history of the division between Cooperatives and Independents are his narrow focus upon the *Christian Standard* as the "heavy" in the story and Corey's own bias as one of the victims of the "attack."[8] However, Corey documents his version of the history copiously and provides a fairly extensive list of the issues which became controversial.

In the years between 1900 and 1907 there was considerable effort among various denominations to form some kind of organization to carry out cooperative Christian work. Many in the Campbell-Stone movement believed that such federation would be a step in the right direction toward the cherished ideal of Christian union. J. H. Garrison, for example, supported federation out of dedication to the notions of Christian union and the evangelization of the world.[9] The *Christian Standard* articulated another, and perhaps more widely held, opinion within the movement when it strongly denounced federation as "not a union in Christ, but union in denominationalism, union in an order of things which Christ and his apostles condemn as carnal and as an enemy to Christian union or the union in Christ."[10] Thus, at the very beginning of the "fifty years of attack and controversy," restoration was in tension with union; liberty to engage in federation was being affirmed on one side and denied on the other. Whether federation was conceived as promoting or hindering the ultimate mission of the Church, of course, was determined by the judgment of whether or not the historic churches were to be viewed as authentically Christian.

The second recipient of a *Christian Standard* attack was the Campbell Institute, "a small group of young men who had gone beyond the college course and the biblical training provided for Disciples and had taken university graduate and seminary studies."[11] There were at least two things wrong with the Campbell Institute from the conservative restorationist perspective. First of all, since this perspective tended to deny the authenticity of Christian institutions outside the Campbell-Stone movement, schools of higher learning that were established and nurtured by the historic churches were automatically suspect. The seminaries which Campbell Institute members had attended included Yale, Harvard, Union, Rochester, Chicago, and Princeton.[12] Secondly, the Campbell Institute was accused of being "inspired by the three evil spirits of evolution, higher criticism, and the new theology."[13] The Campbell Institute signaled an assumption on the part of its members that, in preparing to minister in the pursuit of the unity of the Church and the conversion of the world, one must be open to the points of view of the historic churches. A consequence of acting on this assumption was the increasing incidence of historical-critical thinking among Disciples.

The third controversy that Corey describes is one over "tainted" money. The Foreign Christian Missionary Society, one of the cooperative agencies which had arisen among those Disciples who deemed it appropriate to organize for mission, had been offered and had accepted some gifts from John D. Rockefeller. Rockefeller was a Baptist and supported the Baptist missionary agencies as well. The *Standard* articulated the belief that Rockefeller's money was "tainted" by the methods which the oil magnate had used to acquire it, and was, therefore, not fit to be used for Christian work. One of the *Standard*'s contributors in the attack on the Rockefeller gifts was Thomas W. Phillips, one of Rockefeller's competitors.[14] Corey, who was a secretary of the Foreign Christian Missionary Society, takes no exception to the notion that Rockefeller had used harsh methods and business practices to secure his fortune, but sympathizes with "the officers of the Foreign Christian Missionary Society [who] felt that this money was as good as any money, since there were no conditions attached to it, and that to use it for a great cause need not be any commendation of Mr. Rockefeller's principles."[15]

It was the attack by the *Standard* upon the Rockefeller gift that led to the confrontation between the *Christian Standard* and Archibald McLean, who was president of the Foreign Christian Missionary Society in the early days of the twentieth century. This confrontation is noteworthy, in part, because McLean "rolled up his sleeves and gave it to the *Standard*, blow for blow."[16] Without detailing the attacks and counter-attacks, it is important to note that McLean, by defending himself and his organization, very likely fanned the flames of ill feeling at the *Christian Standard*. This may have been a factor in the later virulent denunciation of the UCMS by the *Standard*.

Corey characterizes the years between 1907 and 1910 as "fairly quiet," though he does describe two "attacks" made by the *Christian Standard* in this period. The first was the *Standard*'s opposition to the participation of Disciples in a "Union Christian University" in Nanking, China. The *Standard*'s objection here was the same as it had been to federation—that such participation entailed a recognition of the Christian character of non-Campbell-Stone denominations.[17] The other issue that emerged between 1907 and 1910 was in connection with the centennial celebration of Thomas Campbell's *Declaration and Address*. This celebration was held in Pittsburgh in 1909.

Writing from the point of view of the Independents, James DeForest Murch calls Pittsburgh "the crest of a wave which was to break in fifty years of controversy and division." Murch stresses that criticism of the missionary societies arose relative to their "*centralization of authority*" and reports, more ominously, that "delegates noted the *rise of liberalism in Christian doctrine* in several of the addresses, notably those of Samuel Hardin Church, Perry J. Rice, and Herbert L. Willett. . . . These happenings were symptomatic of a disease which was infesting all Protestantism."[18] Church was an advocate of "open membership." Willett was an historical-critical Bible scholar and Rice was the president of the Campbell Institute. Both the approach to the Bible represented by Willett and the closely related rapprochement with the historic churches represented by Rice and Church were intolerable to conservative restorationists.

The threat that the assumptions of Campbell-Stone restorationism would be drowned in a tide of Protestant liberalism had much to do with the next target selected for attack by the *Christian Standard*—Guy W. Sarvis. Sarvis was a young missionary candidate slated for work in China. He went to do some preparatory graduate study at the University of Chicago. There he became the pastoral assistant of Edward Scribner Ames at the Hyde Park (Disciples) Church. Sarvis's critics must have been horrified at the prospect of having Ames's views taken to the mission field.[19] Ames, who was "a disciple of John Dewey and a master in the new discipline of psychology of religion," "scandalized many of his brethren with a famous article on 'My Conception of God' as 'the idea of the personified, idealized whole of reality.'"[20] The Sarvis controversy, then, was yet another skirmish in the battle over theological liberalism and the place it would take in the thought of the Campbell-Stone movement. This was a battle which not only involved the traditional ideals of restoration and union relative to the validity of those Christian institutions which nurtured theologies such as Ames's, it also involved the differing interpretations of the ideal of freedom of opinion.

One of the most persistent problems that the heirs of Campbell and Stone have had with their basic ideals is the determination of how those ideals should be embodied in structures. Alexander Campbell himself had hoped that his co-workers in the movement would create a delegate assembly, but he died without seeing his hopes realized. Details of the movement's structural evolution will be set forth later in this study. However, at this point it may be noted that before 1912 there was a national convention which was "in fact a series of separate, and only indirectly related, annual meetings of . . . three [Disciples] missionary organizations." In 1912 the national convention of Disciples at Louisville approved a plan for the reorganization of the convention. The *Christian Standard* opposed the idea of a delegate assembly for the Disciples of Christ, and the plan (which had been approved at Louisville) was not implemented.[21]

> In 1917 a compromise was effected which resulted in the . . . International Convention. A new constitution was adopted . . . which provides for a mass assembly of any and all persons who may wish to register. However, it also provides for a Committee on Recommendations which is a delegate body and composed of members elected by the various state conventions.[22]

Opposition had forced the idea of a delegate assembly for the Campbell-Stone movement to be abandoned once again. In its place was put this bicameral compromise. The opposition to the International Convention of the Disciples of Christ, the bicameral body which was the movement's extra-congregational national structure until Restructure, came from the *Christian Standard* in terms of its being "an ecclesiasticism" and its representing "denominationalism."[23]

Though Corey believes that the most significant "attacks" by the *Standard* were those made upon the missionary societies, he assigns secondary importance to those made upon Transylvania College and The College of the Bible.[24] The College of the Bible episode was part of "The Battle over the Book."[25] Alexander Campbell, the most influential of the founding four of the Campbell-Stone movement, had claimed that his college (Bethany) placed the Bible at the center of its curriculum. The very name "College of the Bible" says much about the early Disciples' view of ministerial education. One of the central convictions of early Disciples was that there is an absolute distinction between human opinion and divine revelation. The Bible was understood to be unequivocally in the latter category.

A method of study that gained prominence in the United States in the early years of the twentieth century shook the traditional Disciples assumption to the core by blurring that distinction. That method was "higher criticism," "the study of the authorship, dates of writing, meaning, etc. of the books of the Bible, using the techniques or findings of archaeology, literary criticism, comparative religion, etc."[26] The University of Chicago was particularly influential in introducing this pattern of thought into Disciples circles.[27]

The question which arose after a time of Disciples' exposure to institutions like Chicago was, What about their own schools? Would they remain firmly anchored in the traditional approach of Alexander Campbell and his students (such as J. W. McGarvey) or would they become influenced by the style of thought represented by scholars of the University of Chicago (such as Herbert L. Willett)?[28] It was over this question that the *Standard* found occasion to concern itself with The College of the Bible. The crisis came in 1917 when changes occurred in the faculty. Before this time, there had been rumblings—the controversies surrounding the Campbell Institute, Guy Sarvis, and the Pittsburgh speakers. This time, however, the *Christian Standard* faced the horrifying possibility of liberals teaching at The College of the Bible:

> As long as these [liberal] views were confined to a small group of intellectuals not teaching in Disciple seminaries, this view could be seen by the proponents of Disciple scholasticism as that of a radical fringe. When it captured the stronghold of Disciple scholasticism, the College of the Bible, the situation became quite different.[29]

The most important upshot of the changes at The College of the Bible and Transylvania College was the ultimate success of the liberal faculty members. Among Cooperatives, the decision was made to remain in the mainstream of twentieth century educational, theological, and scientific thought as reflected in historical-critical methods. This decision led directly to the establishment of an alternative set of educational institutions by the Independents. Writing about the "Church of Christ Number Two" in 1956, A. T. DeGroot publishes a roster of "forty independent or semi-independent Disciple colleges with founding dates."[30] Only two on the list, Johnson Bible College (1893) and Minnesota Bible College (1913) were founded before the storm over The College of the Bible. This, then, is the point of divergence between Cooperatives and Independents on the issue of ministerial education.

After the storm over The College of the Bible had broken and abated, the *Christian Standard* concentrated its efforts upon the missionary societies of the Disciples. Corey devotes the bulk of his book to the conflict between the *Standard* and these societies. In 1919 the Christian Woman's Board of Missions entered into a comity agreement with other denominations on the mission field in Mexico. The by-now familiar issue of "recognizing the denominations" arose once again as the *Standard* equated comity with federation.[31] The next major antagonist that the *Christian Standard* tackled was the UCMS. The denunciation of the UCMS by writers among the Independents continued until Restructure.[32]

Basically, the opposition of the Independents to the UCMS revolved around two issues. The first was open membership. The Independents made much of accusing the UCMS missionaries of having fellowship with unimmersed persons on the mission field. Again, the Independents saw the UCMS as countenancing the weakening of a cardinal point in the *restoration* doctrine—the insistence upon immersion of believers as the only legitimate initiation into the Church. The second issue was that of "centralization." Since the UCMS had brought into one agency three former missionary societies, it was suspected of being an oppressive ecclesiastical machine. The existence of such an agency—especially taken together with the creation of the International Convention in 1917—was regarded as a threat to the principle of *liberty*. The issues were now in place. The Independents would continue up to and beyond Restructure to emphasize restoration and liberty from ecclesiastical control in a ways that defined their commitments to Christian union, mission, and liberty of opinion.

Edwin V. Hayden published a response to Corey's book entitled *Fifty Years of Digression and Disturbance*. Hayden offers an Independent perspective and sees the issues at stake between his group and Cooperatives as involving "the acceptance or rejection of Christ as the Head of His church, the Bible as the Word of God, and the New Testament plan for conversion and Christianity." Hayden identifies "four major digressions" of the UCMS: federation, the acceptance of the historical-critical view of the Bible, open membership, and comity agreements.[33] Hayden's response rearticulates and defends the fundamental ideological position of the *Christian Standard*.

Of course, the *Christian Standard* did not monopolize the journalism of that portion of the Campbell-Stone movement not in the Southern Churches of Christ. On the opposite side of virtually all of the "attacks" made by the *Standard* stood the "defenses" of the *Christian-Evangelist*.

Just before the 1919 International Convention the *Christian Standard* called for a "Restoration Congress."[34] In 1921 the *Standard* reported that the St. Louis Restoration Congress passed a resolution "urging all churches to discontinue fellowship with the United Christian Missionary Society and the General

Convention until present abuses are rectified."[35] In October 1927 the first North American Christian Convention was held.[36] Thus, by 1927, there was not only a recognizably separate journalism (reminiscent of that which developed in the North and South just after the Civil War) and separate educational institutions embodying divergent educational rationales, but also separate national conventions for Cooperatives and Independents.

Despite the separate journals, schools, and conventions, the International Convention neither had nor desired any mechanism by which to exclude congregations. Therefore many congregations which did not support the International Convention and the UCMS continued to be listed in the *Year Book* of the Christian Churches (Disciples of Christ) until the late 1960s when Independents conducted a campaign encouraging congregations to withdraw from the *Year Book* listing.[37] Thus for at least the forty years from 1927 to 1967, and in many ways extending farther back to the turn of the century and the beginnings of the "attacks" of the *Christian Standard*, a second real schism in the Campbell-Stone movement existed yet awaited full articulation and recognition.

The existence and reality of a second schism without the full articulation of it created difficulties for the portion of the Disciples of Christ who were attempting to cooperate through the International Convention, the UCMS, and the other cooperating agencies. One expression of these difficulties was the publication of a pamphlet by the International Convention entitled *What Brotherhood Cooperation Means*. The purpose of the pamphlet was to distinguish clearly between the "so-called Independents and Cooperatives."[38] The pamphlet identifies differences in the names, assemblies, publishing houses, educational programs, literature, youth programs, higher education, ministry, benevolences, lists of acceptable ministry, missionary programs, senses of history, and pension plans of the two groups. In addition, differences in the attitudes toward denominationalism, the basis of Christian unity, inclusivity/exclusivity, cooperation, freedom, and the nature of the church are discussed.[39] The assumption of the pamphlet is that a second schism had occurred in the Campbell-Stone movement and that its nature needed to the clarified. The fact that such a pamphlet would appear in the 1960s bespeaks the confusion that had characterized the extracongregational life of the Disciples for forty years.

An hypothesis of W. E. Garrison relative to the mainspring of this second division touches closely the focus of this work upon the fundamental *ideals* of the Campbell-Stone movement and their divergent interpretation in the second generation and beyond. Writing of his father, J. H. Garrison, W. E. Garrison said:

It was not a system of doctrine that had convinced and converted him, but rather the vision of a simple evangelical Christianity within the hospitable fellowship of which all Christians might find their brotherhood in loyalty to the one Christ and in their recognized membership in his one Church.

In addition to this constitutive conviction and objective, the Disciples of Christ had a body of opinions, patterns of thought, forms of expression and modes of procedure which were, in general, characteristic of the entire group.... Some Disciples never learned to distinguish between these two: the basic conviction and purpose which justified their existence as a religious body; and the opinions and practices which had characterized the movement at its beginning as conditioned by the time and place.

J. H. Garrison was among those who began early to see this distinction.[40]

The idea that there was an important distinction to be made among the traditional values of the Campbell-Stone movement is echoed in Stephen J. Corey's book. The distinction is that between *means* (instrumental values) and *ends* (ultimate values). Speaking of the Independents, Corey writes, "On the platform of 'Restorationism' as a means towards an end, this later schism has subordinated the great goal, or end, of Christian unity to that means."[41]

Alfred T. DeGroot concluded in 1940 that *"the principle of restoring a fixed pattern of a primitive Christian church is divisive and not unitive."*[42] This was a forthright public statement of a fact that the experience of the Campbell-Stone movement in the years 1866 to 1940 had made apparent. DeGroot's conclusion was included in the influential textbook *Disciples of Christ: A History*. In this work, which was the standard Cooperative text for a generation, DeGroot's collaborator W. E. Garrison comments that even Walter Scott had "perceived that the rigidity of the restoration program was divisive rather than unitive in its effects."[43] DeGroot's conclusion was noted by other writers. For example, Whitley quoted it in his 1959 *Trumpet Call of Reformation*.[44] James DeForest Murch denounced it in his 1962 *Christians Only*.[45] Ironically, DeGroot's conclusion was perhaps more influential than he desired. In 1960 he wrote a defense of the *Restoration Principle*. The principle was not here described in characteristically Campbell-Stone terms, however, but in terms of the restoration of the ethical faith *of* (rather than faith *in*) Jesus.[46]

DeGroot's 1960 interpretation and defense of the restoration principle was certainly late if David E. Harrell, Jr. is correct in saying that "the naive optimism of early Disciples history vanished in the years after the Civil War. Post-war leaders ... lost their confidence in the dual plea for restoration and union. The plea was simply impractical." Harrell concludes that Disciples chose either restoration or union.[47] He writes of the early weakening of the restoration platform and its jettisoning by some in the movement.

> [There was] a new candor and irreverence toward the restoration tradition in Missourian George T. Smith's declaration *in 1893*: "A principle may set aside an apostolic precept. It may brush aside an apostolic decree. We do that constantly. We follow the apostolic example whenever we like it; when we do not, we depart from it."[48] (Italics mine.)

The weakening which Harrell points to as beginning in the late nineteenth century achieved new proportions by the 1940s and 1950s.

Part of the disaffection with the restoration method of seeking Christian unity might be rooted in the appearance on the scene of a more promising means to the same end. Underscoring the important distinction between means and ends, methods and goals, Paul A. Crow, Jr., points out that "methodologies change as the world changes." Although restoration was "a valid nineteenth century methodology," in the twentieth century it "is not an adequate method for Disciples or anyone else."[49]

As Cooperative Disciples increasingly internalized the conclusions of DeGroot and others with regard to the inadequacy of restoration as a means of achieving Christian union (for the sake of mission), they also were exploring another possible avenue to Christian union—participation in the modern ecumenical movement. In 1957, W. E. Garrison wrote:

> The modern "ecumenical movement" is now over forty years old, if its beginning is reckoned from the World Missionary Conference at Edinburgh in 1910.... Within these four decades there have been many conferences, countless meetings of commissions and committees, extended and repeated discussions of areas of agreement and points of disagreement among the churches, and fruitful co-operative activities of many kinds and for many purposes. ...
>
> All this has produced three very valuable results: first, more intimate acquaintance and a more genuine sense of Christian brotherliness across sectarian barriers; second, some habits and techniques of co-operation in practical service, in thinking together on the deepest

problems that confront man in the contemporary world, and in common worship; and third, a better understanding by each group of the convictions and traditions of all the others.[50]

In the years between 1910 and the writing of these words in 1957, Cooperatives had, through their representatives, *experienced* the developments Garrison described.

Almost simultaneous with the birth of the modern ecumenical movement, an ecumenical consciousness was born in the individual who best represents Disciples of Christ ecumenism in the early twentieth century—Peter Ainslie. Finis S. Idleman, Ainslie's biographer, records that "the year 1910 saw a distinct widening in the conceptions of Peter Ainslie." Before that year, Ainslie had been primarily concerned with the affairs of his own denomination and parish. "He had followed the traditional paths of his religious group. During the first twenty years of his ministry in Baltimore he had, for the most part, preached a gospel of exclusiveness."[51] Idleman suggests that Ainslie's "widening" was brought about by his election to the post of president at the Centennial Convention at Pittsburgh in 1909. In his presidential address to the Topeka, Kansas, convention of 1910 his new conceptions were made public.

In his address, Ainslie spoke of the apostles, Paul, Luther, Calvin, the Wesleys, and the Campbells, and stressed Christian unity with those who had gone before in history. Making the same essential point with respect to his contemporaries, Ainslie continued: "But standing on God's balcony, we look about us today and yonder are millions in all parts of the world witnessing for Jesus." These, too, should be regarded as Christians "whatever their names."[52] Ainslie called for the creation of a foundation among the Disciples of Christ devoted to the pursuit of Christian unity, and the Council on Christian Union was incorporated late in 1910.

In 1911, the publication of the *Christian Union Quarterly* was begun under the editorship of Peter Ainslie.

> The *Quarterly* at once took its place as the most significant and influential American periodical devoted entirely to the cause of Christian unity. . . . At no time was it a mere house organ to propagandize the Disciples' "historic position" as the only way unity should or could be attained. It was, on the contrary, an open forum for the presentation of various views—a kind of journalistic "faith and order" conference long before the first Faith and Order Conference met at Lausanne.[53]

Peter Ainslie symbolizes a change that was destined to become characteristic of the leadership of the Cooperative wing of the Campbell-Stone movement. The change was one from emphasizing the restoration *means* to that of emphasizing Christian union as an *end*. Thus, a member of the Campbell-Stone movement who was initially "widely known and honored because of his ardent devotion to the [Restoration] Plea"[54] changed into a committed leader of the ecumenical movement.

Ainslie's significance is not only symbolic; he helped to involve the Disciples of Christ in the Faith and Order movement. In fact, the 1920 planning conference on Faith and Order at Geneva grew out of the efforts of Ainslie and Episcopal Bishop Charles H. Brent. Disciples were present at the Faith and Order conferences at Lausanne (1927) and Edinburgh (1937); the Life and Work meetings at Stockholm (1925) and Oxford (1937); and the conferences on World Christianity sponsored by the International Missionary Council at Jerusalem (1928) and Madras (1938).[55] Therefore, by the time A. T. DeGroot wrote about the divisiveness of the restoration methodology in 1940, some Cooperative Disciples had considerable exposure to an alternative method of seeking both Christian union and greater effectiveness in the mission of the Church universal.

That Peter Ainslie was a pioneer, one far beyond most of his peers in the Campbell-Stone movement with regard to ecumenical commitment, is clear. But Ainslie was a Disciple whose attitude toward the churches other than his own both foreshadowed and helped to usher in a new interpretation of the Campbell-Stone ideology. The full, forthright expression of Disciples' recognition of the relative, historical character of the Campbell-Stone movement—a character which places Disciples on a no-better-than-equal footing with the historic churches—came most dramatically in the work of the Panel of Scholars in the late 1950s and early 1960s. Ainslie anticipated that expression when he wrote: "And we propose to recognize, in all our spiritual fellowships, the practice of equality of all Christians before God."[56]

One way of assessing the status of Disciples' commitment to Christian union and the other basic ideals of the movement by the middle of the twentieth century is to examine the reports of the Commission on Restudy of the Disciples of Christ. This commission was created in 1934 at the Des Moines International Convention as a response to the "tensions long rife" within the Campbell-Stone movement and as an "effort to preserve" its internal unity.[57]

> Commission personnel included leading ministers and laypersons and represented almost every shade of opinion. The Commission submitted to the International Convention of 1946 a report outlining the principle

[*sic*] areas of tension. Diverse views were presented and possibilities for the future were suggested. The work of the Commission was considered closed after its 1949 report to the convention.[58]

The 1946 report of the Commission addresses several "causes of unrest and dissension among our people." The first of these is the issue of whether the Campbell-Stone movement is a denomination or a movement. The report stresses the historical commitment to movement status and denounces the acceptance of denominational status as a defeat of the movement's purposes. Possible positions on this issue are identified: 1) refusing denominational status and being nonpartisan; 2) accepting denominational status but speaking against denominationalism and seeking common ground for all Christians; or 3) accepting the fact that the Disciples had become a denomination like others. This last position was identified as being the view of only a "few."

Another issue addressed was that of "local church autonomy." Agreement was expressed that this principle should be affirmed. The divergence on this issue was that "some" saw agencies and conventions as tending to compromise this principle while "others" saw agencies and conventions as exercising leadership which the churches desired and followed voluntarily. On the issue of the New Testament Church, there was agreement as to the normative character of the New Testament for evangelism and church life. But there was disagreement as "some" saw the New Testament as providing a "divinely authoritative pattern for the form and organization of the local church"—a pattern which they sought to restore. "Others" discerned only "principles" and not "forms" in the New Testament. On the subject of "unity and restoration," there was an affirmation of the commitment to unity and a confession of the poor record of the Disciples on performing up to this ideal. This poor record was attributed to a lack of clarity and agreement as to the "fundamental purpose of our movement." Specifically, the dissension which had arisen in the half-century before 1946 was blamed upon the "falling apart" of the two concepts of unity and restoration, which "have been held together in a parity of mutual dependence." Unity only through restoration is identified in the report as the Disciples' historic plea. Symbolic of this affirmation is the fact that the report expresses, with little tendency toward modification, an understanding of immersion and immersion only as being the norm of the Campbell-Stone movement, in spite of the contrary practice of "a considerable number of churches." The admission of unimmersed persons into congregations is seen as "a cause of tension."[59]

The subsequent reports carry much the same content as the 1946 report. The thrust of each of them is a reaffirmation of the historic restorationism of the Campbell-Stone movement, with a slight softening of the literalistic interpretation of restoration—evidence of a minority view in dissension. An example of the softening of the interpretation of restorationism is the conclusion to the 1948 report, which emphasizes restoration of the New Testament *gospel*, not just the New Testament *Church*.[60]

In the 1940s few Disciples were ready to disavow entirely the commitment to both restoration and unity. However, what had been evolving since at least the days of J. H. Garrison and J. W. McGarvey was a divergence in the relative emphases assigned to the four historic values of the movement. The situation may be charted as follows:

Independents

1. *Restoration* is *primary*; the New Testament presents a straightforward pattern for Christian faith and Church, the acceptance of which leads to . . .

2. Christian *union*, which is derivative; for any union apart from the "restored" pattern is not "Christian." Therefore, . . .

3. *Mission* is delimited to the extension of the restoration plea. Comity agreements with the historic churches and/or fellowship with the unimmersed are unacceptable on the mission field.

4. *Liberty* is most prominently interpreted ecclesiastically, That is, strict congregationalism is the embodiment of liberty. Liberty of opinion is severely curtailed by the biblistic emphasis.

Cooperatives

1. Christian *union* is *primary* and is seen as an essential prerequisite to the success of the Church's evangelistic . . .

2. *Mission*, which is to be pursued in partnership with the historic churches, even nonimmersionists.

3. *Restoration* must not be viewed legalistically, for such an approach hampers the progress of union and mission and denies . . .

4. *Liberty*, which is viewed in terms of liberty of opinion and freedom *of* (as opposed to *from*) association and organization. Such liberties are widened by an increasingly historical-critical view of scripture.

Twentieth-Century Conflicts

The increasing polarization of the Independent and Cooperative Disciples reflected a development that was observable in many Christian groups in the same era. In *Righteous Empire: The Protestant Experience in America*, Martin E. Marty writes of "The Two-Party System: A Division Within Protestantism." Marty identifies the two parties as "private Protestantism" and "public Protestantism." The first "accented individual salvation out of the world, personal moral life congruent with the ideals of the saved, and fulfillment or its absence in the rewards or punishments in another world in a life to come." It is also called conservative, evangelical, and, in its more militant forms, fundamentalist. The second "was public insofar as it was more exposed to the social order and the social destinies" of humanity. This party goes by the names liberal, mainline, and, especially in the early twentieth century, modernist.[61] The effects of this basic bifurcation in American Protestantism, which Marty sees as having taken place in the years between 1857 and 1908, may have been prolonged in the Campbell-Stone movement. However, just as the division between the Churches of Christ and the remainder of the Campbell-Stone movement had a sectional dimension which places it in some connection with other sectional church schisms, the second division in the Campbell-Stone movement was undeniably related to the two-party system which has become one of the enduring features of American Protestantism.

The fact that the second schism in the Campbell-Stone movement belongs within the context of the situation of Protestantism in general may be seen in the positions of the movement's parties with respect to the Bible and the modern ecumenical movement. Not only were the Bible and ecumenism related to the movement's cherished ideals (restorationism and Christian union, respectively), but also the stance of the movement's two parties vis-a-vis the Bible and the modern ecumenical movement paralleled the positions of the two parties in Protestantism.

Writing in the *Christian Standard* in 1959, Henry E. Webb offered his understanding of the historical-critical biblical scholarship embraced by Cooperatives and the dissenting view of the Independent Disciples:

> The theory of evolution had become popular, and many scholars made free application of its principles to the Scriptures... Critics declared that what men had once believed was the Word of God was really only the record of the strivings of an especially sensitive people in their gropings after religious verities in the context of a prescientific and extremely credulous era. The Christianity reflected in the Scrip-

tures (which incidentally were redated into later times), was held to be a synthesis of Hellenized Judaism and oriental mysticism.

With such an approach to the Bible, Webb wished to take sharp exception: "We do not worship the Bible, we are not bibliolaters; but we realize clearly that everything that we or anyone else knows about the Christ we do worship comes to us from the Scriptures."[62]

The polarization in American Protestantism led to two parallel structures of multidenominational relationship. The more liberal party organized the National Council of Churches. The more conservative party formed the American Council of Christian Churches and the National Association of Evangelicals.[63]

Independent scholar James DeForest Murch combined opposition to Restructure of the Disciples with a denunciation of the Consultation on Church Union (COCU) and the World and National Councils of Churches in his book on *The Free Church*.[64] Murch did give leadership to the multidenominational National Association of Evangelicals. However, this may have been made possible by the fact that the National Association of Evangelicals did not claim a churchly character in a way that forced the issue of members' ecclesiology but "operate[d] more as a holding corporation or accrediting agency."[65] Murch could conscientiously work with *individuals* through an agency to preserve and protect the basis of his restorationism (and derivative commitment to Christian union)—a conservative view of the Bible.

In sharp contrast to Murch's view was the behavior of the leaders of the Cooperatives. They had been charter members of the Federal Council of Churches and continued to support the National and World Councils.[66] As the Consultation on Church Union unfolded, they became involved in that as well.

Through the pioneering work of Peter Ainslie and others and the participation of Disciples in the ecumenical movement, the Cooperative segment of the Campbell-Stone movement was gradually finding its way toward ecumenism as an alternative to unity through restoration. After 1948 there was a change in the orientation of the Faith and Order movement that portended a parallel change among Cooperative Disciples.

> Early in the 1950's the Faith and Order Commission of the World Council of Churches discovered that its historic procedure of comparative studies of each other's thought and practices was leading the churches nowhere. Gradually, through the 1950's the center of attention became the Christ who is the One Lord of the church.[67]

Twentieth-Century Conflicts

Cooperatives participated in that shift, and a deepened seriousness about the ecumenical movement was reflected in their literature and life.[68]

It was perhaps the experience of the increasing involvement in the ecumenical movement and the accompanying broadened vision of Christian faith and the Church that enabled several scholars among Cooperatives to move beyond the grudging criticism and reinterpretation of restorationism that DeGroot had suggested to a forthright disavowal of that value. That forthright disavowal of restorationism was undeniably a watershed in the evolution of ideology in the Campbell-Stone movement and itself suffices to make *The Renewal of Church: The Panel of Scholars Reports* a significant document.

In 1956 the UCMS and the Board of Higher Education of the Disciples of Christ created the Panel of Scholars "to restudy the doctrines of Disciples of Christ, justifying their conclusions on the basis of the best available scholarship."[69] The Panel met semiannually beginning in 1957, and their reports were published in 1963. The general editor of the three-volume *Reports*, W. B. Blakemore, summed up the Panel's work in terms that were strikingly reminiscent of the simultaneous direction of the ecumenical movement: the Panel had discovered that "Christ is our tradition."

> There were two dominant results of the discovery that Christ is our tradition, that he is the center of our teaching. One result was negative, the other positive. The negative result was the recognition that whatever the historic significance for Disciples of "restorationism," it is not our tradition.... We are fundamentally a Christian movement, and not a restoration movement.[70]

That assessment was driven home in the *Reports* by numerous authors and articles. Taken together, these articles were nothing less than a systematic repudiation of the restoration methodology for seeking Christian union and a redefinition of the "nature of the unity we seek."[71]

The restoration method was repudiated by examining and finding erroneous three key assumptions of restoration ideology: 1) that the method is biblical, 2) that it is trans-historical (not a nineteenth-century methodology but a "timeless" methodology), and 3) that it is potentially effective (in bringing about Christian union and the evangelization of the world).

The examination of the first assumption was made by Dwight E. Stevenson, Professor of Homiletics at The College of the Bible.[72] One of the most telling passages in his paper contains a list of five of Alexander Campbell's "presuppositions" or "basic assumptions":

1. Congregational independency is only a relative term; the church embraces all local congregations everywhere in the world. This unity of the whole church must have institutional expression
2. The New Testament recognizes this; moreover, it gives us in express command or approved precedent all that we need to guide the modern church in matters of organization
3. In the New Testament church, organization is everywhere the same, every congregation being developed on the same pattern, and the unity of the whole church being expressed in the same way throughout all its districts
4. The offices of the New Testament church were definite in name, number, and functions
5. The New Testament pattern for church organization was essentially static, and was meant to remain so for all subsequent time

Stevenson then poses the question, "How do these presuppositions fare in the light of modern biblical knowledge?"[73] After surveying "modern biblical knowledge" about church organization in New Testament churches in Jerusalem, Antioch, the churches established by Paul, and those established after Paul, Stevenson concludes: "Of the five [of Alexander Campbell's presuppositions] which we attempted to articulate, only the first stands. The remaining four are wholly untenable in the light of biblical scholarship."[74] Thus, the restorationist assumption that the New Testament contained a definite, single, and fixed pattern for the Christian Church is negated by the modern understanding of the Bible.

The transhistorical character of the restoration method was challenged by Ralph G. Wilburn, Dean and Professor of Historical Theology at The College of the Bible.[75] Wilburn stresses the rootage of the restoration idea in late sixteenth- and seventeenth-century Church of England Independency, the deep influence of the Haldanes upon Alexander Campbell (through Greville Ewing), and the influence of both the Haldanes and Sandeman upon Walter Scott (through George Forrester). The chief argument of Wilburn's article is that phenomena must be understood relative to history.

Wilburn notes the development of: "1) the scientific development of biblical criticism; 2) a new understanding of the historical character of human existence; and 3) the theological growth of ecumenicity." He construes these historical developments as having laid bare the "fundamental errors in the Disciple restoration plea."[76] These five errors reflect the incompatibility of the restoration "plea" with the ideas entailed in the historical developments identified. The five errors are: 1) "a false presupposition of the orthodox view of the Bible";

2) "the failure to deal critically with the problems of biblical interpretation"; 3) "inadequate awareness of the historical character of the church"; 4) "the separatist attitudes of sectarianism"; and 5) "the neglect of theology."[77]

Wilburn did identify several "elements of truth in the Disciple restoration plea." These elements, however, had been "distorted . . . by the restoration idea." Wilburn ended his discussion with several "suggestions toward theological reconstruction." In this section he bluntly states that "the restoration idea is basically a false concept."[78] Thus, Wilburn goes much farther than DeGroot had gone. Wilburn's is not merely a reluctant admission that restorationism had failed to be unitive, but rather a critique of the idea itself principally on historical grounds.

The assumption that restorationism is potentially effective is denied by Ronald Osborn. Osborn sets the stage for the Panel's treatment of the restoration theme in his Preface to the first volume of the *Reports*. Osborn offers a wide-ranging critique of the restoration idea. He outlines the restoration "plea" and identifies elements of "dominant Christian thought today" which challenge or rebut each point of the "plea." In most cases the "plea" is found to be at odds with contemporary "dramatic movements toward unity." Restorationism, especially as embodied in the insistence upon baptism by immersion, is "an ecumenical stumbling block." The anticlericalism, anti-intellectualism, antidenominationalism, anticreedalism, and simplistic view of the Bible inherent in the restorationist ideology are all found wanting when exposed to patterns of thought current in a wider Christian context.[79] Osborn's most important criticism is his implication that restorationism is ineffective, even counterproductive, in the quest for Christian union.

The repudiation of the restoration idea by members of the Panel of Scholars was not the only ideological development reflected in the work of that body. The Panel not only represented a decisive shift to the mission-union pole of traditional Campbell-Stone ideology but also a reinterpretation of the ideal of liberty, especially as it related to polity.

The thinking of members of the Campbell-Stone movement on issues of polity had long been dominated by fierce congregationalism and a fear of all organization beyond the local level.[80] Part of the background of this thinking is the view that there are only three types of ecclesiastical polity—episcopal, presbyterial, and congregational. For members of the Campbell-Stone movement this meant that any move away from an "ideal type" congregationalism was certain to be construed as a move in the direction of presbyterial or episcopal structure. In this connection, W. B. Blakemore's "The Issue of Polity for Disciples Today" takes on its significance.

Stevenson, Wilburn, and Osborn had cleared the way for the jettisoning of restorationism. Similarly, Blakemore sought to unburden Disciples of a notion of liberty that precluded all possibilities for structure other than congregationalism. He wrote:

> Does the term "congregational polity" any longer represent a valid and viable conception?
> As we work our way through to a more adequately Christian conception of church polity, can the term "congregational polity" serve to designate that more adequate conception?
> The thesis of this paper is that the answer to both the above questions is "No."[81]

Blakemore's paper identifies no fewer than five types of polity which had all been called "congregational." The first of these he called "radical congregationalism," which he identified with the dissolution of the Mahoning Association in 1830. A second type of congregationalism permits "associations of Christians other than local congregations as 'means' of carrying on various desirable religious works." These are construed as associations of individuals, "not as associations of congregations." A third type of congregationalism recognizes "the inevitability of supralocal organizations and asserts that while this level of organization in none of its parts may be called 'church,' it should all be under the control of the congregation." Blakemore believed that "through the greater part of the history of Disciples of Christ the second conception has been the one which has accompanied the development of their co-operative life."

Blakemore viewed the Cooperative Disciples as having shifted to the third conception of congregationalism. This shift was problematic because "the third interpretation of congregational polity is neither coherent nor has correspondence to reality ... and ... has no relevance for ecumenical activity."[82] Blakemore maintained that the debate among proponents of congregational, presbyterial, and episcopal forms of church polity had come to an "impasse"; he suggested that "confusion over polity has stemmed from the 'tyranny' of certain general notions about organization, specifically the ideas of 'a fundamental unit' and 'a single locus of power.'"[83]

Taking his cues from a work on *Congregationalism* by Douglas Horton, Blakemore suggested that a fourth type of congregationalism is one which extends the recognition of the "autonomy of the local congregation" to "associations and councils" by construing them as "congregations." This seemed to Blakemore to be a step in the right direction, though he saw "the autonomy of the local congregation" as a "shibboleth" and believed that the "insight that the term 'autonomy' may protect is that the powers of any particular level of association originate with it and do not derive from elsewhere."

Blakemore suggested that a fifth type of congregationalism would be one that "rather than seeing a single locus of power or a fundamental unit" recognizes that "an act of association or cooperation is actually productive of new power that did not exist prior to the act of cooperation." This notion escapes the "tyranny" of the idea that power must come either from the "top down" or the "bottom up." However, with regard to the church, each association may not truly be described as "autonomous" because "while no specific organization is prior to the local congregation which emerges, we must assert that what is prior is that very *concrete* entity: the *Church of Christ* on earth." Blakemore saw this fifth type of congregationalism as one in which all levels of organization participate in the Church universal. As a consequence, organizations and persons acting as part of the Church never attempt to "represent" in a literal way anything other than their own best consciences under the lordship of Christ.[84]

The polity described in Blakemore's article for the Panel of Scholars is strikingly similar to that which emerged in the process of Restructure. In the *Provisional Design for the Christian Church (Disciples of Christ)* produced during Restructure the levels of churchly organization are called "manifestations." There is no notion of one "manifestation" as the "fundamental unit" or the "single locus of power." Each has, as Blakemore had suggested, its own inherent, not derivative, legitimacy as part of the Church universal.

There is a disagreement as to the impact of the Panel of Scholars' thought upon the subsequent Restructure of the Cooperative Disciples as well as upon the general significance of the Panel's work.[85] However, as Restructure proceeded it seemed to assume both the repudiation of restorationism as a method of attaining Christian union and as a method of determining church polity. Furthermore, the polity which emerged from Restructure was something other than the congregationalism that Blakemore had identified as being traditional among members of the Campbell-Stone movement. Whether the Panel of Scholars really laid the groundwork or merely reflected an ideology that had evolved among Cooperatives, this much is clear—by the dawn of the 1960s Cooperatives were ready to *build* a forthrightly denominational structure (without claiming to be restoring anything) against a backdrop of continued ecumenical commitment and ecumenical awareness.

The impending process of Restructure, then, might be described as having internal and external dimensions. The basic internal dimension of Restructure was the effort to create a single, unified, churchly denomination, the Christian Church (Disciples of Christ), out of the Cooperative vestige of a larger and always loosely organized Campbell-Stone movement. The basic external dimension was the determination that the new unified denominational body would take its place among the historic churches (other denominations) and seek Christian unity through participation with these others in the ecumenical movement. The fact that Cooperatives increasingly had viewed the related aims of Christian union and mission as the movement's authentic *raison d'etre* meant that the internal and external dimensions would be especially closely related to each other.

Part of the plausibility of the shift represented in the *Panel of Scholars Reports* rested upon the vitality of the wider ecumenical movement in which denominations sought Christian union and the advance of God's mission. The dawning years of the 1960s brought dramatic developments which both heightened the hopes of ecumenists and deepened the fears of those who opposed the movement. The first of these dramatic developments happened in Rome just before the decade of the 1960s began:

> Pope John XXIII announced, on January 25, 1959, his intention to convoke an "ecumenical Council for the whole Church, not only for the spiritual good and joy of the Christian people but also to invite the separated Communities to seek again that unity for which so many souls are longing in these days throughout the world."[86]

The announcement was greeted with a reaction that included high hopes among ecumenists. Enthusiastic press reports misled the naive into a vision of a great gathering of all Christian denominations.[87] For the more knowledgeable Catholics, the Pope's announcement seemed to imply something analogous to the Councils of Lyons (1274) or of Florence (1439) in which the representatives of the East (Orthodox) and West (Roman Catholic) had tried to come together to unite Christendom.[88] Neither of these expectations proved accurate.

As the sessions of Vatican II unfolded, it became clear that it was something between an ecumenical council in the sense of the early, enthusiastic hopes and simply a Roman Catholic ecumenical council. "Observers" from the Eastern Orthodox churches, Anglicans, and even Protestants[89] were in attendance. The observers were treated with such collegiality, the Council's sixteen documents were so preoccupied with ecumenism, and the stress on the vision of the Church as the people of God was so great that the Council in part justified the hopes of those early naive enthusiasts.[90]

Twentieth-Century Conflicts

Although the theology of the Roman Catholic Church still did not permit it to recognize the other Christian communities as equals, the language of the Second Council's *Decree on Ecumenism* is quite conciliatory:

> In subsequent centuries much more serious dissension appeared and quite large Communities became separated from full communion with the Catholic Church—for which often enough, men of both sides were to blame. However, one cannot charge with the sin of separation those who at present are born into these Communities and in them are brought up in the faith of Christ, and the Catholic Church accepts them with respect and affection as brothers....
> ... They therefore have a right to be called Christians.[91]

Such language as this, the exhortation to have study and dialogue with the members of "separated Communities," the exhortation to pray with members of these communities, and the opening of the door to worship in common, were the features of the *Decree* that made the largest impression upon ecumenically minded Protestants during the 1960s and that added momentum to their thinking in terms of the whole Church. That momentum was reflected within the leadership of Cooperative Disciples.

The second dramatic development in the ecumenical arena in the early days of the 1960s was the "Blake proposal" and the formation of the Consultation on Church Union (COCU). One of the most controverted aspects of the history of the Restructure process among Disciples of Christ is the degree to which Restructure and COCU were related.[92] Because COCU was in the background during much of the time that Restructure proceeded, both the prehistory of COCU and its development in the 1960s will be briefly discussed.

COCU did not really spring entirely and without precedent from the mind of Eugene Carson Blake. There had been many efforts to achieve organic unity from the plurality of denominations in the United States in the early twentieth century. The "Philadelphia Plan" had been initiated in 1918 as an endeavor to gather evangelical churches into a federation which would eventually point toward the goal of full union. This plan, and its proposed "United Churches of Christ in America," died in the 1920s and gave way to a plan of E. Stanley Jones that advocated "union with a federal structure" leading to the fully United Church of America. This plan's advocates were invited to join forces with the American Conference on Church Union. This Conference had originated in a "small meeting of churchmen in New York City in 1946." They convened their first major gathering in 1949 in Greenwich, Connecticut, and their plan became known as the Greenwich Plan. Charles Clayton Morrison of the *Christian Century* was a central figure in the Greenwich group. The Greenwich plan was abandoned in 1959.[93]

It was not long after the demise of the Greenwich plan that delegates gathered in San Francisco in 1960 for the Fifth General Assembly of the National Council of Churches of Christ in the United States of America.[94]

> On Sunday, December 4, at the very verge of the Assembly, Eugene Carson Blake preached in Grace Cathedral (Protestant Episcopal) on the theme, "A Proposal Toward the Reunion of Christ's Church." His purpose became immediately evident: to develop a "plan of church union both catholic and reformed" between four American denominations. These churches were the United Presbyterian Church in the U.S.A., the Protestant Episcopal Church, the Methodist Church, and the United Church of Christ.[95]

The response to Blake's sermon and to the endorsement of his proposal by James A. Pike, Bishop of the Episcopal Diocese of California, was immediate and varied. The most concrete and consequential response, however, was that of several presbyteries of the United Presbyterian Church in the United States of America.

> Numerous presbyteries overtured the 173rd General Assembly of the United Presbyterian Church to invite the Protestant Episcopal Church, meeting in General Convention in Detroit in the same year [1961], to join with it in an invitation to the Methodist Church and the United Church of Christ to enter into the exploration of the establishment of a united church.[96]

This invitation, and the response of the Episcopal and Methodist Churches, was the beginning of COCU.

The name, "Consultation on Church Union," was adopted at the meeting in Washington, D. C., 9-10 April 1962. Invitations were extended to churches in North America to send two observer-consultants to future COCU meetings. Invitations were sent to the International Convention of the Christian Churches (Disciples of Christ), the Polish National Catholic Church, and the Evangelical United Brethren to become full partners in COCU. When they had answered their invitation affirmatively, Evangelical United Brethren and Disciples representatives were immediately named to the Consultation's executive committee. The Polish National Catholic Church settled upon observer-consultant status.

By the time COCU met in Oberlin, Ohio, 19-21 March 1963, it was composed of: 1) the United Presbyterian Church in the United States, 2) the Protestant Episcopal Church, 3) the Methodist Church, 4) the United Church of Christ, 5) the Evangelical United Brethren, and 6) the International Convention of Christian Churches (Disciples of Christ). The first report of the Consultation meeting in Oberlin contained the consensus that 1) the Old and New Testaments have unique authority; 2) Jesus Christ is the center of the Holy Scriptures; and 3) the Holy Scriptures are taken to be canonical, that is, the norm of the total life of the church (worship, witness, teaching, and mission). The recognition of three relationships between Scripture and tradition also came out of the Oberlin meeting: 1) Scripture itself is included in tradition; 2) Scriptures are interpreted in light of tradition; and 3) Scriptures are the "supreme guardian and expression of tradition."[97]

The next meeting of the Consultation was held at Princeton, New Jersey, 13-16 April 1964. There the Consultation approved a statement on "One Ministry" which attempted to affirm the traditions of episcopacy, presbytery, and diaconate, and which pointed to the need for further study. Another statement, "One Baptism," was approved, which affirmed both the traditions of infant and adult baptism.[98] By this time COCU recognized the difficulty of the ecumenical undertaking and acknowledged the possibility of future difficulties. But also at Princeton, Roman Catholic observer-consultants were welcomed to COCU for the first time.[99]

During 5-8 April 1965, COCU met at Lexington, Kentucky. Two reports on ordained ministry were adopted.[100] These reports reflected a general agreement to include the historic episcopate (Apostolic succession) in the ministries of the new body.[101] The African Methodist Episcopal Church was welcomed as a full COCU partner. A special commission was appointed to draw up an actual "Plan of Union."[102]

When the Consultation next met, in Dallas, Texas, 2-5 May 1966, it adopted "an open letter to the churches involved in the union justifying the merger as an expression of God's will." A timetable was also proposed for the merger, which called for "creation and ratification of a union plan within thirteen years, followed by some thirty years of federation during which a constitution ... [would] be prepared."[103] At the Dallas meeting two new full partners were welcomed—the African Methodist Episcopal Zion Church and the Presbyterian Church in the United States. The Lutheran Church, Missouri Synod, sent observer-consultants.[104]

When COCU met in Cambridge, Massachusetts, 3-4 May 1967, it was joined by its tenth new member, the Christian Methodist Episcopal Church. At this meeting the role of the observer consultants was considerably expanded. "Guidelines for the Structure of the Church" were received and the timetable which had been adopted at the Dallas meeting was modified.[105]

The Cooperative Disciples were very much involved with COCU and it had not yet come to its most disappointing days. Therefore, the formation of COCU and its largely optimistic and progressive development during the years of Restructure, together with the ecumenical enthusiasm generated by the Second Vatican Council, added credibility to the growing conviction among Cooperatives that ecumenism rather than restorationism was the more promising route to Christian union and missional faithfulness.

---

1. J. Brooks Major, "The Role of Periodicals in the Development of the Disciples of Christ, 1850-1910" (Ph.D. dissertation, Vanderbilt University, 1966), 144; McAllister and Tucker, *Journey in Faith*, 253.

2. McAllister and Tucker, *Journey in Faith*, 446-47.

3. Oliver Read Whitley, *Trumpet Call of Reformation* (St. Louis: Bethany Press, 1959), 147.

4. Alfred T. DeGroot, *Church of Christ Number Two* (Birmingham, England: By the Author, 1956), 4.

5. DeGroot, *Grounds of Divisions*, 204-205.

6. Ibid., 185.

7. Stephen J. Corey, *Fifty Years of Attack and Controversy: The Consequences Among Disciples of Christ* (St. Louis: Christian Board of Publication for the Committee on Publication of the Corey Manuscript, 1953), 14-61.

8. Ibid., 11.

9. J. H. Garrison, "Church Federation," 449-50.

10. "It Is Not Union in Christ," *Christian Standard* 42 (17 February 1906):251, quoted in Corey, *Attack and Controversy*, 15.

11. Corey, *Attack and Controversy*, 17.

12. Ibid.

13. J. W. McGarvey, "Biblical Criticism: The Little 'Scroll' Again," *Christian Standard* 42 (10 November 1906):1697, quoted in Corey, *Attack and Controversy*, 18.

14. Corey, *Attack and Controversy*, 20.

15. Ibid.

16. Ibid., 22.

17. Ibid., 31-32.
18. Murch, *Christians Only*, 214.
19. Corey, *Attack and Controversy*, 36-37.
20. Ronald E. Osborn, "Theology Among the Disciples," in *Interpretative Examination*, ed. Beazley, 102.
21. Corey, *Attack and Controversy*, 43.
22. Loren E. Lair, *The Christian Churches and Their Work* (St. Louis: Bethany Press, 1963), 133.
23. "Why Protest?", *Christian Standard* 52 (23 December 1916):371, quoted in Corey, *Attack and Controversy*, 44.
24. Corey, *Attack and Controversy*, 46.
25. McAllister and Tucker, *Journey in Faith*, 364.
26. *Webster's New World Dictionary*, 2nd College ed., s.v. "higher criticism."
27. See Boring, "The Disciples and Higher Criticism," 63-64.
28. Ibid., 29-70.
29. Beazley, "Who Are the Disciples," 40, n. 37.
30. DeGroot, *Church of Christ Number Two*, 32-33.
31. Corey, *Attack and Controversy*, 58.
32. James DeForest Murch, *The Free Church: A Treatise on Church Polity with Special Relevance to Doctrine and Practice in Christian Churches and Churches of Christ* (Washington, D.C.: Restoration Press, 1966), 110-11, 116-17.
33. Edwin V. Hayden, *Fifty Years of Digression and Disturbance: A Review of Stephen J. Corey's Book, "Fifty Years of Attack and Controversy"* (Joplin, Missouri: By the Author, 402 N. Wall Ave., 1953), 3, 6.
34. McAllister and Tucker, *Journey in Faith*, 380.
35. Edwin R. Errett, "Louisville Congress Makes History," *Christian Standard* 57 (17 December 1921):2997, quoted in McAllister and Tucker, *Journey in Faith*, 383.
36. McAllister and Tucker, *Journey in Faith*, 383.
37. Kenneth L. Teegarden, General Minister and President of the Christian Church (Disciples of Christ), personal letter, 27 January 1982.
38. Commission on Cooperative Policy and Practice, International Convention of Christian Churches (Disciples of Christ), *What Brotherhood Cooperation Means* (St. Louis: Christian Board of Publication, n. d.), 19.
39. Ibid., 19-20, 3-15.
40. Winfred E. Garrison, Foreword to *J. H. Garrison*, by Tucker, 9-10.
41. Corey, *Attack and Controversy*, 8.
42. DeGroot, *Grounds of Divisions*, 220.
43. DeGroot and Garrison, *The Disciples of Christ*, 553.

44. Whitley, *Trumpet Call of Reformation*, 209.
45. Murch, *Christians Only*, 352.
46. DeGroot, *Restoration Principle*, 14.
47. David Edwin Harrell, Jr., "Peculiar People: A Rationale for Modern Conservative Disciples," in Robert O. Fife, David Edwin Harrell, Jr., and Ronald E. Osborn, *Disciples and the Church Universal*, The Reed Lectures for 1966 (Nashville: Disciples of Christ Historical Society, 1967), 39.
48. Harrell, *Social History*, 2:14.
49. Crow, interview.
50. Winfred E. Garrison, *The Quest and Character of a United Church* (New York: Abingdon Press, 1957), 12.
51. Finis S. Idleman, *Peter Ainslie: Ambassador of Good Will* (Chicago: Willett, Clark & Co., 1941), 60.
52. Peter Ainslie, "Our Fellowship and the Task," President's Address to the American Christian Missionary Society, Topeka, Kansas, 14 October 1910, 2 (mimeographed), Peter Ainslie Personal Papers File, Disciples of Christ Historical Society, Nashville, Tennessee.
53. Winfred E. Garrison, *Christian Unity and Disciples of Christ* (St. Louis: Bethany Press, 1955), 162.
54. Idleman, *Peter Ainslie*, 60.
55. McAllister and Tucker, *Journey in Faith*, 422.
56. Peter Ainslie, Introduction to *The Equality of All Christians before God: A Record of the New York Conference of the Christian Unity League Held at St. George's Church, New York City* (New York: Macmillan Co., 1930), 10; On Disciples' changing concepts and practices with regard to Christian unity, see Douglas A. Foster, "The Disciples' Struggle for Unity Compared to the Struggle Among Presbyterians, 1880-1980" and Anthony L. Dunnavant, "Disciples Leaders' Changing Posture Regarding the United States and 'Denominationalism,' 1880-1980," in *A Case Study of Mainstream Protestantism*, ed. Williams, 171-93, 236-59.
57. This is the way that Henry E. Webb characterizes the creation of the Commission. Webb's is a very full and sympathetic account of the Commission's work (Webb, *In Search of Christian Unity*, 339, 339-54).
58. McAllister and Tucker, *Journey in Faith*, 401.
59. Commission on Restudy of the Disciples of Christ, *Report of the Commission* (San Francisco: International Convention of Disciples of Christ, 1948), 11-15.
60. Commission on Restudy, *Report*, 26-27.
61. Martin E. Marty, *Righteous Empire: The Protestant Experience in America* (New York: Dial Press, 1970), 177, 179.

62. Henry E. Webb, "The Authority of the Scriptures," *Christian Standard* 94 (22 August 1959):469.

63. Ernest R. Sandeen, "Fundamentalism and American Identity," *Annals of the American Academy of Political and Social Science* 387 (January 1970): 60.

64. Murch, *Free Church*, 120-130.

65. Sandeen, "Fundamentalism and American Identity," 60.

66. McAllister and Tucker, *Journey in Faith*, 16, 423-24.

67. W. B. Blakemore, "Where Thought and Action Meet," in Blakemore, gen. ed., *Panel of Scholars Reports*, 3:17.

68. Examples of the literature would include Winfred E. Garrison's three books *A Protestant Manifesto* (New York: Abingdon Press, 1952), *Christian Unity and the Disciples of Christ* (St. Louis: Bethany Press, 1955), and *The Quest and Character of a United Church* (New York: Abingdon, 1957).

69. Willard M. Wickizer, "A Statement Concerning the Panel of Scholars," in Blakemore, gen ed., *Panel of Scholars Reports*, 1:8.

70. Blakemore, "Where Thought and Action Meet," 17.

71. Ralph G. Wilburn, "The Unity We Seek," in Blakemore, gen. ed., *Panel of Scholars Reports*, 3:335-62.

72. "Panel of Scholars Membership," in Blakemore, gen. ed., *Panel of Scholars Reports*, 2:11.

73. Dwight E. Stevenson, "Concepts of the New Testament Church which Contribute to Disciple Thought about the Church," in Blakemore, gen ed., *Panel of Scholars Reports*, 3:38-39.

74. Ibid., 39-49.

75. "Panel of Scholars Membership," 11.

76. Ralph G. Wilburn, "A Critique of the Restoration Principle: Its Place in Contemporary Life and Thought," in Blakemore, gen. ed., *Panel of Scholars Reports*, 1:215-16, 219, 226.

77. Ibid., 226-33.

78. Ibid., 223, 241.

79. Ronald E. Osborn, "Crisis and Reformation: A Preface to Volume I," in Blakemore, gen. ed., *Panel of Scholars Reports*, 1:25-26.

80. Willard M. Wickizer, "Ideas for Brotherhood Restructure," in Blakemore, gen. ed., *Panel of Scholars Reports*, 3:113.

81. W. B. Blakemore, "The Issue of Polity for Disciples Today," in Blakemore, gen. ed., *Panel of Scholars Reports*, 3:52.

82. Ibid., 62.

83. Ibid., 67.

84. Ibid., 64-80.

85. Howard E. Short, private interview, St. Louis, Missouri, 8 July 1982; Kenneth L. Teegarden, private interview, Indianapolis, Indiana, 13 July 1982; James O. Duke with Joseph D. Driskill, "Disciples Theologizing amid Currents of Mainstream Protestant Thought, 1940 to 1980: Sketchbook Observations," in *A Case Study of Mainstream Protestantism*, ed. Williams, 146-50.

86. The Second Vatican Council, *The Decree on Ecumenism*, trans. The Secretariat for Promoting Christian Unity (Glen Rock, New Jersey: Paulist Press, 1965), 7.

87. "The Ecumenicity of Vatican II," *America* 114 (1 January 1966):8.

88. Second Vatican Council, *Decree on Ecumenism*, 7.

89. Despite the fact that Anglicans in the United States for the most part belong to the "Protestant Episcopal Church," Roman Catholics and others frequently and justifiably distinguish between Anglicans and Protestants.

90. "Ecumenicity of Vatican II," 8.

91. Second Vatican Council, *Decree on Ecumenism*, 7.

92. James DeForest Murch, *Adventuring for Christ in Changing Times: An Autobiography of James DeForest Murch* (Louisville: Restoration Press, 1973), 393-94; Robert W. Burns, private interview, Atlanta, Georgia, 10 June 1982.

93. William J. Schmidt, "COCU in the Crucible," *Catholic World*, August 1968, 214.

94. The National Council is the direct descendant of the Federal Council of the Churches of Christ in America, which was organized in 1907 "for the prosecution of work that can be better done in union than in separation." It was composed of most major Protestant denominations and one Eastern Orthodox body; its constituents numbered well over 25,000,000. Vergilius Ferm, ed., *An Encyclopedia of Religion* (Paterson, New Jersey: Littlefield, Adams & Co., 1959), s.v., "Federal Council of the Churches of Christ in America," by Luther Allan Weigle.

95. Schmidt, "COCU in the Crucible," 215.

96. COCU, *The Official Reports of the Four Meetings of the Consultation* (Cincinnati: Forward Movement Publications, 1966), 7.

97. Ibid., 7-9.

98. Ibid.

99. Schmidt, "COCU in the Crucible," 217.

100. COCU, *Official Reports*, 9.

101. Schmidt, "COCU in the Crucible," 217.

102. COCU, *Official Reports*, 10.

103. "Ecumenism: From Handholding to Engagement," *Time*, 13 May 1966, 86.

104. Schmidt, "COCU in the Crucible," 217.

105. COCU, *Church Union 1967: Principles of Church Union, Guidelines for Structure, and a Study Guide* (Cincinnati: Forward Movement Publications, 1967), 63-89.

CHAPTER IV

STRUCTURE IN THE CAMPBELL-STONE MOVEMENT IN ITS FIRST GENERATION

Thus far the main focus of this study has been the ideological tradition in the Campbell-Stone movement as centered in commitment to the ideals of restoration, unity, liberty, and mission. As the relative importance of and interpretation of these fundamental ideals changed so did the embodiment of the movement's ideals in organizational structure.

A logical place to begin a survey of the structural traditions of the Campbell-Stone heritage would be with the first of the four founders active in the United States, Barton W. Stone, and with the earliest of the primary documents of the movement, the *Last Will and Testament of the Springfield Presbytery*. The *Last Will and Testament* is a document that obviously relates to structure. It is a repudiation of churchly structures believed by its authors to be unauthorized by the New Testament. These structures included "Church Sessions, Presbyteries, Synods, General Assemblies, etc."[1] The *Last Will and Testament* was a strongly congregational document—it advocated the independence of each "particular church" and stressed only spiritual rather than organizational or structural unity among churches.

> *Item*. We *will*, that each particular church, as a body, actuated by the same spirit, choose her own preacher, and support him by a free will offering, without a written *call* or *subscription*—admit members—remove offences; and never henceforth *delegate* her right of government to any man or set of men whatever.[2]

The constitutive principle of the Church was, to Barton Stone, "the indwelling of the Holy Spirit in each believer and member of the church."[3] The "church" usually meant the "congregation."[4] Stone was suspicious of extracongregational structures. His renowned commitment to Christian union was a commitment that was not pursued organizationally but "spiritually" and through "fellowship." Stone did believe in a broad view of Christian fellowship. His fellowship extended to unimmersed persons.[5] In short, Stone was not so much interested in creating structures to embody Christian union as in *eliminating* structures so that Christians' "spiritual union" could emerge.

Loren Lair has commented about the "Christian Church movement" of Barton Stone: "Its emphasis was upon the independence of the local church, the Scriptures as the basis of authority, and conferences for the sake of fellowship and mutual edification. However, there was no strong emphasis or motivation for cooperative work and organization."[6] A Dale Fiers goes even further and suggests that "Barton W. Stone, the theologian and theorist of the Christians, was not a man profoundly concerned with polity." It may certainly be said that Stone did little to encourage the development of extracongregational polity in the Campbell-Stone movement. Fiers implies that those who have used the *Last Will and Testament of the Springfield Presbytery* as the "cornerstone of a full-blown polity which saw all organization beyond the local congregation as evil and as forbidden by [the] New Testament" go beyond Stone's intention.[7] The Stone "Christians'" conferences did retain at least one function that made them somewhat presbyterial; they were involved in the ordination of elders.[8]

The important point which clarifies Stone's view of churchly structure may be stated in terms of the classical Campbell-Stone values of restoration, union, liberty, and mission. To Stone, history showed that churchly structures had taken away the liberty of "common people" under Christ and had substituted clerical rule.

> While . . . [Jesus] reigned and ruled alone in the first centuries of the world, religion in her loveliest forms dwelt on earth; but . . .
> . . . the clergy changed the laws and government of the king of Zion at the council of Nice, A.D. 325, and the many took the government from the shoulders of Zion's king and laid it on their own. . . . Finally [they] put it on the shoulders of one man, the Pope. . . . but they have substituted themselves in his stead. . . . The difference between Papists and Protestants, is, that the Papists are ruled by one infallible Pope, and the Protestants by many.

It was this usurpation which was responsible for division and strife among Christians and indeed among all people.

The triumph of the Church's mission and the consummation of her unity awaited only the restoration of the absolute monarchy of Jesus Christ.

> To [Jesus Christ] . . . is given authority over all flesh—he is the one—the only lawgiver of all—of the whole world. All, Jews and Gentiles are under his government, and bound to obedience to his laws. They are not to add to, nor diminish from, his laws—they must not change his government, but submit to it cheerfully, fully, and cordially. Were

First-Generation Structure

all to do this, peace, love, and harmony would unite, and keep united the now jarring, wretched world.[9]

How does the absolute monarchy of Jesus Christ function? For Stone it is not primarily through churchly structures, but through the encounter of the individual Christian with the Bible, with belief in its testimony, and with God's gift of the Holy Spirit.[10] In the words of the *Last Will and Testament*:

> *Item.* We *will*, that our power of making laws for the government of the church, and executing them by delegated authority, forever cease; that the people may have free course to the Bible, and adopt *the law of the Spirit of life in Christ Jesus*.[11]

Thus, while Stone continued to support conferences among "Christians" and certainly supported the principle of Christian union, practiced a broad interpretation of Christian fellowship, and even retained at least a quasi-presbyterial understanding of the function of the conference in the ordination of elders, the main thrust of his view was antiecclesiastical. In terms of his cherished values—the union of Christians, the liberty of Christians under Christ's monarchy (administered through the Bible), and eventual triumph of Christ in history (evangelization-mission-millennialism)—the structures of the historic churches were viewed as impediments and as the products of an apostasy.

> Men by the light of truth are beginning to see that Christians have no right to make laws and governments for themselves, and that all should submit to the government and laws of our king. This is a great reformation; and must be done, we must cease to support any other government on earth by our counsels, co-operation, and choice. . . If we do not, it will be done by others—the millenium [*sic*] approaches.[12]

Just as the *Last Will and Testament* relates directly to organization and structure in its announcement of the "death" of one structure—the Springfield Presbytery—and its denunciation of other churchly structures, so, too, the second primary document of the Campbell-Stone movement directly relates to structure in its announcement of the formation of the Christian Association of Washington, Pennsylvania. The implications for the issue of structure in Thomas Campbell's *Declaration and Address of the Christian Association of Washington, Pennsylvania* may be approached by examining three categories of statements contained in that document.

First, there are the statements that the *Declaration and Address* makes about "the Christian Association of Washington, Pennsylvania." These statements, while not necessarily about the Church per se, reveal something about what the author considered to be valid structure for the embodiment of at least some aspect of Christianity. Second, there are statements about the Church universal. Finally, there are statements which relate to the structures of the historic churches.

Most of the statements about the Association itself come in the form of nine resolutions that set forth the character, organization, purpose, and fundamental assumptions of that body. The first resolution states the purpose of the organization as "promoting simple evangelical Christianity, free from all mixture of human opinions and inventions of men." The second resolution provides for finances, based upon subscription, to be paid semiannually, and to be used "to support a pure Gospel ministry, that shall reduce to practice that whole form of doctrine, worship, discipline, and government, expressly revealed and enjoined in the word of God. And, also, for supplying the poor with the holy Scriptures." The third resolution placed upon the Society (Association) the duty of encouraging the formation of others like itself through correspondence and the rendering of "all possible assistance." The fourth resolution states most clearly the Association's self-understanding:

> IV. That this Society by no means considers itself a Church, nor does at all assume to itself the powers peculiar to such a society; nor do the members, as such, consider themselves standing connected in that relation; nor as at all associated for the peculiar purposes of Church association; but merely as voluntary advocates for Church reformation; and, as possessing the powers common to all individuals, who may please to associate in a peaceable and orderly manner, for any lawful purpose, namely, the disposal of their time, counsel and property, as they may see cause.

This resolution not only denies that the Association was a church but suggests that Christians may organize for avowedly Christian purposes in a society that does not claim churchly status. This principle proved to be a prominent one in the history of structure in the Campbell-Stone movement.

The remainder of the resolutions reiterate the determination of the Association to support only a "pure Gospel ministry," provide for a standing committee including officers with delegated powers, provide for meeting times

First-Generation Structure

and agendas, and look toward the promotion of "a pure evangelical reformation, by the simple preaching of the everlasting Gospel, and the administration of its ordinances in an exact conformity to the Divine standard."[13]

These basic resolutions of the Christian Association make clear that: 1) Campbell believed that Christians could organize a reformation movement based upon associations *within* the churches, which would not themselves be churches but would be designed to act as "reforming" bodies upon the churches; 2) such societies were to be based on a principle of voluntaryism; 3) such societies could properly have committees with some delegated powers; and 4) while no claim is made as to the scripturalness of the Association, the Association's avowed purposes are biblistic—to "support a pure Gospel ministry" and "supply . . . the poor with the holy Scriptures."

The roots of this kind of society or interdenominational voluntary association in Thomas Campbell's experience were in the Evangelical Society of Ulster. Such societies, for "the support of itinerant preaching" had been "a common feature of the evangelical revival of the 1790s" in the British Isles.[14]

The statements about the Church universal are principally concentrated in the thirteen propositions, which are summarized above (chapter one). These propositions advance basic assumptions about the Church: 1) in the intention of God, and as God constitutes it, the Church is one and consists of those who conform to Scripture both in faith and ethics; therefore, although congregations are geographically separate, they should still manifest unity; 2) the New Testament is the constitution of the Church, beyond which the Church may not go when determining fitness for membership, worship, discipline, or government; and 3) divisions among Christians, which are evil, are caused by a violation of the scriptural constitution. Thomas Campbell's understanding of the nature of the Church as composed of individuals who conform to the constitution (the New Testament) in terms of belief and life and his assumption of the "givenness" of this nature in the intention of God underlay his belief that Christianity, and indeed the Church, continued to exist within the historic churches. What he hoped to do with his Christian Association was not offer an alternative church but to reform the existing churches so that the Church might more clearly emerge from their midst.

It should be remembered that Campbell addressed his document to *"all that love our Lord Jesus Christ, in sincerity, throughout all the Churches,* . . . DEARLY BELOVED BRETHREN."[15] His assumption that the Church did exist among the churches softens what would otherwise be a harsh biblicism in the *Address*. The propositions contain at least two other statements which qualify the *Address*'s biblicism:

> ... It is not necessary that persons should have a particular knowledge or distinct apprehension of all Divinely revealed truths in order to entitle them to a place in the Church. ...
>
> ... If any circumstantials indispensably necessary to the observance of Divine ordinances be not found upon the pages of express revelation, such, and such only, as are absolutely necessary for this purpose should be adopted under the title of human expedients.[16]

The *Declaration and Address* depicts a Church whose character is determined by the New Testament as its constitution, whose membership is determined by conformity to that constitution, and whose unity exists in the intention of God but is hidden by human additions to and violations of that divine constitution. The strict biblicism is qualified by a recognition of the limits of human knowledge and the necessity for the adoption of "expedients" in the Church. Campbell insisted that when "expedients" be adopted they be done so "without any pretense to a more sacred origin."[17] This insistence became a stumbling block to the assertion of the "churchly" character of extracongregational structures in the Campbell-Stone movement, for these structures were viewed as "expedients."

The final category of statements in the *Declaration and Address* which relate to structure and organization is that of statements which reflect the condition of the historic churches. The first of these conditions is division:

> Grievously affected with those sad divisions which have so awfully interfered with the benign and gracious intention of our holy religion, ... we cannot suppose ourselves justifiable in withholding the mite of our sincere and humble endeavors to remove them.

Thomas Campbell's intention that the removal of division be embodied in actual structures is reflected in the Appendix to the *Declaration and Address*:

> We are speaking of the unity of the Church considered as a great, visible, professing body, consisting of many co-ordinate associations; each of these, in its aggregate or associate capacity, walking by the same rule, professing and practicing the same things.[18]

The implication is clear that the churches were divided structurally and, in Campbell's view, needed to achieve greater structural unity. The *Declaration and Address* also implies that the juridical or judicial structures of churches were ill-constituted. Given the experience of Thomas Campbell with his presbytery, this seems a reasonable inference to draw from the following words:

> We are ... of opinion that as the Divine word is equally binding upon all, so all lie under an equal obligation to be bound by it, and it alone; and not by any human interpretation of it; and that, therefore, no man has a right to judge his brother, except in so far as he manifestly violates the express letter of the law.... Every such judgment is an express violation of the law of Christ, a daring usurpation of his throne, and a gross intrusion upon the rights and liberties of his subjects.

Later in the same paragraph, Campbell rejects both the "opinions" and the "inventions of men as of any authority, or as having any place in the Church of God."[19]

The *Declaration and Address* is implicitly antiecclesiastical in its suggestion that structures which exist between the *individual* and the Church universal impede the Church's unity. As has been seen in Campbell's advocacy of an associational principle among associations, he viewed the Church as being constituted in aggregate fashion by its smaller units. To him, the basic unit was the individual. "By the Christian Church throughout the world, we mean the aggregate of . . . professors, . . . even all that mutually acknowledge each other as Christians, upon the manifest evidence of their faith, holiness, and charity." This was the structure that Thomas Campbell preeminently advocated. To Campbell, the theological and ecclesiological developments of the postapostolic era were the "rubbish of the ages."[20]

Still, the historic churches were not all bad. They were not beyond reformation. It was their reformation which was Thomas Campbell's aim. He considered his movement one for which the churches had laid the groundwork:

> Have not greater efforts been made, and more done, for the promulgation of the Gospel among the nations, since the commencement of the French revolution, than had been for many centuries prior to that event? And have not the Churches, both in Europe and America, since that period, discovered a more than usual concern for the removal of contentions, for the healing of divisions, for the restoration of a Christian and brotherly intercourse one with another, and for the promotion of each other's spiritual good, as the printed documents upon those subjects amply testify?

Perhaps it was naivete, but Campbell also declared: "The prayers of all the Churches, nay, the prayers of Christ himself . . . are with us." Campbell was certainly anxious to express his intention toward the churches:

> We have no intention to interfere, either directly or indirectly, with the peace and order of the settled Churches, by directing any ministerial assistance with which the Lord may please to favor us, to make inroads upon such; or by endeavoring to erect Churches out of Churches, to distract and divide congregations.[21]

While Thomas Campbell praised the reforming and unifying tendencies which he saw working in the historic churches, he also expected his reformation to commend itself to the churches. He reminded his readers that "we have our educational prejudices and particular customs to struggle against as well as they." However, these must be overcome. No longer could "an external name, a mere educational formality of sameness in the profession of a certain standard or formula of human fabric, with a very moderate degree of what is called morality" be the basis for churchly order. What Campbell called for was a "Church constitution and managements, . . . exhibit[ing] a complete conformity to the apostolic Church."[22] While he was not so naive as to believe that *all* within the churches would receive his *Address* favorably ("for there will always be multitudes of weak persons in the Church, and these are generally most subject to bigotry; add to this, that while division exist, there will always be found interested men who will not fail to support them"),[23] it was to be to Christians within the churches that Campbell addressed his reformation, commending the churches for their own tendencies in his reforming direction, and expecting the prayers, cooperation, and commendation of all authentic Christians within these bodies.

In sum, the *Declaration and Address* presents the principles of: 1) biblicism, as seen in the purposes of the Association and in the affirmation of the New Testament as the constitution of the Church; 2) individualism, as seen in the individualistic voluntaryism which is the organizing principle of the Association and in the identification of individuals as the proper objects of Campbell's address (since morally or ethically Christian individuals in aggregate were, in his view, the Church); and 3) freedom of organization, as seen in the creation of the Association and in the statement about "expedients." The *Declaration and Address* reflects an awareness of the structural divisions of the historic churches and a belief that the churches' judicial structures were "unauthorized" and their postapostolic structures "rubbish." However, the churches' recent missionary

First-Generation Structure 101

and cooperating trends were judged praiseworthy, and the "authentic" members of the churches were counted on to support the reformation. The historic churches, corrupted by history, had become lax and formal, and were a mixture of the pious and impious; but these bodies were reformable and it was from among them that Thomas Campbell expected the Church to emerge.

In 1810 and 1811 in the Campbell branch of the Campbell-Stone movement there were two major developments which had serious implications for the issue of structure. The first major development was the rejection of the Christian Association by the Presbyterian Synod of Pittsburgh and the Association's reconstitution as an independent congregational church. This development contradicted the insistence of the *Declaration and Address* that the Association was not a church and tended toward contradicting that same document's insistence that the Association was not "endeavoring to erect Churches out of Churches."[24] Part of the explanation for those contradictions lies in the fact that by 1811 Thomas Campbell's dominant leadership role in the new church was being eclipsed by the role of his son, Alexander. The emergence of Alexander Campbell as the primary leader of the Campbell branch of the movement was the second major development. This meant that it would *not* be the author of the *Declaration and Address* but the eventual editor of the *Christian Baptist* and *Millennial Harbinger* whose ecclesiological thought would have the most impact on the structure of the Campbell-Stone movement.

Another major ecclesiological development related to Alexander Campbell's emergence as the primary leader of the movement was the change in the movement's outlook with regard to the historic churches brought about by the adoption of immersion as the only mode of baptism. "No longer was it simply a matter of persuading churches to unite on the beliefs which Christians already held. It would be felt necessary to persuade them also to accept immersion which at that time only the Baptists believed to be commanded."[25]

During the years from 1815 to 1830 the Brush Run Church and other congregations influenced by the Campbells belonged to various Baptist associations. In 1815 the Brush Run Church joined the Redstone Baptist Association, with the reservation that the Brush Run congregation should remain free to follow the Bible as opposed to creeds. There was opposition to the presence of the Campbell "reformers" among the Baptists from the beginning, and the situation was exacerbated by Alexander's 1816 "Sermon on the Law," with its emphasis on the difference between the Old and New Testaments, and, later, by his writings in the *Christian Baptist*.[26]

The writings of Alexander Campbell in the *Christian Baptist* with regard to the legitimacy of extracongregational cooperative structures have long interested historians of the Campbell-Stone movement. In 1884, F. M. Green attempted to make sense of the early antiecclesiastical Alexander Campbell in light of the later Campbell who advocated and participated in extracongregational structures.

> The history which lies between the years 1823 and 1830, is noisy with the roar of immense conflict. . . .
> Much that was good in the religious systems of the day received iconoclastic treatment along with the bad in whose company unfortunately it was found. It would not be true to the facts to say that Mr. Campbell's words were always the fittest to describe what he assailed so bitterly and vigorously. . . .
> The *Christian Baptist* was the "thunder-hammer" of his might which he used with but little regard for the consequences; the *Millennial Harbinger* was the full-orbed power of the righteous man who desired to "deal justly, love mercy, and walk humbly before God."[27]

Although the style of writing has changed, the substance of Green's statement has been often repeated in studies of Alexander Campbell.

In his study of the thought of Alexander Campbell on the structure of the Church, D. Ray Lindley also identifies two distinct periods in the career of Alexander Campbell:

> Thus we have seen that until the third decade of the 19th century Campbell's career was marked by a violent antiecclesiasticism. That antiecclesiasticism rooted back both in Campbell's historical experience and his psychological make-up. It was absolutistic in its sweep, and sought to brush aside all existing Christian sects with their media of propagation. . . .
> Beginning in the middle of the third decade, and reaching its peak in the fourth and fifth decades of the 19th century, Campbell applied himself to the constructive period of his career, and struggled to create the type of Christian community which would meet the dictates of what he considered to be both reason and revelation.[28]

In the first part of Lindley's book, the antiecclesiasticism of Alexander Campbell is treated under two headings. "The Mother of Harlots and Her Progeny" details Campbell's view of the Roman Catholic Church and the Protestant denominations. The second heading is "The Tools of Ecclesiastical Tyranny," in which category the early Alexander Campbell placed the clergy, creeds and confessions of faith, church courts, theology and orthodoxy, Sunday schools, and missionary organizations.[29]

On the pages of the *Christian Baptist*, especially, Campbell ridiculed the notion of church government:

> After all that has been said upon the subject of church government, lodged in human hands; after all the angry contests, whether an episcopacy similar to a monarchy; whether a presbytery similar to an aristocracy, or an independency similar to a democracy, be instituted by God, or authorized in the New Testament—it might perhaps appear, upon an impartial examination of the scriptures, that the whole controversy is . . . a sound and nothing else; that there is no such thing as "church government," in the popular sense of the terms.[30]

In the same periodical, three years later, Campbell himself entered the "angry contests": "The Grecian and Roman republics, the commonwealth of Israel in its primitive integrity, the republics of America, and the congregations of christians in this one instance are essentially the same. *In their first origin the people did everything, both elect and ordain.*"[31]

It was not so much the notion of a church government, nor the method of arguing for a church government from an analogous political system that offended Campbell. It was instead the despotic character of existing churchly structures that he opposed:

> That "monster horrific, shapeless, hugh, whose light is extinct," called an ecclesiastical court. . . .
> Whether such an alliance of the priests and the nobles of the kirk be called a session, a presbytery, a synod, a general assembly, a convention, a conference, an association, or annual meeting, its tendency and result are the same. Whenever and wherever such a meeting either legislates, decrees, rules, directs, or controls, or assumes the character of a representative body in religious concerns, it essentially becomes "the man of sin and the son of perdition."[32]

During his *Christian Baptist* editorship, Campbell attacked and attempted to pull down those structures which he regarded as illegitimate additions to the "ancient order":

But to come to the things to be discarded, we observe that, in the ancient order of things, there were no creeds or compilations of doctrine in abstract terms, nor in other terms other than the terms adopted by the Holy Spirit in the New Testament. *Therefore, all such are to be discarded.*[33]

What Alexander Campbell wrote of creeds he also believed of churchly structures. Lindley has summarized Campbell's thought: "If the Antichrist of ecclesiasticism used the clergy as its high priests, and creeds as its shibboleths, it used its ecclesiastical courts as its sanhedrins in its tyranny over the free spirit" of humanity.[34]

Not surprisingly, during the days of the *Christian Baptist* Alexander Campbell seemed to equate the "church" with the local congregation. He published approvingly the following:

> When they refer to any circumscribed or limited situation, as a town or city, they, in all cases, use the singular number, as the church at Ephesus, at Corinth, at Cenchrea, . . .
> But when they come to speak of a certain district of country, in which there was a number of such assemblies, they as invariably use the plural number, as "the churches of Galatia."[35]

If each congregation is "the church" and collectively they are "the churches," what is to be the structure of their interrelation, the embodiment of the Church universal? The Campbell of the *Christian Baptist* replied: "The church . . . a society of disciples . . . meeting together in one place, with its bishop or bishops, and deacon or deacons, . . . is perfectly independent of any tribunal on earth called ecclesiastical."[36] The early Campbell shunned the notion that the unity of Christians would have structural expression. He preferred to speak in terms of a union in Christ:

> The societies called churches, constituted and set in order by those ministers of the New Testament, were of such as received and acknowledged Jesus as the Lord Messiah, the Saviour of the World, and had put themselves under his guidance. The ONLY BOND OF UNION among them was faith in him and submission to his will.[37]

The structural implications of this statement are far from clear. Like Barton W. Stone, Alexander Campbell liked to speak in terms of the kingship of Christ:

First-Generation Structure

"There is no other authority recognized, allowed, or regarded, by a society of christians, meeting in one place as a church of Jesus Christ, than the authority of its king or head."[38] How was this kingship exercised? First, through the apostles; after their deaths, through the Bible; and finally, through the Holy Spirit "in accordance with" the Bible.[39]

During his iconoclastic period, Campbell would certainly not have suggested that the Church universal, or the kingdom of Christ, might find expression in extracongregational structures. He opposed these. Not only did he oppose judicial structures, but also theological schools and missionary societies. In each case he opposed these institutions by denying that the local churches needed them and suggesting that the churches functioned better without them:

> The New Testament... churches were not fractured into missionary societies, bible societies, education societies; nor did they dream of organizing such in the world.... They dare not transfer to a missionary society, or bible society, a cent or a prayer, lest in so doing they should rob the church of its glory, and exalt the inventions of men above the wisdom of God.[40]

This denunciation of the society idea is interesting in light of both the prior and the subsequent history of the Campbell-Stone movement.

Alexander's father, Thomas, had participated in an evangelical society in Ireland and subsequently launched the Campbell's branch of the movement as a society with a strict denial that it was a church. A little over a decade later, Alexander *still differentiated* societies from churches, but implied that the former had no right to exist. Three decades after this denial, Alexander Campbell was the president of the American Christian Missionary Society. This reversal on the society issue, together with Alexander's turnabout with regard to theological schools,[41] contributed to the lack of clarity as to the ecclesiological values of the Campbell-Stone movement. The ecclesiological impact of the emergence of Alexander Campbell as the primary leader of the movement lay largely in 1) the strengthening (through the *Christian Baptist*) of the antiecclesiasticism, anticreedalism, and anticlericalism which had been introduced at the very beginnings of the movement and which are apparent in the *Last Will and Testament* and the *Declaration and Address*, and 2) the confusion over polity resulting from Campbell's reversals.

Like Campbell, Walter Scott exhibited little consistency on the matter of extracongregational structure. In 1827 Scott wrote to Barton W. Stone in qualified support of extracongregational structures as they existed among the Campbell "reformers":

> I care not whether a religious convocation be termed a conference, association, or annual meeting; but as to the propriety of the brethren occasionally meeting for religious edification, instruction, and information, from different parts of the community, within proper and limited bounds, there should exist no doubts whatever. . . .
>
> Many are under the impression that we associate for the purpose of legislating or making laws for the rule and government of our churches. Nothing is more foreign from our views. I acknowledge one lawgiver and believe the great Head of the church as left a perfect code of laws for the government of his people.

Scott's advocacy of "conferences" is carefully qualified in the by-now familiar terms of the Bible's being the Church's "perfect code" and Christ's being the Church's "Head"; yet he thought it appropriate that the conferences meet to "worship together and strengthen the bonds of union, . . . attend to ordination," and "arrange appointments" for preaching.[42]

Scott's qualified support of extracongregational structures was not his last word on the subject, however. In 1830 Scott at least acquiesced in, and perhaps instigated, the dissolution of the Mahoning Association. And in 1843 Scott wrote that "church cooperation is alike unscriptural and unphilosophical," and that "the cooperation of the scriptures is not the cooperation of churches as a sect but of individuals as a church."[43] This utterance sounds very much like the Alexander Campbell of the *Christian Baptist*, though it came after Campbell's tones on church cooperation had undergone a marked change. Scott was destined to undergo another change.

In 1854 the *Millennial Harbinger* reprinted an address that had been made to the American Christian Missionary Society by its "much beloved and highly gifted Vice President, Elder Walter Scott."[44] In this address the great evangelist of the Campbell-Stone movement called for a multilevel cooperation in the great task of evangelism. Speaking for "our organization," Scott expressed a desire "to enjoy *town, city, county, district and state co-operation*" for "the perfection of the good cause" of evangelism. He also advocated the "exercise . . . [of] the combined power of all the churches by *delegation*, without destroying their individual and separate independence."[45] (Italics mine.)

This older Scott had moved to the advocacy of a kind of organization he had earlier denounced. No longer was he speaking of the cooperation of

First-Generation Structure

individuals, but of churches by delegation in an organization of multiple levels. The kind of organization that Scott advocated in this address was not adopted by the Campbell-Stone movement until Restructure and the creation of the Christian Church (Disciples of Christ) in the *Provisional Design* in 1968.[46] Part of the reason for that long delay is that like Alexander Campbell (the great journalistic leader of the first-generation Disciples), Walter Scott (the great evangelist of first-generation Disciples) helped to confuse the movement's early adherents with his apparent vacillations on polity.

Some of Scott's apparent self-contradiction on matters of polity might be explained in terms of the particular circumstances from which his actions or utterances arose. The motivation for the dissolution of the Mahoning Association may have been the growing disaffection between "orthodox" Baptists and the Campbell "reformers." This is the contention of McAllister and Tucker:

> In 1826 ten orthodox churches in the Redstone Association excluded thirteen congregations which refused to subscribe to the Philadelphia Confession. Three years later the Beaver Association in Pennsylvania severed its relationship with the Campbell-Scott dominated Mahoning Association in Ohio.... Before the close of 1830 practically all Baptist associations in Kentucky . . . had taken a public stand against the Reformers and excluded them.[47]

Alexander Campbell had not endeared himself to the Baptist associations in the pages of the *Christian Baptist*. In 1827 he wrote:

> Numerous complaints have been forwarded to this office from different parts of the country, of certain great stretches after dictatorial power, on the part of some leading members of Regular Baptist Associations, within the last two years. . . . We are happy to learn that in . . . almost every instance, Haman has been hung upon the gallows erected for Mordecai the Jew.[48]

As D. Ray Lindley points out, the Baptists were included in Alexander Campbell's blasts at the "daughters of 'The Mother of Harlots'" after the Baptist associations had begun to spurn him.[49] In short, both Scott and Alexander Campbell may have been mainly seeking freedom from a "tyrannical" association with a particular group of Baptists rather than intending to denounce associations in general in the years just prior to 1830.

Despite the fact that the *Christian Baptist* contained plenty of support for the idea of a vigorous congregationalism, by the 1830s Alexander Campbell no longer supported the notion. In an 1831 series of *Millennial Harbinger* articles on church cooperation, Campbell argued that the churches of the Apostles were organized in districts, and more significantly, appealed to a broad principle of doing "whatsoever things are true, . . . just, . . . benevolent."[50] Campbell attended the 1831 "fellowship" meeting of the Mahoning Association, which conducted no business, and offered there the suggestion that the churches might organize county meetings.[51]

In 1832 another milestone occurred in the history of the Campbell-Stone movement—the union of the Campbell "Disciples" and the Stone "Christians." "The Christians had been expanding as a separate communion since the dissolution of the Springfield Presbytery in 1804." The dissolution of the Mahoning Association in 1830 terminated the association of the "reformers" (Campbell's Disciples) with the Baptists and cleared the way for possible union of the Disciples with Stone's group. After several "grass-roots" initiatives, Campbell and Stone became involved in "an extended and sometimes heated interchange" on the issue of the union of the two groups. This interchange was carried in the *Christian Messenger* and the *Millennial Harbinger*.

> Stone opened the correspondence by stating flatly that no reason existed to prevent union as far as the Christians were concerned. In essence the Reformed Baptists—as he called them—had accepted the doctrine taught by the Christians for a number of years. Stone's candor upset Campbell. Other antisectarian reformers were pioneers clearing forests and burning brush, Campbell replied, but only he and his followers had restored the ancient gospel. Stone was unwilling to concede the point. . . . If the union of Christians and Disciples had depended solely upon the goodwill between Campbell and Stone, it never would have been accomplished.[52]

However, the union did not depend entirely upon the good will of the two principal leaders of their respective movements.

John T. Johnson, a preacher of the Campbell Disciples, became a close friend of Barton W. Stone and helped to push the process of union.[53] Another follower of Campbell, "Raccoon" John Smith, played a prominent role in the union which was effected in Lexington, Kentucky, 1 January 1832.[54] Stone and Smith, acting on behalf of the two groups at this gathering, agreed upon

First-Generation Structure 109

union based on "the ancient gospel and order of things as presented in the words of the Book."[55]

> In a moment charged with emotion Smith and Stone clasped hands. Then, at the proposal that all who were willing to accept union on the basis indicated should follow suit, members of one group reached for members of the other to offer them the "right hand of fellowship." Elders, teachers, and members joined in this act and thus, "ratified and confirmed the union."

Alexander Campbell was in Virginia at the time, "writing favorable observations" on news of the union as it reached him. The union encountered some "rocky moments," and some of the Stone "Christians" did not enter into it (one group eventually became part of the Congregational Christian Churches and finally the United Church of Christ; another group maintained its distinctive identity). However, "the process of union worked remarkably well."[56]

The union of 1832 not only introduced new vigor into the Campbell-Stone movement, but also new tensions.[57] There was some personal tension between Alexander Campbell and Barton Stone, reflected in their correspondence preceding the union. More seriously, there were several differences in the emphases of the two movements. McAllister and Tucker suggest the following differences: 1) the (Campbell) Disciples laid more stress on restoring primitive Christianity than did the (Stone) Christians; 2) the Disciples equated baptism with immersion, while the Christians tended to tolerate unimmersed Christians; 3) the Disciples observed the Lord's Supper weekly while the Christians observed it less frequently; 4) the Christians were less anticlerical than the Disciples; 5) the Christians were more tolerant of emotional revivalism than the Disciples; and 6) the Christians preferred the name "Christian" and the Disciples the name "Disciples."[58] In his analysis of the "Nature of the Church among the Disciples of Christ," Allen Eikner suggests that the united movement tended to take on Campbell's positions.[59] Although Eikner's suggestion appears correct on the basis of McAllister and Tucker's list in light of the subsequent history of the Campbell-Stone movement, initially the union brought new ambiguities and tensions.[60] Eva Jean Wrather places the union in the context of the organizational struggles of the movement when she writes:

> A new element to the problem of cooperation was introduced when the Campbell Reformers and . . . Stone "Christians" joined forces. . . . Ecumenically satisfying as this merger might have been, these "Christians"—born of the Great Revival of the West—were not

only committed to a wholly subjective concept of faith emphasizing the miraculous intervention of the Holy Spirit evidenced in the conversion "experiences" of the frontier camp meeting, . . . but they were also thoroughly imbued with that same frontier spirit of rampant individualism which had activated the rebellious Mahoning messengers of 1830. From the standpoint of Campbell's [post-1830] crusade for order and discipline, the union compounded the need for redoubled effort.[61]

Campbell's efforts on behalf of the order of the movement were exerted from his position as editor of the *Millennial Harbinger*. In 1835 he brought out the *Millennial Harbinger* "Extra on Order" and the first edition of his principal book—what was later entitled *The Christian System*. W. E. Garrison summarizes this principal book by describing Campbell's concept of the "kingdom of God." This was a kingdom "like any other," with "its constitution, its king, its subjects, its laws, and its territory." The Bible, of course, contains the constitution, and

> exhibits . . . three successive revisions for the successive dispensations. Here the influence of the Covenant Theology is seen, which, as Campbell applied it, both softened the rigors of Calvinism and focused attention on the New Testament as containing the whole constitution for the kingdom in its Christian dispensation. The King is Christ. The subjects are those who believe in him and give him their allegiance. . . . The laws of the kingdom are of two kinds: positive and moral. . . The positive laws also are of two kinds: laws for the naturalization of aliens, to wit, faith, repentance and baptism; and laws for citizens of the kingdom, . . . the weekly celebration of the Lord's Supper, and assembly on the first day of the week for this purpose and for worship and edification. All other laws of the kingdom are moral, that is, such as are approved by the enlightened conscience. The territory of the kingdom is the whole earth.[62]

The "Extra on Order" reflected Campbell's tendency to think in terms of "order" and "system." Together, the *Christian System* and "Extra on Order" called on "all creation to attest the glorious system and order of God's entire universe." The "Extra on Order" suggested that "evangelists and other general ministers or 'public officers' of the church . . . are to be chosen and ordained by a plurality of the churches." It was here that Campbell articulated the idea that "the relation between congregations and their overseers, at the local or

First-Generation Structure

national levels, should be considered as a *covenant*, a relation which would most effectively safeguard both order and liberty."[63]

Between 1835 and 1849, Alexander Campbell provided a continual editorial influence in favor of some form of extracongregational churchly life and organization. Sometimes Campbell's support of church consultation and cooperation came in the form of reporting on meetings of messengers. For example, in April 1835 the *Millennial Harbinger* contained a report of a "General Meeting of Messengers" which included comment on the rationale for cooperation among congregations:

> From all which we learn, that in those days there were consultations and co-operations in all things which transcended the knowledge and power of one congregation to effect. And this leads us now to take a more enlarged view than was expressed during our meeting, of all the relations in which the congregations stand to each other and to the world....
>
> In the conversion of the world co-operation is necessary upon any hypothesis.... Co-operation in reference to the internal affairs of the congregations, is wholly out of the question.[64]

Campbell found himself frequently in the position of editorially taking "a more enlarged view" than that expressed by some Disciples at their meetings in the 1830s. This fact led to utterances such as the following:

> We want co-operation. Some of our brethren are afraid of its power; others complain of its inefficiency. Still we go for co-operation...
>
> I have found a large class of men, professors too, who will sit still for a year rather than rise up crooked. They are conscientious men; but they do nothing right lest they should do something wrong.[65]

This legalistic mind-set of some within the Campbell-Stone movement was, in part, rooted in the *Declaration and Address*.

> In the *Declaration and Address* [Thomas] Campbell proposed that followers of Christ accept the New Testament as the church's *constitution*.... Strict constructionists or scholastics among the Disciples insisted that the church's organization and elements of worship must be derived from explicit scriptural commands and precedents.[66]

Alexander Campbell's "large class of men" were clearly of the same mind as the second-generation "scholastics" referred to here by McAllister and Tucker. But if this "class" found its ideology in the *Declaration and Address*, no less did that document provide the principle which the younger Campbell advanced in opposition to the "strict constructionists." That principle was expressed in the *Declaration and Address*'s thirteenth proposition, which allowed for the adoption of human expedients.[67]

The theme of Alexander Campbell in the second half of the 1830s and throughout the subsequent decade was that cooperation among churches was necessary and that the manner of that cooperation was *not* mandated by Scripture and should, therefore, be adopted as a human expedient.

> Co-operation among christian churches in all the affairs of the common salvation, is not only inscribed on every page of apostolic history, but is itself of the very essence of the christian institution.
> ... There is too much squeamishness about the *manner* of co-operation. Some are looking for a model similar to that which Moses gave for building the tabernacle. These seem not to understand that this is as impossible as it would be incompatible with the genius of the gospel.[68]

To Campbell, the manner of cooperation was an "inessential" matter, not covered fully and expressly in the New Testament. In 1842 he wrote of the "probability, at least," that

> ... The Christian Lawgiver enacted as of essential and vital importance to church organization just so much as is detailed in the books of the New Institution, *and all beyond that is matter of Christian prudence and discretion, illuminated by the records of human experience and directed by the exigencies of society.*[69] (Italics mine.)

Alexander Campbell was clearly moving in the direction of advocating church organization which went beyond the New Testament "constitution."

Campbell began to contend for a moderation of the extreme congregationalism and independency that his earlier writings had helped to nurture. In 1838 he suggested:

> There are extremes of Congregationalism and monarchial despotism. There is popery and a fierce democracy. Neither of these are the

First-Generation Structure 113

Christian Institution. Mobocracy may become as tyrannical as unlimited monarchy. Both are to be eschewed for the same reasons. Louis XIV., though a persecuting tyrant, was no more to be feared than the organs of the popular assemblies in the "age of reason" and "the reign of terror."[70]

One area in which Campbell rejected a radical localism and total congregational autonomy was in the oversight of the ministry. He found biblical foundation for three offices of the ministry: bishops or elders, deacons, and evangelists. "The evangelist was a traveling preacher who made converts, brought them into community, and got them to elect local officers, elders or bishops and deacons. He then moved on."[71] The evangelists belonged to a "class of public functionaries" whose responsibility was beyond the local level.[72]

Since, to Campbell, the *raison d'etre* for church cooperation was evangelism or mission, the church's "public" officers were evangelists or missionaries. Because of the existence and necessity of officers whose function took them beyond the level of a single congregation, Campbell reasoned that there must be "some common tribunal" for this public ministry.

If the New Covenant made no provision for the induction of its public agents—if it have given them no public care for one another,; if it have allowed every community to do what seems right in its own eyes-if it have given to its public functionaries to go and come, and operate when, where, and as they please—and if they are only amenable, directly or indirectly, to the particular community from which they take their departure; then, indeed, the Great Prophet and Lawgiver of the church has been more negligent of the interests of his kingdom, . . . than any other author of a new order of society that ever lived.[73]

The public ministry was not limited to the establishment of congregations. The local churches were to have "messengers" to attend to "the increase, preservation, and prosperity" of the kingdom of Christ, and the bishops or elders of the various congregations were to cooperate in supralocal functions—"oversight over the church" and "*cultivat*[ing] *the whole district more or less occupied by the congregations which created them, and over which they preside*."[74] This public ministry, then, is not confined to evangelists, but is to be discharged also by the bishops or elders, who may no longer be termed strictly local officers.

> We want an efficient Christian organization—an able, faithful, conscientious and benevolent ministry—Bishops and deacons—Elders in every church, who will co-operate with all the Elders of all the churches in a given district, and who will labor in the word and teaching and provide for all the exigencies of times and circumstances.[75]

The desire for cooperation in mission, for oversight of the public ministry of evangelists, and for oversight of the churches by the cooperative effort of bishops had been articulated by Campbell by 1842. Late in that year he offered:

> FIVE ARGUMENTS FOR CHURCH ORGANIZATION.
> *Great need for a more rational and scriptural organization.*
> 1. We can do comparatively nothing in distributing the Bible abroad without co-operation.
> 2. We can do comparatively but little in the great missionary field of the world either at home or abroad without co-operation.
> 3. We can do little or nothing to improve and elevate the Christian ministry without co-operation.
> 4. We can do but little to check, restrain, and remove the flood of imposture and fraud committed upon the benevolence of the brethren by irresponsible, plausible, and deceptive persons, without co-operation.
> 5. We cannot concentrate the action of the tens of thousands of Israel, in any great Christian effort, but by co-operation.
> 5. [sic] We can have no thorough co-operation without a more ample, extensive, and thorough church organization.[76]

As if to answer his own challenge, Campbell suggested in an 1843 article a "Project of a Scriptural System of Church Organization and Cooperation Submitted to the Candid Consideration and Criticism of All the Intelligent and Faithful Everywhere."[77]

> This "project" assumes an island of Guernsey to which Christianity is brought by an Evangelist who founds six churches. The article then suggests how these churches might cooperate in carrying out the mission committed to them by Christ....
> In this "project" a view evolves of the church as a "community of communities."[78]

Early in 1845, Campbell offered another "project" that had come out of a meeting in Steubenville, Ohio, in October 1844. "Church Organization" was treated under the headings, "Organization," "Church Edification," and "Co-operation." Under the heading of "Co-operation," both the necessity and manner and the limitations of structures beyond the congregation were outlined. "It is the duty of all the congregations in any city or district to co-operate in accomplishing in that district, state, or nation, whatever they could not otherwise accomplish" in carrying out the mission of the church. This requires that the churches' "deputies, messengers, or representatives" meet and consult occasionally. "These meetings, being voluntary expedients in matters of expediency . . . have no authority to legislate in any matter of faith or moral duty, but to attend to the ways and means of successful co-operation in all the objects of duty before them."[79]

Campbell was calling for meetings of messengers on state and national as well as district levels. But for the members of the Campbell-Stone movement such organization was not to be on the *national* level until more than a century after Campbell called for it.

---

1. *Declaration and Address; Last Will and Testament*, 20-21.

2. Ibid., 18. Stone's own words also reflected a reluctance to support extracongregational organization and an insistence that unity in spirit is the desirable form of unity. See B[arton] W[arren] Stone, "Christian Union," in *Works of Elder B. W. Stone, to which Is Added a Few Discourses and Sermons (Original and Selected)*, comp. James M. Mathes, 2nd ed. (Cincinnati: Moore, Wilstach, Keys & Co., Printers, 1859), 328, and B[arton] W[arren] S[tone], "The 7th Interview between an Old and Young Preacher," *Christian Messenger* 14 (September 1845 [1844]):145, both quoted in Eikner, "Nature of the Church," 148.

3. Stone, "Letter to the Church of Christ," 119.

4. Stone's view of the "church's" proper order focused upon the organization of the congregation. See, for example Editor [Barton Warren Stone], "A Letter, to the Disciples and Followers of Christ, Called Christians, in the United States of America," *Christian Messenger* 5 (January 1831):9-10, quoted in Eikner, "Nature of the Church," 142.

5. DeGroot, *Restoration Principle*, 150.

6. Lair, *Christian Churches and Their Work*, 45.

7. A Dale Fiers, "Structure—Past, Present, and Future," in *Interpretative Examination*, ed. Beazley, 151.

8. DeGroot, *Disciple Thought*, 151.
9. Stone, "Reflections of Old Age," 124-25.
10. Eikner, "Nature of the Church," 138-42.
11. *Declaration and Address; Last Will and Testament*, 18.
12. Stone, "Reflections of Old Age," 125-26.
13. *Declaration and Address: Last Will and Testament*, 24-27.
14. Thompson, "Irish Background to *Declaration and Address*," 23-24. The character of the Christian Association as built on the model of the Evangelical Society of Ulster, at least in part, had not been well remembered by Disciples until Thompson's work and additional descriptions of these roots by Hiram Lester (Hiram J. Lester, "The Case Against Sectarianism," *The Disciple* 17 [3: March 1990], 10-12).
15. *Declaration and Address; Last Will and Testament*, 27.
16. Ibid., 47-48.
17. Ibid., 48.
18. Ibid., 28, 68.
19. Ibid., 23, 24.
20. Ibid., 78, 49.
21. Ibid., 31, 33, 57-58.
22. Ibid., 35, 79, 34-35.
23. Ibid., 37.
24. Ibid., 58.
25. McAllister and Tucker, *Journey in Faith*, 119.
26. Ibid., 120, 122, 131.
27. F. M. Green, *Christians Missions and Historical Sketches of Missionary Societies among the Disciples of Christ, with Historical and Statistical Tables* (St. Louis: John Burns Publishing Co., 1884), 61-62.
28. D. Ray Lindley, *Apostle of Freedom* (St Louis: Bethany Press, 1957), 73-74.
29. Ibid., 5.
30. Editor [Alexander Campbell], "The Clergy—No. II," *Christian Baptist* 1 (November 1823):71-72, quoted in Lindley, *Apostle of Freedom*, 79.
31. Editor [Alexander Campbell], "A Restoration of the Ancient Order of Things—No. XIV. The Bishop's Office—No. III," *Christian Baptist* 4 (August 1826):8.
32. [Alexander Campbell], "Essays: On Ecclesiastical Characters, Councils, Creeds, and Sects—No. III," *Christian Baptist* 1 (June [July] 1824):223-24, quoted in Lindley, *Apostle of Freedom*, 64.

33. Alexander Campbell, "A Restoration of the Ancient Order of Things. No. II," 153.

34. Lindley, *Apostle of Freedom*, 64.

35. Philalethes [pseud.], "For the Christian Baptist: Extracts from Tassey's Vindication: Of 'The Supreme and Exclusive Authority of the Lord Jesus Christ in Religious Matters,'" *Christian Baptist* 4 (March 1827):157-58, quoted in Lindley, *Apostle of Freedom*, 154.

36. Editor [Alexander Campbell], reply to a letter, *Christian Baptist* 1 (June 1824):216, quoted in Lindley, *Apostle of Freedom*, pp. 182-83.

37. [Alexander Campbell], "The Christian Religion," *Christian Baptist* 1 (July 1823):14, quoted in Lindley, *Apostle of Freedom*, 121.

38. Alexander Campbell, "Clergy—No. II," 72, quoted in Lindley, *Apostle of Freedom*, 80.

39. Lindley, *Apostle of Freedom*, 84-86.

40. Alexander Campbell, "Christian Religion," 14, quoted in Lindley, *Apostle of Freedom*, 72.

41. In the first volume of the *Christian Baptist*, Campbell wrote: "When the bishop rests from his labors, the church, of which he had the oversight, by his labors, and by the opportunity afforded all the members of exercising their faculties of communication and inquiry in the public assembly, finds within itself others educated and qualified to be appointed to the same good work. The church of the living God is thus independent of theological schools and colleges for its existence, enlargement, comfort and perfection; for it is itself put in possession of all the means of education and accomplishments, if these means be widely used" (Alexander Campbell, reply to a letter, 217, quoted in Lindley, *Apostle of Freedom*, 185). By 1840 (twenty years after the above pronouncement), Campbell was directing his efforts toward the establishment of Bethany College (Lindley, *Apostle of Freedom*, 214).

42. Philip [Walter Scott],"For the Christian Messenger," *Christian Messenger* 1 (January 1827):49-51, quoted in West, *Search for the Ancient Order*, 1:152-53.

43. Scott, "Organization and Co-operation," 54, quoted in Neth, *Walter Scott Speaks*, 93-94.

44. A[lexander] C[ampbell], "The American Christian Missionary Society," *Millennial Harbinger*, ser. 4, 5 (February 1855):76, editor's note.

45. Scott, "American Christian Missionary Society: Address," 81.

46. Fiers, "Structure—Past, Present, and Future," 157.

47. McAllister and Tucker, *Journey in Faith*, 144.

48. Editor [Alexander Campbell], "Associations," *Christian Baptist* 5 (November 1827):99.

49. Lindley, *Apostle of Freedom*, 5, 45.

50. Editor [Alexander Campbell], "Co-operation of the Churches, No. IV," *Millennial Harbinger* 2 (October 1831):436, quoted in Wrather, *Creative Freedom in Action*, 18.

51. Wrather, *Creative Freedom in Action*, 18.

52. McAllister and Tucker, *Journey in Faith*, 147.

53. Ibid., 151.

54. Ronald E. Osborn, "Remembering after 150 Years: Sesquicentennial of an Ecumenical Triumph," *Discipliana* 41 (Winter 1981):53.

55. John Augustus Williams, *Life of Elder John Smith* (Cincinnati: Standard Publishing Co., 1904), 455, quoted in Osborn, "Remembering after 150 Years," 53.

56. Osborn, "Remembering after 150 Years," 53-54, 59.

57. Ibid., 54.

58. McAllister and Tucker, *Journey in Faith*, 148-49.

59. Eikner, "Nature of the Church," 161.

60. These tensions may have proven divisive (see Hughes, "Apocalyptic Origins of Churches of Christ").

61. Wrather, *Creative Freedom in Action*, 19.

62. Winfred E. Garrison, *Variations on a Theme: "God Saw that It Was Good"* (St. Louis: Bethany Press, 1964), 76-77.

63. Wrather, *Creative Freedom in Action*, 19.

64. J. T. M'May and A[lexander] Campbell, "Report of the Proceedings of a General Meeting of Messengers, from Thirteen Congregations, Held in Wellsburg, Va. on Saturday, the 12th of April, 1834," *Millennial Harbinger* 6 (April 1835):167, 169.

65. A[lexander] C[ampbell], "Co-operation," *Millennial Harbinger*, n.s., 2 (June 1838):269.

66. McAllister and Tucker, *Journey in Faith*, 237.

67. *Declaration and Address; Last Will and Testament*, 48.

68. Editor [Alexander Campbell], "Co-operation," *Millennial Harbinger* 6 (March 1835):120-21.

69. A[lexander] C[ampbell], "The Nature of the Christian Organization, No. VIII," *Millennial Harbinger*, n.s., 6 (November 1842):512-13.

70. A[lexander] C[ampbell], "The Senatorial Government of the Church," *Millennial Harbinger*, n.s., 2 (February 1838):128.

71. Fiers, "Structure—Past, Present, and Future," 155, n. 15.

72. A[lexander] C[ampbell], "The Nature of the Christian Organization. No. II," *Millennial Harbinger*, n.s., 6 (February 1842):62.

First-Generation Structure

73. Ibid., 63, 64.

74. A[lexander] C[ampbell], "The Nature of the Christian Organization. No. IV," *Millennial Harbinger* n.s., 6 (April 1842):183.

75. Ibid., 185.

76. Alexander Campbell, "Five Arguments for Church Organization," *Millennial Harbinger*, n.s., 6 (November 1842):523.

77. Alexander Campbell, "Church Organization, No. XII," *Millennial Harbinger*, n.s., 7 (February 1843):82, quoted in Fiers, "Structure—Past, Present, and Future," 155.

78. Fiers, "Structure—Past, Present, and Future," 155-56.

79. A[lexander] C[ampbell], "Church Organization," *Millennial Harbinger*, ser. 3, 2 (February 1845):61, 62, 65, 66-67.

CHAPTER V

THE EMERGENCE OF THE SOCIETY CONCEPT AS THE BASIS OF POLITY IN THE CAMPBELL-STONE MOVEMENT

This chapter focuses upon developments in the polity of the Campbell-Stone movement in the period 1849 to 1917. The beginning point for a consideration of this period is with the place of D. S. Burnet in the history of Disciples polity. His place is a controversial one. On the one hand, Burnet's biographer Noel L. Keith regards Burnet's efforts and accomplishments as the foundation of subsequent extracongregational life in the Campbell-Stone movement, and sees Burnet's "society system" in this light:

> The term *Society* system was used early by Disciples of Christ to describe the organizations which became united by common interests and purposes for fostering programs of education, missions, benevolence and publishing. It was in the early development of the society system that the modern organizations among Disciples of Christ had their roots.[1]

On the other hand, Burnet's society system can be viewed as having supplanted the possible development of a polity more along the lines advocated in the late 1830s and 1840s by Alexander Campbell and thus as having delayed substantially the development of a churchly structure among the Disciples of Christ.

It has been noted earlier that the Campbell side of the Campbell-Stone movement was launched as a voluntary association (the Christian Association of Washington, Pennsylvania). Therefore, this form of organization was not introduced to the movement by D. S. Burnet. Nor was the voluntary-associational form in any sense unique to the Campbell-Stone heritage. It was a form that flourished in American Protestantism in the early nineteenth century.[2] However, in spite of the already present character of the society concept in the Campbell-Stone movement and around it, the importance of Burnet is clear as a promoter of this form of organization among Disciples.

D. S. Burnet "was a man whose mind and temperament directed his energies along organizational lines. . . . Known as the man who held the first located pastorates among the Disciples," Burnet was an acquaintance of Walter Scott and served as Scott's successor as president of Bacon College.[3] In January 1845, Burnet let the representatives from four Disciples congregations in Cincinnati in the formation of the American Christian Bible Society. This society sought support from the entire Campbell-Stone movement and initially was opposed by Alexander Campbell—perhaps, in part, because it would compete with his own causes. However, Campbell had also advocated a more churchly structure of messengers. With the establishment of the American Christian Bible Society, two different *concepts* of organization and cooperation vied for acceptance by the Campbell-Stone movement.[4]

As his movement approached its first general convention in 1849, Alexander Campbell again took up the subject of "Church Organization" in the pages of the *Millennial Harbinger*. In February of that year he wrote: "There is now heard from the East and from the West, from the North and from the South, one general, if not universal, call for a more efficient organization of our churches." He added his own voice to the call in the familiar terms of the missionary imperative: "But we want organization—the setting in order of the things wanting to perfect the church and convert the world."[5] When Campbell returned to the topic in April, he concentrated upon the use of the word "*ekkleesia*" in the New Testament:

> But the most important fact is, *that it is used in the singular number, in two distinct senses,*—one indicating a single community, meeting in a single place—the other indicating the congregated multitude of all these communities, as existing in all ages and nations. We have then, the church universal, and a church particular.[6]

The next issue of the *Millennial Harbinger* brought with it Campbell's assertion that the two senses of "church" created two classes of officers within the Church. This assertion was an expansion of his earlier description of the existence of a "public ministry." "The public interests of the aggregate Christian community in every one nation, province or empire ... require public agents, whether called evangelists, messengers, delegates, or ... missionaries." Campbell returned to two familiar ideas in his advocacy of church organization. The first of these ideas was that the churches were free to organize through the making of covenants. Campbell wrote that "the congregational or Baptist associational form of cooperating and uniting" was "more acceptable to my views than any other form of co-operation in Christendom."[7]

> Their whole moral or ecclesiastic authority is purely convention-al, ... depending on covenanted stipulations which have but the sanc-tion of a solemn agreement amongst the churches of a given district. ... These covenants or constitutions have, of course, no other authority

The Society Concept

> than the voluntary agreement of the parties or churches entering into them. But like all other covenants, are morally binding in the fair construction of their respective items or articles of agreement.[8]

The second idea was that the covenants are made under the category of "temporal expediency."

> But as are the temporalities of Christianity in any country or age, as are the conditions of surrounding society, are the duties of the whole Christian profession in existing circumstances in such province or empire. These must be necessarily contingent and ... are wisely left open to human wisdom and prudence, and ever to be matters of conventional and covenant agreement.[9]

It was in the context, then, of having offered a view of churchly structure as properly being a *delegate convention* (in its organization) and *covenantal* (in its binding power and authority) that Campbell issued the call for a convention of national scope.

Alexander Campbell published his call for a convention in August 1849 in the *Millennial Harbinger*. He called for a convention in the image of the covenantal, delegate body he had taken pains to describe:

> It should not be a Convention of Book-makers or of Editors, to concoct a great book concern; but a Convention of messengers of churches, selected and constituted such by the churches. ... It is not to be composed of a few self-appointed messengers, ... but a *general* Convention.

Curiously, Campbell was "also of opinion that Cincinnati is the proper place for holding such a Convention."[10] In light of the fact that D. S. Burnet had established a Bible Society and a Tract Society, Campbell may have had Burnet in mind when he made the comment about "Book-makers" and "Editors."[11] If it is true, as Noel L. Keith suggests, that "the real clash was between two growing centers of strength of the brotherhood, Bethany and Cincinnati,"[12] Campbell's action played into the hands of Burnet. The convention certainly took on Burnet's view of organization—"to further the work of the societies"—and not Campbell's—"a convention of the churches with messengers appointed by and for the churches."[13]

The convention was planned to "coincide with the annual meeting of the Bible Society and a Sunday School and Tract Society organized in Cincinnati."[14] About two hundred persons attended the 1849 convention. "There were one hundred fifty-six delegates enrolled, representing one hundred local churches from eleven different states. One state meeting, Indiana, sent a 'messenger.'"[15] On October 23, the gathering listened to an address by D. S. Burnet, "and concerned itself with the annual meeting of the American Christian Bible Society." L. L. Pinkerton presided over an election of officers. Alexander Campbell was elected president, although he was not present. Burnet was elected one of four vice-presidents and presided over subsequent sessions in Campbell's absence.[16]

Noel Keith suggests that Burnet had something to do with Campbell's election, for strategic purposes:

> It is highly probable that he [Burnet] must be credited with the diplomacy that took for himself a secondary position in the organizational movement. He seems clearly to have fostered Campbell's position with the societies in order that the Disciples of Christ might cooperate to a better advantage.[17]

At the second session of the General Convention of the Christian Churches in the United States of America the question arose as to what "constituted a delegate."[18]

> The convention . . . was mostly composed of preachers and workers who had come on their own initiative out of interest and concern. . . . The convention voted to allow all present to participate fully and freely in the business of the meeting. The first national convention became a mass meeting in spite of Campbell's desire that it be a gathering of elected "messengers."[19]

Thus the convention moved away from the concept of being a body constituted by the representatives of the congregations, or of district or state cooperations.

Two other developments signaled the defeat of the kind of church organization for which Alexander Campbell had been contending in the *Millennial Harbinger*. The first of these was the repudiation of extracongregational oversight of ministers; the second was the adoption of the society concept.

The Society Concept

It has been noted that one of Campbell's motivations for his advocacy of churchly organization beyond the congregation was the prevention of "the flood of imposture and fraud committed upon the benevolence of the brethren by irresponsible, plausible, and deceptious persons." One of his other "arguments for church organization" was "to elevate and improve the Christian ministry."[20] Campbell also argued for supralocal church organization, in part, because he believed in the existence of a "public" order of ministry. One of his hopes for the convention must have been for the creation of some structure for the oversight of the "public" ministry. This hope was specifically disappointed. A resolution was offered which recommended that preachers not be recognized as such unless sanctioned by two or more churches.[21] This would have been a step in the direction that Campbell had advocated explicitly in 1842.[22] "After much discussion upon the matter a resolution was adopted which seems somewhat vague."[23] The original resolution was weakened to the point that total local congregational independency in the matter of ordination remained intact:

> WHEREAS, It appears that the cause of Christianity has suffered from the imposition of false brethren upon the churches, therefore,
>
> *Resolved*, That we recommend to the churches, the importance of great care and rigid examination, before they ordain men to the office of evangelists.
>
> *Resolved*, That this convention earnestly recommend to the congregations to countenance no evangelist who is not well reported of for piety and proper evangelical qualifications, and that they be rigid and critical in their examination of such report.[24]

The second development which indicated the defeat of the type of churchly structure advocated by Campbell was the adoption of the society concept. This came in the form of the convention's creation of the American Christian Missionary Society (ACMS), the "only agency of the churches recognized by the convention." It alone was "envisioned as capable of administering all the cooperative work of the churches."[25] Therefore, the *national* polity of the Campbell-Stone movement was basically determined by the structure of the ACMS. The Society elected officers, including Alexander Campbell as president and twenty vice-presidents, chosen on the basis of geographic distribution.[26] But the ACMS was a society of *individuals*, and the basis of membership was monetary: "Life memberships (at $20 each) and life directorships (at $100 each) were offered. Any church could appoint a delegate for a $10 annual contribution."[27]

The business of the Society was to be conducted by an Executive Board composed of the officers, directors, and twenty-five managers elected by the Society.[28] The base of operations was clearly established as Cincinnati:

> ART.VI. Two of the Vice-Presidents, the Treasurer, the Secretaries, and at least fifteen of the managers, shall reside in Cincinnati or its vicinity. . . .
> ART.XI. The annual meeting shall be held in Cincinnati on the Wednesday after the third Lord's day in October, or at such other time and place as shall have been designated by a previous annual meeting.[29]

Through 1868, the convention met annually at Cincinnati and the society concept which D. S. Burnet had pioneered in that city was the order of the day.[30]

In light of the frustration of a number of his goals for the first national convention of the Campbell-Stone movement, Alexander Campbell's editorial reaction is interesting: "Our expectations from the convention have more than been realized. We are much pleased with the result, and regard it as a very happy pledge of good things to come." Campbell lifted up the convention's recommendation of periodic meetings at the district level:

> The suggestions deferentially submitted to all the brotherhood, for their concurrence and action in reference to the necessity and importance of periodically meeting, in given districts, large or small, . . . for consultation and practical effort in the advocacy of the cause in all their localities, must, we think, meet the approbation of all the intelligent and zealous brethren and churches everywhere.

He also gave his support to the societies established by the convention:

> The Christian Bible Society . . . now approved by all the churches present, and commended by them to all the brethren, removes all my objections to it in its former attitude. . . . The Christian Missionary Society, too, . . . will be a grand auxiliary to the churches. . . .
> . . . We thank God and take courage, and commend these instrumentalities to the prayers of all the holy brethren, and to the blessing of the Lord.[31]

The Society Concept

Perhaps Campbell is best described as having acquiesced to the organizational direction his movement was taking. In 1850 Campbell "occupied his president's chair" in the ACMS,

> and thereafter every autumn, with few exceptions, he was present in Cincinnati to deliver his annual presidential address. . . . As the decade of the 1850's advanced, he had given himself more and more to ecumenical and scholarly pursuits, content to leave in younger hands the task of working out the details of the structure which had begun to emerge from the convention of 1849.[32]

Loren Lair sees the first convention as a series of what he calls "compromises": 1) the convention did not recognize those whom churches had sent as messengers as such; 2) the Bible and tract societies did not place themselves under the direct auspices of the convention; 3) the convention was made into a missionary organization; 4) the organization was constituted as a society of individuals; 5) the society was not financed through the churches; and 6) the society was managed, in part, by individuals selected on the basis of a monetary contribution.[33] The theme that ties together all these "compromises" is that the society concept supplanted the ideal of a churchly organization. Ironically, the *local congregation*—that entity which alone was widely accepted as authentically "church"—was bypassed when the convention became a mass meeting of and created a society of self-selected individuals.

To suggest that the society idea championed by D. S. Burnet prevailed at Cincinnati in 1849 and that Alexander Campbell turned his attention away from structural matters, however, is not to suggest that controversy about structure came to an end. The creation of the ACMS was greeted with hostility by leaders such as the Kentucky preacher Jacob Creath, Jr., and with "grave doubts" by Tolbert Fanning.[34] Opposition to the Missionary Society became one of the distinguishing features of the Churches of Christ as they emerged as a separate body.[35] However, there clearly remained in the movement those who were committed to carrying forward the vision of the mature Alexander Campbell on churchly structure. It was this group which made the next major attempt to establish a representative structure for the Campbell-Stone movement—the Louisville Plan of 1869.

Before the 1869 convention was held the Campbell-Stone community endured the shocks of the Civil War (1861-65) and the death of Alexander Campbell (1866). Although scholarly debate continues as to the exact role and magnitude of these traumas relative to the first major schism in the movement, it is clear that division was on the horizon.

An analysis of the various state organizations in the movement prior to 1869 would reveal a trend toward the adoption of conventions on the mass-meeting or popular-assembly principle combined with the organization of missionary societies based upon categories of paid memberships for individuals. On the national level, the ACMS continued to function as "the avenue of brotherhood expression." Although the meetings of the ACMS in the 1850s and 1860s were given a "representative character" by the presence of "annual delegates" from local congregations, they were "properly . . . business meetings of members of the Society" and "lacked . . . the wider geographical representation" of the 1849 General Convention. At the 1853 meeting of the ACMS, for example:

> there were 66 delegates listed. Eleven came from Cincinnati, and all but five were from the tri-state area: Ohio, Kentucky, and Indiana. In 1859, however, the Society was in the midst of a period of prosperity and 216 delegates were enrolled: 74 from Ohio, 74 from Kentucky, 41 from Indiana, and 7 from other states.

In part, the lack of geographical representation, which worsened during the Civil War years, contributed to further troubles for the Society:

> In 1861 there were no delegates from the southern states and income dropped to one-third of the previous year. Intense emotion stirred by the war led the Society to vote a resolution of loyalty to the Union. This action not only antagonized the southern brethren but alienated others. Benjamin Franklin, who had given support to the Society, was never thereafter its friend. J. W. McGarvey and Moses E. Lard became its severe critics. Opposition to the Society reached its height. It was evident that some drastic change was necessary if a general cooperation was to continue.

The "drastic change" which was to be suggested in 1869 was a return to the "delegate" or "messenger" concept which had been championed by Alexander Campbell in the *Millennial Harbinger* two decades earlier. One of the objections that had been raised against the society concept was the "requirement of a cash payment . . . to participate."[36] The difficulties into which the ACMS had fallen presented the Campbell-Stone movement with an opportunity to organize itself into some kind of national body based on a principle other than that of paid membership.

"In 1869 a committee of twenty representative men was appointed by the Society to develop an acceptable plan of cooperation."[37] The committee did run the ideological gamut from staunchly legalistic conservatives like Moses E. Lard and Benjamin Franklin to the more liberal William K. Pendleton and William T. Moore. The plan which this ideologically diverse committee presented was passed by the convention with only two dissenting votes.[38]

> The plan which was presented and adopted created the General Christian Missionary Convention and a uniform system of cooperative organization at district, state, and national levels. It provided for state conventions composed of delegates from the churches and a general convention composed of delegates from the states. These conventions and their administrative boards were concerned with the whole field of brotherhood cooperation in their respective areas.[39]

Under the Louisville Plan (so named because it was adopted at the annual meeting held, for the first time outside Cincinnati, in Louisville), "funds received for missionary purposes" were to be distributed "on a basis of 50% for the district, 25% for the state, and 25% for the national."[40] The plan placed the cooperative work of the Disciples on a congregationally supported rather than individually supported basis, and seemed to diminish the feature of the society as just a collection of individuals.[41] The former members of the ACMS were to be retained in the General Christian Missionary Convention, but the delegates would presumably be preponderant.[42]

The Louisville Plan "appeared ideal in principle but in reality it proved a disaster."[43] The first casualty in the new system was the principle of delegate representation:

> The first annual assembly was held in 1870. Seventy-four delegates were present from 14 states. There were 600 visitors present who were invited by the Convention to participate in the deliberations, a precedent which was continued and nullified the principle of delegate representation.[44]

The second feature of the plan to fail was the financial aspect. "Adopted within a short time by eleven state meetings and thirty-six district organizations, the plan was ignored from the outset by most of these groups. Receipts for missionary work reached a new low."[45] When neither the delegate representation nor the financial support envisioned in the plan proved to be forthcoming, the Louisville Plan died and the *idea* of a delegate assembly for the Disciples of Christ languished. Since at least the mid-1840s two basic concepts—the delegate convention and the society of contributing individuals—had contended for the minds of Disciples as they attempted to organize beyond the level of the congregation. When the ACMS had seemed a failure the movement naturally turned to its other traditional option. When the General Christian Missionary Convention failed, the Campbell-Stone movement returned with equal facility to the society concept: "In 1876 the General Convention was compelled to turn to individuals for direct support and in 1881 it was replaced by the American Christian Missionary Society, which had kept a paper existence through the eleven years."[46]

The failure of the Louisville Plan and the subsequent return to the society concept of organization for Disciples on the national level strengthened the already observable trend away from representative bodies and toward societies at the state level.

The pattern wherein both the representatives of congregations and dues-paying members would be included in the structure was the form which the society concept took in the states. When F. M. Green wrote his *Christian Missions and Historical Sketches* in 1884, he included constitutions of Disciples missionary societies for the states of Ohio, West Virginia, Michigan, Arkansas, Missouri, Iowa, New York, Nebraska, North Carolina, Kansas, Illinois, Wisconsin, Colorado, and Indiana. All but Arkansas and Kansas reflected the adoption of the society concept insofar as provisions were made for paid memberships.[47]

Part of the process of popularizing the society type of structure was the direct influence of the Christian Woman's Board of Missions and the ACMS in the years before it adopted the Louisville Plan. The ACMS had not met with spectacular success on the foreign missions field:

> By 1870 only three missionaries had been sent out under the ACMS. Dr. J. T. Barclay reached Jerusalem on February 7, 1851 and continued until October 1861. Alexander Cross, a black man, reached Monrovia, Liberia, in January 1854, but died after two months of service. Julius O. Beardslee ... began work in Jamaica in 1858 and continued until 1866 when the work had to be abandoned for lack of support.... Following the Franco-Prussian War (1869-1870) a mission to Germany was recommended but nothing came of it.[48]

With this poor record and the apparent failure of the Louisville Plan before her, Caroline Neville Pearre began to work early in 1874 to realize a personal vision for what became the Christian Woman's Board of Missions (CWBM). She began with a local organization in Iowa City, Iowa, and a wide correspondence with Disciples of Christ women. She also wrote to Thomas Munnell, corresponding secretary of the ACMS, to Isaac Errett, editor of the *Christian Standard*, and to J. H. Garrison, editor of the *Christian*. With the editorial support of Errett and Garrison, Pearre was able to call together seventy-five women from several states gathered at the meeting of the General Christian Missionary Convention in Cincinnati in October 1874. On October 22, 1874, the CWBM adopted its first constitution. It provided for individual memberships on the basis of membership in an "Auxiliary Society," which was "any number of ladies contributing annually," or on a basis of a direct contribution—one dollar for an annual membership and twenty-five dollars for a life membership.[49] The CWBM intended, from its beginning, to encourage local cooperative organization for mission work. "Within a short time, by-laws were written and a sample constitution prepared for the use of local groups which the women hoped would be organized in every congregation across the country." The level of success with local and state organizations was such that "by 1876 the women had the money to send out their first missionaries."[50]

Encouraged by the creation of the CWBM, the men organized the Foreign Christian Missionary Society (FCMS) in 1875. It, too, was a society composed of three different membership categories based upon the size of the member's financial contribution.[51] These two societies began to put the foreign missions work of the Campbell-Stone movement on a more stable and permanent footing. However, the more obvious early achievements in "missions" for the movement came within the United States.

Between 1851 and 1898 the ACMS undertook missionary or evangelistic work in the following states (or territories), Alabama, Arizona, Arkansas, California, Florida, Georgia, Idaho, Kansas, Louisiana, Maryland, Michigan, Minnesota, Mississippi, Nebraska, New England (Massachusetts, Connecticut, and Maine), New Mexico, North Dakota, South Dakota, Oklahoma, Oregon, Texas, Utah, Virginia, Washington, Wisconsin, and Wyoming. The CWBM was especially active in Montana and Colorado. Grant K. Lewis reports that "the minutes of the American Christian Missionary Society of 1853 record that 'the activity of the state organizations of Kentucky, Ohio, Indiana, Illinois, and Missouri have well-nigh relieved us of any care for their population.'"[52] These states were the "sending" states, and from them the early evangelists of the ACMS and CWBM went forth to the mission field of the American continent.

The society concept of organization, which had evolved as one alternative for the Campbell-Stone movement by 1845, and which was confirmed by the disastrous results of the Louisville Plan, was part of the "gospel" planted in the younger Disciples churches of the American mission field.

The success of missionary efforts by members of the Campbell-Stone movement in the American West was accompanied by failure in the East. This pattern continued through the period 1875 to 1900. As W. E. Garrison observes, "the planting of the cause in new areas enjoyed the advantage of support from the resources of older commonwealths which had been frontier territory a generation earlier." The result was a growing strength in the Western states, especially Kansas and Oklahoma.[53]

In the United States Census of 1890, the Disciples of Christ was reported as having 641,051 members in 7,246 congregations. However, only 18,782 members in 56 congregations existed in cities with populations between 100,000 and 500,000. In the four cities with over 500,000 people—New York, Chicago, Philadelphia, and Brooklyn—the Disciples could claim only 14 congregations with 2,493 members collectively. Even in the category of cities having a population of 25,000 to 100,000, the Disciples showed only 94 congregations and 21,459 members.[54] Therefore, of their 7,246 congregations and 641,051 members, only 164 congregations and 42,734 members were in large cities (with populations of 25,000 or more). That is, more than 93 percent of the membership of the Disciples of Christ was in towns of fewer than 25,000 persons, villages, and rural areas.

In 1890 the great numerical strength of the Campbell-Stone movement still lay in the states of Missouri, Indiana, Kentucky, Illinois, and Ohio. These states together claimed 369,654 of the 641,051 reported members—over 57 percent of the total. But the westward direction of the movement's growth was evidenced by 1890 in several ways. First, Missouri with 97,773 members, had supplanted Kentucky as the state having the most Disciples. Second, the states which followed the aforementioned five in numbers of Disciples were primarily to the west of those five—Texas, Tennessee, Iowa, Kansas, and Arkansas. Third, small but significant growth was observable in the West and clearly not observable in the East. For example, together the states of California, Colorado, Nebraska, Oregon, and the Indian Territory (eastern Oklahoma) showed 23,592 members in 1890. But the eastern states of Connecticut, Delaware, Maine, New Jersey, Rhode Island and Vermont together claimed only 1,127 Disciples.[55] In short, the Census of 1890 confirms Garrison's observations about the tendency of the Campbell-Stone movement to "follow the frontier."

In general, then, the second generation of the Campbell-Stone movement was a time of expansion and growth westward. It was a time when mission was executed if not conceived primarily in terms of proselytizing nominal Christians

The Society Concept

on the American frontier. The relative success of this strategy for mission fitted well with and confirmed the structural, ecclesiological status quo which had emerged from the struggles of the first generation. This ecclesiological status quo consisted of the ideas that the supralocal, or "public," ministry should be composed of itinerant "evangelists," and that the basic supralocal structure should be a "missionary society." However, this status quo did not persist undisturbed indefinitely.

In a sense the success of the second-generation structure of the Campbell-Stone movement contributed to its own eventual disruption, for as the movement grew within a changing social environment, the movement changed as well. However, the impact of environmental changes were not reflected in uniform change throughout the Campbell-Stone movement.[56] The processes of differential change within the movement are observable in at least four areas: 1) the multiplication of society-type structures with functions other than mission meant that the earlier conception of the evangelist as *the* legitimate extracongregational structure corresponded to reality to a lesser and lesser degree; 2) leaders of the movement gradually came out of isolation in terms of their theological education; 3) the advent of a more sustained effort on the foreign missions field tended to weaken the identification of evangelism with the proselytizing of Christians; and 4) the movement's urban membership became larger and more influential.

The entire period from 1849 to 1917 was not uniform in the rate of the development of national structures among Disciples. The years between 1874 and 1917 contained the greater portion of organizational development in the Campbell-Stone movement at the national level. Predictably, given the rootage of supralocal organizations among the Disciples in the missionary society, the organizational "boom" of the last quarter of the nineteenth and early years of the twentieth centuries began with the establishment of missionary societies.

The organization of state societies, the Christian Woman's Board of Missions, and the Foreign Christian Missionary Society was only the beginning. The formation of the latter two in 1874 and 1875 was followed closely by the organization of the Board of Church Extension in 1883, the National Benevolent Association in 1887, the Board of Ministerial Relief in 1895, the Council on Christian Union in 1910, the Christian Board of Publication in 1911, and the Board of Education in 1914. The development of this range of organizations took the Campbell-Stone movement a considerable distance away from a polity in which the only public minister was the evangelist and the only supralocal structure the missionary society.

The origin of the Board of Church Extension was tied to the "success of evangelists, under the auspices of the American Christian Missionary Society." New congregations requested help from the ACMS for funds to construct meetinghouses. The national and state journals of the movement also gave voice to this need to such an extent that the issue came before the Disciples national Convention in 1883.

The Convention responded by authorizing "the appointment of a committee to raise money for building purposes. During that Convention $3,500 was pledged." The "Church Extension Fund" made its first loan in 1884, and by 1888 "12 churches in 9 states were assisted and the Fund grew to $6,000." At the 1888 Convention the enterprise was organized as a "seven-member Board of Church Extension." Under the leadership of George W. Muckley "Church Extension grew significantly and by 1912 the Fund had reached the $1,000.00 mark."[57] The Board operated independently of the Convention (appointing its own meetings, electing its own officers, making its own rules for its government), except that the Convention elected the members of the Board and the Board was to report to the Convention's annual meetings.[58] This was the basic structure which persisted until 1919.[59]

The beginning of the National Benevolent Association was more independent of the ACMS than that of the Board of Church Extension. The National Benevolent Association began in February 1886 with a group of women from the First Christian Church in St. Louis who were concerned about the plight of orphans and the aged. These women met informally until January 10, 1887, when they organized the National Benevolent Association in order "to help the helpless, to give a home to the homeless, to provide care for the sick and comfort for the distressed." Martha Younkin was a key leader in the NBA and "went to the churches in Missouri and Illinois and Kansas in an effort to interest the women of the Aid Societies in becoming auxiliaries to the Association." The National Benevolent Association's first home was opened in 1889.[60] However, recognition of the Association by the Convention was delayed for twelve years (until 1899) because of "objections . . . to such work."[61] The work was opposed because it was not "preaching the gospel."[62] The character of the opposition to the NBA reveals that the Campbell-Stone movement was having to struggle past the conception that only evangelistic mission was a proper concern for the Church beyond the local level.

The Board of Ministerial Relief emerged in a way that was more similar to the process which gave rise to the Board of Church Extension than that which had produced the National Benevolent Association. On October 23, 1895, the General Christian Missionary Convention held in Dallas, Texas, amended its constitution to create the Board of Ministerial Relief of the Christian Church.

Again, like the Board of Church Extension, the Board of Relief was independent of the Convention except that the nine members of the Board were to be elected annually by the Convention and the Board was to make a yearly report to the Convention. The Board of Ministerial Relief was the ancestor of the Pension Fund of Disciples of Christ, which replaced it in 1928.[63]

The formation of the Council on Christian Union was closely tied to the efforts of Peter Ainslie. Ainslie was the president of the 1910 Topeka, Kansas, Convention which appointed a nine-member "Commission on Christian Union." By 1913 the membership had been increased to twenty-five and an office had been established in Ainslie's home city, Baltimore. The name of the commission was changed several times, eventually becoming the "Council on Christian Unity." The structure of the Council followed the familiar pattern of being composed of individual memberships.[64] However, the Council's board of commissioners was "elected by the national convention" and "the report of its work and finances . . . [was] made annually to the convention."[65]

The chartering of the Christian Board of Publication in 1911 was a milestone in a long and tumultuous process. Much of the tumult related to a rivalry between the publishers of the *Christian Standard* and the *Christian-Evangelist*. In 1882 the Christian Publishing Company, publishers of the *Christian-Evangelist*, underbid the Standard Publishing Company, publishers of the *Christian Standard*, for the contract to publish a revised edition of a hymnal which was owned by the Disciples' General Convention. "The 'hymn book quarrel' betokened something of far greater consequence in the life of Disciples. The *Standard* was striving to protect its predominant position in Disciple journalism, but the *Christian-Evangelist* proved to be an able and ambitious competitor. Inevitably, this rivalry estranged the two papers."[66]

The estrangement came to the fore when the Disciples appointed, at their 1907 Convention, a twenty-five member Publication Committee to explore the possibility of creating a denominational publishing house by "merging the Standard and Christian Publishing Companies." While the Christian Publishing Company was supportive of the idea, Standard Publishing "insisted that the whole scheme was concocted by vain and ambitious men who desired positions of power." Disciples were faced with the question of "whether they should deprive themselves of a denominational publishing house simply because one large private company refused to co-operate."[67]

The situation was complicated by the financial troubles of *Christian-Evangelist* editor, J. H. Garrison. Learning of Garrison's financial situation, Robert A. Long, a wealthy Disciples layman, "purchased the Christian Publishing Company for the purpose of turning it into a 'brotherhood publishing house.'"[68] The publishing company resulting from this purchase, however, was an entity whose essentially private and independent character even the *Christian Standard* applauded.[69] The *Christian-Evangelist* pointed out that the charter of the new "Christian Board of Publication" placed its management in the hands of a board of directors, defined its mission as the promotion of the principles of the Disciples "brotherhood," and arranged for its profits to be "turned over to and paid into the treasury of some one or more of the missionary, benevolent, church extension, educational societies, or other agencies of the Christian Churches (Disciples of Christ) as the board of directors may elect."[70]

That this charter fell short of establishing a "brotherhood publishing house" was certainly the conviction of the *Christian Standard*, which took the opportunity provided by the occasion of the chartering of the Christian Board of Publication to restate its own convictions concerning the proper polity for Disciples. Not surprisingly, what the *Standard* contended for was the view that all organizations beyond the local congregation lacked the sanction of Scripture, were not the "Church" but merely "institutions," and that none had the right to claim the particular sanction of "the brotherhood." The *Standard* insisted "that there should be no invidious distinction among our publishing institutions—or any other institutions, for that matter—by which the brotherhood should be made to appear responsible for one more than for another."[71]

The *Christian Standard* linked the idea of "representative bodies" proposed among Disciples to the proposal of a "brotherhood publishing house." Confronted with such possibilities, the *Standard* reiterated its commitment to the society concept, wherein the only entities other than local congregations are expedient associations or societies of individuals, "as many of them as you please, so long as none of them makes claim to the peculiar sanction of the brotherhood."[72] The flowering of organizations among Disciples in the last quarter of the nineteenth century and the early years of the twentieth, and especially the efforts to coordinate the claims of these organizations upon the movement in the second and third decades of the twentieth century, ran counter to this commitment of the *Standard*. The *Standard* became the center of criticism of ecclesiological development among the Disciples.[73]

Like the Christian Board of Publication, the Board of Education had a history reaching back at least twenty years before its actual formation in 1914. The American Christian Missionary Society had established an educational board of nine members in 1894. This board operated until 1910 "with only mediocre success." Its activities centered around the gathering of information about Disciples colleges, the promotion of higher education in the movement's journals, fund-raising, and finally, the placing of a full-time secretary in the field to pursue the board's goals. In 1910 this board gave way to the Association of Colleges of the Disciples of Christ. At the meeting of the Association in September 1914, the Board of Education was formed in response to the need for an organization which would be able to "help raise and properly distribute" $3,000,000 designated for educational purposes as part of the "Men and Millions" campaign initiated at the 1913 Convention.[74] The purpose of the Board was "to promote Christian education by assisting the colleges and other institutions connected with the Disciples of Christ, to obtain co-operation and unity among the institutions of the church, and to obtain standardization of courses of study in the colleges and schools of the church."[75] "Membership dues in the new board were fixed at $100 per year for the larger institutions, and $50 per year for all others."[76] The organization originally was directed solely by the presidents of the member institutions. However, in 1922 the board was enlarged so that about half would be representatives of the Disciples of Christ at large.[77]

By 1906 the Churches of Christ, which opposed all extracongregational organization, had fully recognized their separate existence. The remaining portion of the Campbell-Stone movement accepted the legitimacy of extracongregational organizations. The new tension in this remaining portion of the movement was not over the legitimacy of organizations per se but over their proper character. The *Christian Standard* of Cincinnati would continue to resist any shift away from the society system. However, by 1914 the Campbell-Stone movement had developed an extensive range of organizations which were ill-fitted to the designation missionary society. Likewise, these organizations had to be staffed and it was clear that the members of these staffs were not all "evangelists." Among some members of the Campbell-Stone movement there appears to have been a recognition that their movement's structures were more similar to the structures of the historic churches than to missionary societies.[78] The growing tendency among those members to view the Disciples of Christ as a church not unlike the historic churches was both manifested in and strengthened by the coming out from isolation of a segment of the Campbell-Stone movement in terms of theological education.

Before the 1890s it was unusual for an "educated" preacher in the Campbell-Stone movement to hold a degree beyond a Bachelor of Arts from one of the movement's own colleges. Gradually this changed as more and more Disciples sought postgraduate theological education. The first member of the Disciples of Christ to do so sought admission to Yale Divinity School in the mid-1870s.[79] Some Disciples had taken courses at Union Theological Seminary in New York even earlier. By 1891, Yale thought it advisable to advertise in Disciples of Christ periodicals. In 1892 there were five Disciples students at Yale,[80] and by 1901 the number had increased to eleven.[81] In 1931, Riley B. Montgomery wrote of the trend in the Campbell-Stone movement toward "better post-graduate and graduate training" of ministers "in the leading universities and seminaries of the country." Of the eleven hundred Disciples who sought such training between 1875 and 1927, 59.18 percent attended the Divinity School of the University of Chicago and 25.73 percent attended Yale Divinity School. The schools attended by the remainder of the eleven hundred, "listed by rank according to number having attended," were: Union Theological Seminary, Vanderbilt School of Religion, Boston University School of Religious Education and Social Service, Harvard Divinity School, and Hartford Seminary Foundation.[82]

Despite the growing influence of the University of Chicago and other universities, such as Yale, the numbers of persons educated for the Disciples ministry at such schools were still proportionately small. Montgomery's 1931 report indicates that of the 590 academic degrees reported by his 565 respondents, "410, or 69.5 per cent, were conferred by Disciple of Christ institutions."[83] As long as these institutions resisted the historical-critical method the general isolation of Disciples ministers in terms of theological education could remain intact. This, however, was not to be. Early in the twentieth century the colleges of the Campbell-Stone movement did begin to accept the historical-critical approach. The most dramatic instance was at The College of the Bible in Lexington, Kentucky (see chapter three). The College of the Bible's acceptance of the historical-critical stance to the exclusion of the conservative position of J. W. McGarvey symbolized the fact that even at Disciples-affiliated institutions, "the era of intellectual isolation in the training of ministers was over."[84]

The growing sense of partnership with the historic churches in the enterprise of theological education was also real and visible in the area of missions. The last quarter of the nineteenth and first quarter of the twentieth centuries brought with them the zenith of American foreign missions activity. Consistent with the trend, between 1876 and 1919 foreign missions work was resumed or initiated by Disciples in ten fields.[85] This renewed participation in and growth of foreign missions activity by Disciples was accompanied by a growing consciousness of and practice of interdenominational cooperation. This was a feature that marked "the whole foreign mission enterprise."[86]

Obviously, the interdenominational character of the zenith of foreign missions in American Protestantism would be anathema to those in the Campbell-Stone movement who were wedded to the conception of evangelism which had characterized the movement's first generation. After all, unimmersed Methodists and Presbyterians were themselves proper *objects* for evangelization according to the conservative restorationist view; they were scarcely to be regarded as

The Society Concept

fitting *partners* in the task of evangelizing the world. But on this issue a different point of view began to be articulated among Disciples in the waning years of the nineteenth century. In his 1884 volume, *Christian Missions and Historical Sketches of Missionary Societies among the Disciples of Christ*, F. M. Green began with a brief discussion of the "History of Christian Missions," which he defined in a tentatively inclusive sense:

> We use the word Christian in its broad, catholic meaning, and not in the narrow sense of a denomination. The history of modern missions scarcely reaches yet three-fourths of a century. It is true, however, taking the old world with the new, that the era of Protestant missions commenced in the eighteenth century. While this is a fact of history, yet *it is not wholly true that the missionary spirit had slumbered in the church from the Apostolic age till then. Every intermediate century had witnessed the diffusion of at least, nominal Christianity*.[87] (Italics mine.)

Even such a hesitant statement as Green's represents a conception of missions that is quite different from that which would construe the gospel as having lain dormant between the time of the Apostles and the birth of the Campbell-Stone movement.

The inclusive, interdenominational approach to foreign missions was given vigorous leadership among Disciples by Archibald McLean. "Widely known as the 'Apostle of Missions,' he was secretary of the Foreign Christian Missionary Society from 1882 until 1900, then its president until . . . 1920."[88] McLean "wrote several books on the history of missions, books ecumenical in scope, and he helped Disciples to see that the New Testament had rather larger concerns than the stereotyped transmission of the doctrinal outlines" inherited from the first generation of the Campbell-Stone movement.[89] Representing the Foreign Christian Missionary Society (FCMS), McLean attended "the first interdenominational missionary conference in London in 1888," and participated in the organization of the Foreign Missions Conference of North America in 1893.[90]

At least as early as 1900 representatives of the other Disciples national missionary society, the Christian Woman's Board of Missions (CWBM), were reflecting a similarly interdenominational outlook by their attendance at the Ecumenical Conference on Foreign Missions.[91] The growth of this outlook was reflected even more dramatically in the World Missionary Conference in Edinburgh, Scotland, in 1910. Archibald McLean chaired a delegation of twenty-three Disciples to this meeting. More significantly, in 1910 the CWBM established in Indianapolis a College of Missions which "provide[d] a complete curriculum that conformed to the recommendations" of the Edinburgh conference.[92] The establishment by Disciples of Christ of such an institution for the training of missionaries represents a dramatic shift away from the old competitive conception of evangelism and mission. The graduates of the College of Missions, who were primarily to be engaged in Disciples missions,[93] were receiving training at an interdenominationally or ecumenically conceived institution.

Both the growth of foreign missions activity by Disciples and its character as part of a much larger enterprise is reflected in the *World Statistics of Christian Missions* published by the Foreign Missions Conference of North America in 1916. By that date the Disciples' CWBM and FCMS could report a combined income of $798,719. They also reported work in China, India, Japan, the Philippine Islands, Africa (Liberia and Congo), Argentina, Mexico, Jamaica, Puerto Rico, Cuba, Canada (among North American Indians), Europe and among Asiatic immigrants to the United States.

The fact that this increased mission activity on the part of Disciples was, indeed, part of the vitality of the general foreign missions effort by North American Christians may be seen in the *Statistics*' tabulation of societies and incomes. Of a total of 699 missionary societies, 223 were in the United States and Canada. The United States alone had 197 societies compared to 84 in Germany and 99 in England. Of the $41,749,173 of income reported by the missionary societies, $21,390,361 had been raised by the societies of the United States and Canada.[94] Winthrop Hudson points out that earlier in the nineteenth century, "Great Britain had taken the lead in the foreign-mission enterprise and the United States had served as a junior partner. At the close of the century this role was reversed."[95]

When the United States became the senior partner in the foreign missions effort, it did so with an exalted understanding of its role. Josiah Strong's 1885 *Our Country* "summoned the churches of America to assume their full responsibility for the Christianization of the world."[96] The Anglo-Saxons, which Strong called "the great missionary race,"[97] were to be the "bearers of two great interrelated ideas—'civil liberty' and 'spiritual Christianity.'"[98]

Strong's statements about the destiny of the United States as the primary representative of the Anglo-Saxon race are strikingly similar to views which had been held in the Campbell-Stone movement since its first generation. Among the Disciples of Christ, "racist views were often combined with the millennial faith in the destiny of the American nation."[99] Alexander Campbell's 1852 article in the *Millennial Harbinger* anticipated Josiah Strong:

> In our country's destiny is involved the destiny of Protestantism, and in its destiny the destiny of all the nations of the world. God has given, in awful charge, to Protestant England and Protestant America—the Anglo-Saxon race—the fortunes, not of Christendom only, but of all the world.[100]

Of course, Campbell was not the only person advancing such a view. The significance of the Anglo-Saxonism of the late nineteenth century foreign missions movement to Disciples is not that Anglo-Saxonism had been uniquely pioneered by Alexander Campbell but that, when Strong and many other Protestant spokespersons sounded themes of Anglo-Saxon missionary destiny, they were speaking in terms thoroughly familiar to Disciples. The idea of a uniquely American role in the evangelization of the world was at least as old among Disciples as Thomas Campbell's *Declaration and Address*.

The Disciples of Christ were part of a much wider surge of interest in foreign missions on the part of American Protestants in the late nineteenth and early twentieth centuries. Part of the reason that Disciples were able to shift from a primarily domestic and proselytizing approach to evangelism to a more foreign-oriented and interdenominationally cooperative approach may lie in the fact that the foreign missions boom was promoted in a rhetoric of Anglo-Saxon superiority and American destiny which was already a part of the Disciples' self-understanding.

Whether or not the shift in Disciples' thinking and action with regard to mission was facilitated by the more general boom and its familiar-sounding propaganda, a shift did occur. By the 1880 meeting of the Disciples' General Christian Missionary Convention, a Committee on New Missions would report:

> We think it very important that the correct and right idea as to the true nature, character, and limitations of foreign mission work be stated, entertained and adhered to in the prosecution of the work. What is that idea? With what end in view, and with what purpose, should foreign missionary societies be established and sustained? Not to change believers from one Protestant faith to another, but to Christianize the heathen; to make known the Christ in his saving power to those who have never heard of him, and to whom he has not been preached. It is to plant congregations of Christian believers in lands distinctively and admittedly pagan, idolatrous and heathen.[101]

Thus, an element of the Campbell-Stone movement was not only supporting missionary societies but shifting its understanding of missions. That shift in understanding was reflected in the results of evangelistic efforts. Between 1902 and 1922, the Disciples experienced a 42.4 percent growth in "homeland" church membership and a 424.0 percent growth in church membership in "foreign fields."[102]

The shift in emphasis was not welcomed by all of the Disciples who remained after the final disaffection and schism with the Churches of Christ.[103] For accompanying the shift in emphasis was the more cooperative and inclusive view of the historic churches—the view that other Protestant and American (Anglo-Saxon) churches were partners in the task of world evangelism. The practical implications of this view proved controversial and ultimately divisive for the remainder of the Campbell-Stone movement. The concrete structural developments in this second major division came in the decade 1917 to 1927. However, it was clear by 1910 that the *Christian Standard* and its ideological constituency was resisting the interdenominational character of the new foreign missions emphasis. Two incidents reported by Stephen J. Corey illustrate this fact. First, the *Christian Standard* opposed the participation of the Disciples in the establishment of the Union Christian University in Nanking, China, in 1910. This was to have been a cooperative effort by Disciples, Methodists, and Presbyterians. Second, the *Standard* strongly supported

> the "Hors de Rome" (out of Catholicism) movement which began in 1909 in Paris, France. It was a venture to establish a church, or churches, of the New Testament faith in the city of Paris, using a division in the Roman Catholic Church and the conversion of some of its priests to Protestantism as the entering wedge.[104]

Thus, there was still an element in the Campbell-Stone movement, after the division with the Churches of Christ, who conceived of missions in the traditionally exclusivistic and proselytizing terms.

The fourth and final area of differential change contributing to the second major polarization in the Disciples of Christ is that in the level and influence of urbanization between 1890 and 1916. Census figures reported in *Religious Bodies: 1916* suggest that caution should be exercised in attributing significance to this factor. The 1890 Census had shown a total of 641,051 members in the Disciples of Christ, of which only 42,734 were in cities of 25,000 or more persons. More than 93 percent of the Disciples were "outside of principal cities."[105]

The Society Concept

By 1916 a very important change had occurred in the enumeration of Disciples in the report—the Churches of Christ were listed separately. The Disciples as a separate body were listed as having 1,226,028 members. Of these, 207,378 were counted as living in cities of 25,000 or more persons. The percentage of membership living in such cities had risen from under 7 to 17 percent.[106] This jump, and the even more dramatic jump in the absolute number of Disciples living in cities (42,734 to 207,378) provide the basis for regarding urbanization as significant. However, the fact that even in 1916 83.1 percent of Disciples were "outside of principal cities" justifies W. E. Garrison's observation that at the beginning of the twentieth century the Disciples were "still a town-and-village rather than a city people."[107] Such a statement would also be true of the Disciples in 1916.

The 1,018,650 members that were listed as "outside of principal cities" in 1916 were, by far, the numerical majority of Disciples. But the separation of the Churches of Christ (who were 95.5 percent "outside of principal cities" in 1916) helped to shift the center of the remaining Disciples both northward and toward the cities.[108]

Although less than 17 percent of the total number of Disciples, the urban Disciples may well have been disproportionately influential. In several of the cities where a concentration of several thousand Disciples were found in 1916, there was also an influential or important agency, publication, or educational institution. Kansas City, with 11,343 Disciples, was the original home of the Board of Church Extension. Des Moines, with 8,808 Disciples, was also the location of Drake University. Indianapolis had the ecumenically inspired College of Missions as well as 8,545 Disciples. Louisville was the site of the Louisville Bible School, an institution for the training of black Disciples ministers, and the home of 5,415 Disciples. Cleveland had 5,267 Disciples, the social settlement Hiram House, and Hiram College nearby. St. Louis was the home of the *Christian-Evangelist* and 4,389 Disciples. Pittsburgh had been the site of the Disciples' 1909 Centennial Convention. The nearest major city to Bethany College, Pittsburgh had 4,185 Disciples. Lexington, Kentucky, with 4,080 Disciples, was the location of Transylvania College and The College of the Bible. Finally, Chicago was not only the site of the Disciples Divinity House of the University of Chicago, of the *Christian Century*, and of the Campbell Institute, but also of 4,066 Disciples.[109] To see the impact of urbanization upon the Disciples of Christ in terms of the direct experience of the majority of its members would be erroneous. But many among the 207,378 members of the Disciples of Christ which the 1916 religious census identified as in cities of 25,000 or more persons *were* concentrated in centers of Disciples influence.

An equation cannot be suggested, however, between urbanization and liberalism. Cincinnati, with 3,354 Disciples, headquartered the *Christian Standard* which, by 1916, was clearly opposed to any trend away from the assumptions of conservative restorationism.[110] Similarly, Canton, Ohio contained 4,225 Disciples who were largely under the leadership of P. H. Welshimer, a "catalyst in the creation of the Christian Church [as distinct from the Disciples of Christ]."[111] Even the predominately rural Churches of Christ had one urban center of strength in 1916. Nashville, Tennessee, was reported to have had 3,946 members of the Churches of Christ in 1916. Only two other cities of 25,000 persons or more showed more than a thousand members of this body—Detroit and Fort Worth.[112] So while an equation cannot be suggested, it seems generally to be the case that the more conservative the wing of the Campbell-Stone movement, the more rural.[113]

Accompanying the increased urbanization of the Disciples membership in this period was their deep involvement in the temperance crusade, which was similar to the foreign missions movement in its interdenominational character. James A. Crain contends that "the drive toward . . . prohibition made a strong impact upon Disciples of Christ," who formed their own Temperance Board in 1907.[114] While this "great Protestant crusade" appealed to both liberals and conservatives,[115] it may have helped drive the wedge deeper between the two emerging groups (Independents and Cooperatives) within the Disciples. Because it was so broadly supported in Protestantism, the temperance movement made partners of Disciples and other Christians. Therefore, like foreign missions, the temperance movement raised the question of what was the proper attitude for Disciples toward the historic churches.

At the very beginning of the period 1849 to 1917, the structural alternatives for the organization of the Campbell-Stone movement at the national level seemed to be either a representative convention of delegates from congregations (the kind of convention that Alexander Campbell had advocated) or some combination of a "mass meeting" convention and a society of interested, dues-paying individuals (the concept championed by D. S. Burnet). The adoption of the society concept in 1849 at the Campbell-Stone movement's first national convention did not represent a final decision between these two alternatives, however. Weakened by the shocks of the Civil War and the death of Alexander Campbell, the Disciples nonetheless attempted again in 1869 to embody the structural vision of the mature Alexander Campbell in the delegate-based Louisville Plan. The failure of the Louisville Plan strengthened the position of the society concept in the organizational tradition of the movement. Regional as well as national structures were, for the most part, organized according to the society concept by the late

The Society Concept

nineteenth century. However, the changing social environment of the Disciples and accompanying changes within the movement itself in the late nineteenth and early twentieth centuries created pressures on the society system.

Although these changes did not occur uniformly throughout the movement, the rise of national societies of diverse functions, the increasing influence of interdenominational postgraduate theological education, participation in broadly Protestant foreign missions and temperance crusades, and the increasing impact of urbanization all put pressure on the status quo of the Campbell-Stone movement. The pressure began to polarize that portion of the movement that remained after the disaffection and departure of the Churches of Christ.

The polarization was between those still deeply committed to the theological assumptions of a conservative restorationism combined with the ecclesiological assumptions of the society system and those whose experiences of cooperation both within the movement and with the historic churches had begun to press them beyond continued commitment to the status quo. Thus, the conventional designations for these emerging groups, Independents and Cooperatives, though based on the attitudes of these groups toward extracongregational organizations within the movement, are also quite descriptive of their respect attitudes toward the historic churches.

The divergence between Independents and Cooperatives among Disciples may be traced at least as far back as the first decade of the twentieth century when the *Christian Standard* opposed developments within the Campbell-Stone movement that contained an element of rapprochement with other churches.[116] The division between Independents and Cooperatives had occurred, in fact, at least by the decade of 1917 to 1927. During this critical decade the Disciples created the International Convention of Disciples of Christ (1917) and the United Christian Missionary Society (1919).[117] The emerging Independents, given direction by the *Christian Standard*, which blasted both of the aforementioned structures, organized a rival body, the North American Christian Convention (1927).[118] Thus a second division in the Campbell-Stone movement was given a concrete structure. For fifty years, from 1917 until the decade of Restructure, this *de facto* separation confused and confounded Disciples.

---

1. Noel L. Keith, *The Story of D. S. Burnet: Undeserved Obscurity* (St. Louis: Bethany Press, 1954), 7, 9.

2. See Conrad Wright, "The Growth of Denominational Bureaucracies: A Neglected Aspect of American Church History," *Harvard Theological Review*

77 (2:1984):177-94; Charles I. Foster, *An Errand of Mercy: The Evangelical United Front: 1790-1837* (Chapel Hill: University of North Carolina Press, 1960).

3. Lair, *Christian Churches and Their Work*, 88.

4. Ibid., 89.

5. A[lexander] C[ampbell], "Church Organization—No. I," *Millennial Harbinger*, ser. 3, 6 (February 1849):90, 92.

6. A[lexander] C[ampbell], "Church Organization—No. II," *Millennial Harbinger*, ser. 3, 6 (April 1849):221.

7. Alexander Campbell, "Church Organization—No. III," 269, 271.

8. Alexander Campbell, "Church Organization—No. IV," 271.

9. Alexander Campbell, "Church Organization—No. III," 270.

10. A[lexander] C[ampbell], "Convention," *Millennial Harbinger*, ser. 3, 6 (August 1849):475-76.

11. Eikner, "Nature of the Church," 105.

12. Keith, *Story of D. S. Burnet*, 80-81.

13. Lair, *Christian Churches and Their Work*, 95-96.

14. McAllister and Tucker, *Journey in Faith*, 174.

15. Grant K. Lewis, *The American Christian Missionary Society and the Disciples of Christ* (St. Louis: Christian Board of Publication, 1937), 7.

16. McAllister and Tucker, *Journey in Faith*, 175.

17. Keith, *Story of D. S. Burnet*, 105-106.

18. Max E. Willcockson, "Our Conventions through a Century," *Christian-Evangelist* 87 (22 June 1949):613; McAllister and Tucker, *Journey in Faith*, 175.

19. McAllister and Tucker, *Journey in Faith*, 175.

20. Alexander Campbell, "Five Arguments for Church Organization," 523.

21. Gary Wayne Mayes, "Restructure in the Light of Structure among the Disciples of Christ" (B.D. thesis, The College of the Bible, 1965), 31-32.

22. Alexander Campbell, "Nature of the Christian Organization. No. II," 63.

23. Mayes, "Restructure in the Light of Structure," 32.

24. "The American Christian Missionary Society: Resolutions, October 24, 1849," in *American Christian Missionary Society*, by Lewis, 9, 10.

25. James A. Crain, *The Development of Social Ideas among the Disciples of Christ* (St. Louis: Bethany Press, 1969), 18.

26. McAllister and Tucker, *Journey in Faith*, 176.

27. Ibid., 177. The monetary arrangements were soon modified, but the basic voluntary-associational form remained.

The Society Concept

28. "Constitution of the American Christian Missionary Society (Adopted October 26, 1849)," in *Christian Missions and Historical Sketches*, by Green, 370.

29. Ibid., 371-72.

30. *Year Book and Directory (1981) of the Christian Church (Disciples of Christ)* (Indianapolis: General Office of the Christian Church [Disciples of Christ], 1981), m132.

31. A[lexander] C[ampbell], "Cincinnati Convention," *Millennial Harbinger*, ser. 3, 6 (December 1849):694-95.

32. Wrather, *Creative Freedom in Action*, 27.

33. Lair, *Christian Churches and Their Work*, 97-99.

34. W. E. Garrison, *American Religious Movement*, 110; West, *Search for the Ancient Order*, 1:162. See also West's chapter, "Growing Opposition," 1:197-213.

35. Winfred E. Garrison, *Religion Follows the Frontier: A History of the Disciples of Christ* (New York: Harper Bros., 1931), 277.

36. McAllister and Tucker, *Journey in Faith*, 177.

37. Willcockson, "Our Conventions through a Century," 613.

38. McAllister and Tucker, *Journey in Faith*, 256-57.

39. Willcockson, "Our Conventions through a Century," 613.

40. Lair, *Christian Churches and Their Work*, 106.

41. McAllister and Tucker, *Journey in Faith*, 257.

42. "Constitution of the General Christian Missionary Convention (Adopted October, 1869)," in *Christian Missions and Historical Sketches*, by Green, 376.

43. McAllister and Tucker, *Journey in Faith*, 257.

44. Willcockson, "Our Conventions through a Century," 614.

45. McAllister and Tucker, *Journey in Faith*, 257.

46. Willcockson, "Our Conventions through a Century," 614.

47. Green, *Christian Missions and Historical Sketches*, xviii, 386-422.

48. McAllister and Tucker, *Journey in Faith*, 258.

49. Ida Withers Harrison, *History of the Christian Woman's Board of Missions* (n.p., 1920), 27-31.

50. McAllister and Tucker, *Journey in Faith*, 262.

51. Archibald McLean, *The History of the Foreign Christian Missionary Society* (New York: Fleming H. Revell Co., 1919), 35-38.

52. Lewis, *American Christian Missionary Society*, 31-109 passim, 38-39, 69, 49.

53. W. E. Garrison, *Religion Follows the Frontier*, 199-200, 247-48.

54. U. S. Department of Interior, Census Office, *Report on Statistics of Churches in the United States at the Eleventh Census: 1890* (Washington, D.C.: Government Printing Office, 1894), 4, 40, 94, 98, 100, 112.

55. Ibid., 40, XVI, XVII.

56. W. E. Garrison, *Religion Follows the Frontier*, xi.

57. Donald E. Mitchell, "Board of Church Extension: A Century of Service," *Discipliana* 42 (Winter 1982):51-53.

58. Commission for the Direction of Surveys, Authorized by the International Convention of Disciples of Christ, *Survey of Service: Organizations Represented in International Convention of Disciples of Christ* (St. Louis: Christian Board of Publication, 1928), 33.

59. Mitchell, "Board of Church Extension," 53; see also, Lani L. J. Olson, *Building a Witness: 100 Years of Church Extension* (Indianapolis: Board of Church Extension of the Disciples of Christ, 1983).

60. *Fifty Years' March of Mercy* (St. Louis: National Benevolent Association, 1937), 5, 6; see also Hiram Lester and Marge Lester, *Inasmuch . . . The Saga of the NBA* (St. Louis: National Benevolent Association, 1987).

61. McAllister and Tucker, *Journey in Faith*, 272-73.

62. DeGroot and Garrison, *The Disciples of Christ*, 506.

63. William Martin Smith, *For the Support of the Ministry: A History of Ministerial Support, Relief and Pensions among Disciples of Christ* (Indianapolis: Pension Fund of Disciples of Christ, 1956), 54, 96.

64. Commission for the Direction of Surveys, *Survey of Service*, 665, 667.

65. Lair, *Christian Churches and Their Work*, 121.

66. Tucker, *J. H. Garrison*, 219-20.

67. Ibid., 230, 231, 232.

68. McAllister and Tucker, *Journey in Faith*, 329-30.

69. "The Christian Board of Publication," editorial, *Christian Standard* 47 (22 April 1911):645.

70. "Our New Charter," editorial, *Christian-Evangelist* 48 (30 March 1911):436.

71. "Christian Board of Publication," 645.

72. Ibid.

73. Tucker, *J. H. Garrison*, 220.

74. Griffith A. Hamlin, "The Origin and Development of the Board of Higher Education of the Christian Church (Disciples of Christ): 1894-1968" (M.S. thesis, Southern Illinois University, 1968), 24-30, 31-32.

75. "Board of Education Formed," *Christian-Evangelist* 51 (10 September 1914):1179.

The Society Concept 149

76. Hamlin, "Board of Higher Education," 32.

77. Commission for the Direction of Surveys, *Survey of Service*, 606; see also Duane Cummins, *The Disciples Colleges: A History* (St. Louis: CBP Press, 1987), 114-127.

78. This recognition is implied by the participation of some Disciples in such interdenominational enterprises as Christian Endeavor, the Inter-Church Conference on Federation, the Federal Council of the Churches of Christ in America, the Foreign Missions Conference of North America and the Home Missions Conference. Also, the renewed interest in the creation of a national convention composed of delegates from the congregations showed that the society concept was seen as inadequate. All of these developments occurred between 1880 and 1912. See McAllister and Tucker, *Journey in Faith*, 279-82, 340.

79. McAllister and Tucker, *Journey in Faith*, 371.

80. DeGroot and Garrison, *The Disciples of Christ*, 376.

81. McAllister and Tucker, *Journey in Faith*, 371.

82. Riley B. Montgomery, *The Education of Ministers of Disciples of Christ* (St. Louis: Bethany Press, 1931), 53-54.

83. Ibid., 89, 95.

84. Garrison, *Religion Follows the Frontier*, 261.

85. Commission for the Direction of Surveys, *Survey of Service*, 515.

86. Winthrop S. Hudson, *Religion in America: An Historical Account of the Development of American Religious Life*, 2nd ed. (New York: Charles Scribner's Sons, 1973), 322-25.

87. Green, *Christian Missions and Historical Sketches*, 23.

88. J. Edward Moseley, "The Christian Church (Disciples of Christ) and Overseas Ministries," in *Interpretative Examination*, ed. Beasley, 242.

89. Ronald E. Osborn, "Theology among the Disciples," in *Interpretative Examination*, ed. Beazley, 100.

90. Moseley, "Overseas Ministries," 242, 243.

91. Lorraine Lollis, *The Shape of Adam's Rib: A Lively History of Women's Work in the Christian Church* (St. Louis: Bethany Press, 1970), 90.

92. Moseley, "Overseas Ministries," 242. The College of Missions "continued until 1927. . . . The institution became affiliated with the Kennedy School of Missions of the Hartford Seminary Foundation . . . in 1928" (243-44).

93. The 1928 *Survey of Service* reports that of the 410 students enrolled since the opening of the College of Missions, 291 were "graduates sent to the fields or under appointment." However, only 14 graduates belonged to other communions. Commission for the Direction of Surveys, *Survey of Service*, 523. The older, competitive approach to mission is closely related to what Don A.

Pittman and Paul A. Williams have called the "homiletical" view of mission ("Mission and Evangelism: Continuing Debates and Contemporary Interpretations," in *Interpreting Disciples*, ed. Richesin and Bouchard, 220-21).

94. Harlan P. Beach and Burton St. John, eds., *World Statistics of Christian Missions: Containing a Directory of Missionary Societies, a Classified Summary of Statistics, and an Index of Mission Stations throughout the World* (New York: Committee of Reference and Counsel of the Foreign Missions Conference of North America, 1916), 18, 54.

95. Hudson, *Religion in America*, 320.

96. Ibid.

97. Josiah Strong, *Our Country: Its Possible Future and Its Present Crisis*, with an Introduction by Austin Phelps, rev. ed. (New York: Baker & Taylor Co. for the American Home Missionary Society, 1891), 209.

98. Hudson, *Religion in America*, 320.

99. Harrell, *Social History*, 1:52.

100. A[lexander] C[ampbell], "The Destiny of Our Country," *Millennial Harbinger*, ser. 4, 2 (August 1852):462, quoted in Harrell, *Social History*, 1:53.

101. Report of the Committee on New Missions, 1880, quoted in McLean, *Foreign Christian Missionary Society*, 79.

102. Commission for the Direction of Surveys, *Survey of Service*, 516.

103. Congregations of the Churches of Christ pursued their own programs of foreign missions, for an account of which see West, *Search for the Ancient Order*, 2:457-59 and 3:305-370.

104. Corey, *Attack and Controversy*, 34.

105. U. S. Census Office, *Report of Statistics of Churches: 1890*, 4, 40; U. S. Department of Commerce, Bureau of the Census, *Religious Bodies: 1916*, pt. 1, *Summary and General Tables* (Washington, D. C.: Government Printing Office, 1919), 121.

106. U. S. Bureau of the Census, *Summary and General Tables* [1916], 121.

107. U. S. Bureau of the Census, *Summary and General Tables* [1916], 121; W. E. Garrison, *Religion Follows the Frontier*, 276.

108. U. S. Bureau of the Census, *Summary and General Tables* [1916], 121.

109. Ibid., 339, 341; McAllister and Tucker, *Journey in Faith*, 165-375 passim.

110. U. S. Bureau of the Census, *Summary and General Tables* [1916], 339; Corey, *Attack and Controversy*, 1-44.

111. U. S. Bureau of the Census, *Summary and General Tables* [1916], 339; Leroy Garrett, *The Stone-Campbell Movement: An Anecdotal History of Three Churches* (Joplin, Missouri: College Press Publishing Co., 1981), 637.

112. U. S. Bureau of the Census, *Summary and General Tables* [1916], 339.

113. On Disciples historical geography see Roger W. Stump, "Spatial Patterns of Growth and Decline among the Disciples of Christ, 1890-1980," in Williams, ed. *A Case Study of Mainstream Protestantism*, 445-68.

114. Crain, *Development of Social Ideas among Disciples*, 39, 58.

115. Hudson, *Religion in America*, 317.

116. Corey, *Attack and Controversy*, 14, 17, 30, 31.

117. McAllister and Tucker, *Journey in Faith*, 17.

118. Corey, *Attack and Controversy*, 43-46, 60, 101; McAllister and Tucker, *Journey in Faith*, 17.

CHAPTER VI

THE EVOLUTION OF STRUCTURE BEYOND
THE SOCIETY CONCEPT

During the period between 1917 and 1958, Disciples polity "was shaped by increasing attempts at coordination and by increasing frustration" with the Convention and agencies as they attempted "to meet the problems which the twentieth century forced upon this loosely organized confederation."[1] The beginning of this period in the structural history of the Disciples is marked by the creation of the International Convention of Disciples of Christ in 1917.[2] This event was the culmination of efforts which had begun several years earlier. The last quarter of the nineteenth century had seen the proliferation of societies among the Disciples, each of which "had a special offering day when appeals were made to the churches and their organizations for support." This approach to "promotion resulted in confusion and resistance on the part of the churches."[3] The leaders of the competing societies and boards began to feel the need for a more coordinated promotional effort. A constitution that would have provided for such coordination was written in 1893 but never made operative.[4] By the early years of the twentieth century, the idea of coordinating the promotional efforts of the individual societies began to develop in the direction of creating a "delegate convention which would coordinate the societies."

A Committee on Reconstruction and Unification was appointed in 1909 and presented a report in 1912 which recommended a delegate convention "to which all national agencies would be organically related." Before the Committee's report was adopted, however, it was modified so that local churches were not limited in the number of delegates they could send to the convention.[5] Even with this modification, which itself virtually negated any proportionality of delegate representation and preserved the traditional "mass meeting" character of national Disciples gatherings, the opposition was not fully satisfied. "The critics of The General Convention were opposed to its constitution and the features that were in it pertaining to a 'delegate convention.'"[6] When the Convention met again the next year, 2,741 persons attended, well under half of whom were actually "delegates." Opposition to the idea of a delegate convention was "intense" and was given leadership by the *Christian Standard*. As a result of this opposition, a resolution was adopted "which placed the Convention only in an advisory position to the societies" and denied the Convention any funds.[7] By 1913, then, both the feature of proportionate delegate representation and of coordination of the societies' promotions, the original impetus to national organizational change, had been removed from the new convention structure. Not surprisingly, when the congregations did not select and send delegates, the opposition was able to bring about a revision of the constitution.[8] The General Convention had not been able to function according to its constitution in any of the years from 1913 to 1916. In 1916, at the Des Moines convention, a new committee was appointed to revise the Convention's constitution.[9]

The "Committee on Revision of the Constitution" appointed in 1916 reported to the Kansas City convention the following year.[10] The committee had been committed to finding a more acceptable shape for organization than the delegate form proposed in 1912.[11] However, they had also been guided by the desire to find "a more orderly business procedure."[12] The committee's proposed new constitution was adopted at the Kansas City convention on October 26, 1917. Three weeks later, the *Christian-Evangelist* summarized the differences between the new constitution and the one it had supplanted:

> 1. It changes the name from General Convention of Churches of Christ to International Convention of Disciples of Christ.
>
> 2. It places the business of the convention in the hands of a committee on recommendations, composed of business men from the various states, territories and provinces. This committee is to sit during the convention and make recommendations to the various agencies submitting the reports. It is to report all such findings to the convention for its approval or disapproval.
>
> 3. It admits to membership in the convention all who attend and enroll, whether they are delegates representing churches or only represent themselves.
>
> 4. It makes provisions for the expenses of the convention by levying as much as one-half of 1 per cent of the general collection of the agencies as is necessary to defray the expenses.

The new convention retained its advisory status with respect to the agencies of the Disciples. The troublesome delegate feature of the 1912 constitution was transferred from the composition of the convention itself to that of the Committee on Recommendations, where a proportionately representative composition was to be determined as follows:

> The committee on recommendations shall be annually constituted of members of Churches of Christ who shall possess good business qualifications and be actively interested in the various agencies of

Beyond the Society Concept

the brotherhood, but not in their employ. It shall be composed of one appointee of each state or provincial missionary convention, or district convention where there is none more conclusive, and of one additional and preferably lay appointee for every 25,000 or major fraction of members of Churches of Christ within the territory of such convention.[13]

The 1917 constitution of the International Convention of Disciples of Christ was a compromise which provided for both a delegate body (the Committee on Recommendations) and a mass meeting (the convention itself).[14]

The attempt at compromise that led to the 1917 constitution at first appeared successful. The *Christian Standard* even applauded the constitution in November of 1917.[15] However, it was not long until "the *Christian Standard* became even more disenchanted with the reorganized convention and attacked it repeatedly."[16]

The International Convention of Disciples of Christ was not the only convention formed by Disciples in 1917. Black Disciples, who had been meeting for fellowship in a national convention intermittently for years, met in Nashville in 1917 under the leadership of Preston Taylor. At this meeting, representatives from the fourteen states which had formed state organizations of black Disciples organized the National Convention of Churches of Christ (later changed to National Christian Missionary Convention). This organization came about, in part, to "relieve frustration with white Disciples leaders who refused to share leadership" with black Disciples. White leaders who were present at the 1917 convention in Nashville tried unsuccessfully to persuade the black leaders to join with whites in the proposed International Convention rather than to form their own convention. Given the Anglo-Saxonism present in Disciples tradition, it is not surprising that black Disciples were "determined to have their own convention." Among the reasons given for the formation of this body were: interest in higher education specifically for black Disciples, general racism in the church, difficulties at national meetings caused by racial discrimination in public accommodations, paternalism on the part of white Disciples leadership, the desire to foster better communication and relationships within the black Disciples community, and the desire to combat racial stereotypes. It was decided that the National Convention would be "auxiliary of the proposed International Convention."[17]

It is also important to note that the cooperative, organizational impulse was being acted upon by hispanic Disciples during this same period. The "State Mexican Sunday School Convention" was active in the years 1916 to 1922 and involved seven hispanic congregations in the Southwest. These conventions were "the first formal effort at the regional level to bring together hispanic congregations" of Disciples in the United States.[18]

Neither the creation of the International Convention nor the organizational efforts of black and hispanic Disciples fundamentally changed the polity of the Disciples of Christ. The delegate representation had been relegated to the Committee on Recommendations whose members would be determined by state, provincial, and district societies. These more local organizations had evolved in the direction of voluntary-associational societies. Therefore, the Committee on Recommendations was indirectly based on the same membership principle. Furthermore, since the right to vote in the International Convention "could be secured simply by registering and paying the designated fee," the International Convention, "was still a society-type organization."[19]

If the changes involved in the formation of the International Convention of Disciples of Christ failed to bring about the abandonment of the society concept, other more significant changes were not far off. By 1917 Disciples were contemplating some kind of unification for their societies.[20] Several factors contributed to this development. According to D. James Atwood, among them was the impact of World War I.[21]

Two classes of factors were significant to the eventual unification of the Disciples' agencies. First are factors which created a climate among Disciples that permitted "a convincing case for unification" to be made. These factors included "the cooperation of Disciple agencies in missionary projects, the recognized need to reduce competition among the agencies, and the spirit of unity generated by such special brotherhood events as the centennial celebration of 1909." Second are those factors that have been seen as more "decisive" by historians of the Disciples of Christ. This class includes joint budgetary apportionment and the Men and Millions movement. In an attempt to "lessen the impact of some of the more unseemly aspects of the 'special day' method of financing," joint apportionment was "begun in earnest in 1915." The joint apportionment plan involved a "general fund to be divided equitably among participating agencies." While this plan made possible some cooperation between the agencies, the idea "lacked the emotional appeal necessary to persuade a large number of Disciples of the need for fundamental institutional change."

Atwood sees World War I as the catalyst that did convince Disciples of the need for change. In fact, he finds evidence which suggests that joint apportionment itself may have been, in part, a response to World War I. The suggestion of linkage between the second class of factors and World War I is even stronger in the case of the Men and Millions movement.[22] The goals of the Men and Millions campaign included the raising of over six million dollars "for missions, education, and benevolence." When "disruptions brought about by a wartime economy put church institutions in a serious financial bind,"[23] the Men and Millions movement, which had not theretofore been generally supported by Disciples, was kept from "financial failure" by its "War Emergency Drive."

Atwood suggests several other ways in which the war was the crucial experience leading to unification. These include: economic necessity brought about by wartime inflation, the perceived need for more effective organization because of the crisis condition of the world, the experience of interdenominational cooperation during the war, the diverting of Disciples' attention away from potentially divisive issues by an increased focus on the war, Disciples' observation of the mobilization process with its organizational and financial aspects, and the use of the war as a pretext for unification by those who desired it anyway.[24]

The agencies of the Disciples of Christ did take definite steps toward unification. The prospects for unification were dimmed by the fact that the agencies were "chartered institutions with legal responsibilities." They had permanent funds and had been beneficiaries of wills.[25] Nevertheless, the managing boards of the Christian Woman's Board of Missions, the Foreign Christian Missionary Society, and the American Christian Missionary Society passed recommendations in support of unification which were approved by the 1917 Kansas City convention.[26] A Committee on Cooperation and Unification submitted a proposal for a constitution and bylaws of a United Christian Missionary Society (UCMS) in September of 1918. The *Christian Standard* remarked that the proposal "contained a number of exceedingly objectionable features, and, moreover, proposed steps which, it has since proved, would have been illegal and would have endangered funds entrusted to various societies for specific purposes."[27] The 1918 International Convention of Disciples of Christ was canceled because of an influenza epidemic. By 1919, a revised proposal for a constitution and bylaws for the new society had been prepared.[28]

The 1919 plan extended unification to include not only the three missionary societies, but also the Board of Church Extension, the Board of Ministerial Relief, and the National Benevolent Association.[29] The *Standard* reported that the revised proposal had worked out the legal problems of the earlier one.[30] The solution was that "the 'old boards' would remain in existence as holding corporations for property and funds that could not immediately be transferred to the new agency, with members of the new board serving also as members of the boards of these 'holding corporations.'"[31] It was not, however, solely, the legal problems of the proposed UCMS which disturbed the *Christian Standard*.

The *Standard* called its readers' attention to "the care with which any allusion to the mission or message of the Restoration movement had been avoided in framing" the constitution of the UCMS, and characterized that constitution as a "chain to link together our organized work."[32]

Two features of the suggested society seemed to offend the *Standard*. The first, and most important, was the idea that the new society would not promote the distinctive ideology of the Campbell-Stone movement, which the *Standard* clearly understood as a primary commitment to the restoration ideal. Secondly, the *Standard* objected to the "growing autocracy of certain groups of Disciples," which manifested itself in the forging of such a "chain" as the proposed constitution of the UCMS.[33]

Less than a month before the *Christian Standard* published the proposed constitution and bylaws of the UCMS, it devoted its front page to the promotion of a Congress under the headline, "To the Rescue of the Restoration Movement." The article maintained:

> That there is an impending crisis in the affairs of the Restoration movement, coincident with the spread of modern rationalism, is apparent even to the most thoughtless.
>
> 1. Under this influence the Scriptural unity of doctrine is disturbed, among other evils, by the attempted introduction of "open membership," threatening the peace of all our congregations, and the very integrity of the Restoration plea.

The article goes on to suggest that a whole list of "evils" stem from this first one. These include: decreases in evangelism both at home and abroad, the halting of "Bible-school progress," a decrease in the number of ministerial candidates, the secularization of the movement's colleges' curricula, and a journalistic tendency to "champion the cause as a separate denomination or sect, rather than as the divine cure for sectarianism." Having listed the evils which constituted the crisis, the article issues an invitation:

> ... We invite all who are resolved to maintain the Restoration plea intact, to meet with us at Cincinnati, O., Oct. 13, 1919, at the Odd Fellows' Assembly Hall, ... to remain in session for two days.
> This call is issued to our ministry generally, and to the manhood and womanhood of the Restoration movement.[34]

Beyond the Society Concept 159

The *Christian Standard*'s 1919 promotion of a Congress with the avowed purpose of opposing the trends evident in the Disciples' agencies, schools, and other journals argues powerfully for an early dating of the separation between Independents and Cooperatives among Disciples. This 1919 article anticipates strikingly the developments which, over the next four decades, would clearly indicate the existence of two separate religious bodies. The article's complaints about decreasing evangelism and the increasingly "denominational" self-understanding among some Disciples would be reflected in years of attacks upon the conduct of the UCMS on the mission field. The article's concern about Disciples' colleges would be reflected in the promotion of an alternative set of institutions. The article's promotion of a Congress would soon give way to the support of a permanent alternative to the International Convention—the North American Christian Convention.

The process by which the *Standard*'s 1919 call is linked to the 1927 creation of the North American Christian Convention is a process which was fueled by continual controversy over open membership. This controversy was brought to the floor of the 1919 International Convention by conservatives who had just attended the "Restoration Congress."

The editor of the *Christian-Evangelist* supported the merger of the Disciples' agencies.[35] The *Christian-Evangelist* reported the accusations that the constituents of the Congress brought with them:

> The abuses charged against the societies—often in almost cruel personalities—ranged from personal grievances and old strifes like the "Transylvania matter" ... to such allegations as "open membership," "infant dedication" on the foreign field, unjustifiable meddling with the local churches and pastors by the secretaries, the ignoring of the deity of Christ, and the willingness to see our own church work supplanted by others.[36]

Although elements of both traditional Disciples antiecclesiasticism and opposition to theological liberalism are present in this list of charges, the open membership issue is referred to in at least three ways: in the direct reference; in the reference to "infant dedication"; and in the last phrase, a clear reference to comity agreements, the conservative objection to which hinged on the baptismal practices of the historic churches. The open membership question was mainly debated in terms of what was being practiced on the foreign mission field; "very few of the home churches practiced open membership." W. E. Garrison points out that the controversy centered around the question of whether or not open membership was being practiced on the mission field rather than whether or not it *ought* to be practiced.[37]

The missionaries of the Disciples of Christ had been, by 1919, involved for some years in various interdenominational missionary enterprises. They had begun to develop a different understanding of the character of Christian mission than that which had characterized the Disciples in their first generation. Basically, the missionaries and mission leaders whose experiences had forged in them an ecumenical understanding of missions were never able to compete, among a segment of Disciples, with the *Christian Standard*'s continued touting of the familiar exclusivistic mission ideology of the Disciples' first generation. They were unable to communicate effectively to all Disciples the essential difference which they perceived between, for example, China in the early twentieth century and the American frontier which Stone, the Campbells, and especially Scott had evangelized.[38]

Despite opposition, the UCMS was formed in 1919 and incorporated on June 22, 1920.[39] For the next several years, the UCMS became the focus of suspicion as to the practice of open membership.[40] By 1922, the Board of Managers of the Society felt compelled to deny "that they employed any missionary who received unimmersed believers into Christian fellowship." At the 1922 International Convention of Disciples of Christ, the Board of Managers issued a policy statement which the convention adopted:[41]

> In harmony with the teachings of the New Testament as understood by this Board of Managers, the United Christian Missionary Society is conducting its work everywhere on the principle of receiving into the membership of the churches at home and abroad, by any of its missionaries, only those who are immersed, penitent believers in Christ.
> Furthermore, it is believed by this Board of Managers, that all of the missionaries and ministers appointed and supported by this Board, are in sincere accord with this policy, and certainly will not appoint and indeed it will not continue in its service any one known by it to be not in such accord.[42]

This statement apparently "antagonized liberals without appeasing conservatives."[43] The controversy did not go away but intensified. Much of the intensification surrounded the activities of John T. Brown.

John T. Brown was an evangelist from Louisville, Kentucky, and a member of the Board of Managers of the UCMS. Brown undertook a trip into the mission fields of the UCMS, returning in time for the 1922 International Convention.

Beyond the Society Concept

Brown's report of this trip to both the Board of Managers and the International Convention included disapproval of some of what he had observed on the mission field, but confidence that the situation would improve. However, after the 1922 Convention, Brown submitted the entire text of his report on the mission fields to the *Christian Standard*, which published the report in a series entitled, "The United Society Has Broken Faith." This series focused on "what was termed open membership on the mission fields."[44]

The UCMS was clearly struggling with a dilemma. The interdenominational approach and understanding of the mission enterprise which some of the Disciples' mission leaders had lived with for a generation was clearly out of step with the perceptions of a segment of the membership. After 1922, the UCMS had a policy statement which contradicted the interdenominational approach by denigrating the baptismal practice of many of the historic churches. Should the UCMS really export the exclusivistic understanding of Christian missions to the foreign fields? Such was the mandate of the 1922 International Convention, but the Executive Committee of the UCMS was pressed by the Society's Foreign Department to state an "interpretation" of the membership policy:

> We interpret the statement with regard to "being in sincere accord" with the policy pronounced to mean that the missionary should be willing to earnestly carry on the work in the manner suggested. We feel that this was not meant in any sense to infringe upon private opinion or individual liberty of conviction "so long as none judges his brother, or insists on forcing his own opinions upon others or on making them an occasion of strife."[45]

If this interpretation "broke faith" with the intention of the 1922 International Convention, it was in order to keep faith with those who were in the mission fields attempting the evangelization of these fields in partnership with other Christian bodies. Of course, this only drove the wedge deeper between the emerging two parties within the Disciples.

The difference between the perspective of the UCMS, which was involved in an increasingly interdenominational and intercultural missions enterprise, and that of the constituency from which the society sought support can be seen in the United Society's account of John T. Brown's visit to China.

> ... Mr. Brown's aggressive and unceremonious procedure led him into glaring breaches of Chinese etiquette and custom. Had he deliberately planned to shock and contravene the most delicate

sensibilities, and to violate the commonest proprieties of the Chinese people, he could scarcely have succeeded better than he did.

Brown's "brusque questions" as to the baptism of some of the members of the Chinese Church and "his summary disposal of their Christian standing" were held up in the account as especially offensive: "The whole Chinese Church remembers it with shame."

> ... Through his reports, alarms, and investigations on "open membership"—a phrase most of them had never heard before, and which is almost untranslatable into Chinese—the impression was given that the Disciples of Christ stood in pharisaic aloofness from other Communions.... They could not follow his argument, except in the point that a Methodist or Presbyterian must not be recognized as a Christian in a Church of Christ.[46]

There were two major mind-sets represented in the Disciples of Christ in the 1920s. One group of Disciples, indeed, wished to remain aloof from other communions. Those who would soon create the North American Christian Convention did not regard themselves as another communion but as "the divine cure for sectarianism."[47] The other mind-set, especially as represented in the foreign missions department of the UCMS and reflected in the account of Brown's visit, included the belief that "conditions on the mission field might justify some arrangement"—something "very much like" open membership—"without committing the home churches to the approval of any change in the customary Disciples practice."[48] The "interpretation" which the UCMS had given the 1922 policy statement was an attempt to live out this belief. This attempt was at the center of the *Christian Standard*'s explanation of "Why We Can Not Support the U.C.M.S."[49]

A commission appointed by the International Convention met in 1925 for the purpose of investigating open membership on the mission field. The commission reported to the 1926 international Convention in Memphis "that it had found no 'open membership' on the foreign field." Some interpreted this to mean that the commission had not found "open agitation" for open membership. According to Robert O. Fife, a scholar who represents the perspective of the North American Christian Convention's constituents:

> a significant number of members of the Memphis Convention were deeply dissatisfied with the manner in which the issue was

Beyond the Society Concept

handled. In consequence, a mass meeting was held in an adjacent theatre. There a committee was selected to arrange for a "North American Christian Convention" to meet the following year. The discontent of many was expressed by Edwin Errett when he wrote [in the *Christian Standard*] that Memphis was a "Convention of BAD FAITH."

In October 1927 the first North American Christian Convention was held in Indianapolis, with about three thousand in attendance. "The 'North American' met irregularly until 1951, when action was taken to make it an annual assembly."[50] With the formation of the North American Christian Convention, Disciples who were dissatisfied with the International Convention and the UCMS had an alternative national expression.

By 1925 a Christian Restoration Association had come into being and had begun to publish the *Restoration Herald*. This association and its publication were especially committed to "the cause of so-called 'independent missions.'" The Christian Restoration Association supported a missionary competing with the UCMS missionary in the Philippines, reopened a closed UCMS mission in Tibet, and instituted foreign missions work elsewhere.[51]

The "disenchanted Disciples" also provided an alternative "approach to ministerial education" (see chapter three). Therefore, by the end of the 1920s, the Independents had established rival colleges, convention, and approach to missionary support. These were placed alongside the journalism of the *Christian Standard* as the expressions of a constituency hostile to and independent of the International Convention of Disciples of Christ and its agencies. However, because the polity of the International Convention contained no effective device for defining its constituency the division remained unclarified and the terminology "Independents" and "Cooperatives" became conventional.

There were other significant developments in the structure of the International Convention and its agencies in the 1920s in addition to the disaffection of part of their constituency. One such development was the creation of the Commission on Budgets and Promotional Relationships. This Commission was part of the continuing effort to coordinate the fund raising activities of the societies of the Disciples of Christ. Like the organization of the International Convention of Disciples of Christ in 1917, "the organization of the UCMS in 1920, intended to help reduce the multiplicity of appeals to the congregations for financial assistance, did little to relieve promotional pressures."[52] However, it was from the UCMS that the impetus came to create the Commission on Budgets and Promotional Relationships. Upon the recommendation of a group that included members of Disciples "national boards, state secretaries, pastors, and local church leaders" that was called together by the promotional secretaries of the UCMS, the Executive Committee of the International Convention appointed a temporary commission, and in 1923 the Convention called for

> ... the appointment of a permanent Commission on Budgets and Promotional Relationships to which shall be submitted all the budgets of the cooperating agencies. With respect to state missions, this Commission shall deal directly with the Missionary Society in each state. When such budgets shall have been reviewed and approved by the commission, they shall be recommended to the churches. Full report of the actions of this Commission shall be made to the succeeding International Convention for its review and approval.

The composition of the Commission was to be determined by nomination by the Executive Committee of the International Convention, referred to the Committee on Recommendations, and finally passed by the full convention. There was also a proviso that none of the Commission's twelve members "shall be an employee of any of the cooperating agencies."[53]

The intention behind the formation of the Commission on Budgets and Promotional Relationships was to replace "competitive promotion" with "cooperative, unified promotion."[54] Like earlier efforts at promotional coordination the work of the Commission was not fully successful. The creation of the Commission is significant, however, in two regards. First, taken in conjunction with the creation of the International Convention with its Committee on Recommendations and the formation of the UCMS, the election of the Commission on Budgets and Promotional Relationships illustrates that a significant segment of the Disciples of Christ was still struggling to evolve beyond the society concept of polity. Secondly, the origin of the commission in the UCMS illustrates that Cooperative Disciples had a "center of gravity" in their cooperative work. No longer simply an aggregate of individuals with a whole range of societies, Cooperative Disciples now had the UCMS as a focal point. In the years following the creation of the UCMS the pattern represented in the formation of the Commission on Budgets and Promotional Relationships, the impetus for coordination coming from within the UCMS, would become familiar.

In the decade 1917 to 1927, the divergence in organization represented in the consolidation and coordination efforts on the part of Cooperatives on the one hand and the creation by Independents of an alternative set of structures mirrored the ideological polarization within the movement. The open membership controversy reflected sharply differing views on the restoration, unity, and mission ideals. On one side were those wedded to "the mission of restoring a specific pattern of doctrine and practice believed to be that of primitive Christianity."[55] For the Independent group, restoration was regarded as the sole legitimate route to Christian union, and missions could, therefore, be conceived of only in exclusivistic terms. On the other side were those Cooperatives for whom the primacy of the unity and mission ideals had softened the adherence to restorationism.

There was also a basic parting of the ways on the ideal of liberty. W. E. Garrison points out that the "repudiation of any sort of control by the group as a whole" was characteristic of those who were disaffected with the International Convention.[56] The divergence on the ideal of liberty, then, expressed itself in the insistence of the Independents on retaining the society concept of polity in its atomistic form, while the Cooperative party edged toward greater coordination. Ideological and structural division went hand in hand and were largely a *fait accompli* by 1927. In 1931 Garrison observed:

> The supporters of the United Society and the adherents of the "free agencies" and the Restoration Association constitute two groups which read different religious papers, promote two different sets of missions, colleges, and benevolent institutions, attend two different national conventions (with some overlapping), do not freely interchange ministers, and have different attitudes toward cooperation and comity with other religious bodies. In a denomination which has never professed to have any solidarity except such as results from and expressed itself in fellowship and actual cooperation in the advancement of common ideals, this comes near to constituting an effective division.[57]

The tension which continued to exist for three decades was between an "effective division" and an officially recognized one. The official ecclesiology of the Disciples failed to address the reality; but the sociological reality was that, with the passage of time, Cooperatives and Independents increasingly went their "own preferred way."[58]

One possible dimension of the sociological process of division may be seen indirectly by looking at urbanization. If studies that have found a link between rurality and religious conservatism[59] reflect a relationship that also existed in the early twentieth century, the ideology and structural developments among Cooperative Disciples suggest further urbanization. In 1916, eleven cities of 25,000 persons or more had 4,000 or more Disciples of Christ.[60] In all, 65,812

Disciples were in these large cities. By 1926, the same eleven cities showed 87,542 Disciples of Christ. This increase of 21,730 Disciples in the denomination's main urban centers is not itself remarkable. However, what is striking is that over 65 percent of that urban growth was in two cities, Kansas City and Indianapolis. Thirty-six percent of the increase was in Indianapolis alone.[61]

Urbanization was not the only social process which made an impact on the Disciples of Christ in the 1920s. It would be an error to interpret the history of the Disciples during this period solely in terms of factors which were unique to the Disciples. Part of the theological, ideological, and structural controversy of the 1920s can legitimately be classified under the more widespread phenomenon of the fundamentalist-modernist controversy.[62]

Another more widespread phenomenon that made its impact on the Disciples is what Robert T. Handy has called "the American religious depression."[63] Handy identifies the religious depression with the years 1925 to 1935. He distinguishes between the religious depression and the economic depression of the 1930s, though an "intimate relationship between them seems beyond doubt." Handy lists several indicators of the religious depression, including a decline in contributions and volunteers for missions, falling church attendance, lowered social status of ministers, a slump in the social gospel, and a conspicuous increase in scientism, behaviorism, and humanism in the thought of the time. Particular importance is attached to the disillusionment which resulted from the identification of Protestantism with American culture, "which left the churches quite exposed to cultural crosscurrents."[64]

As the religious depression blended into the economic, several developments occurred. First, some religious leaders were surprised when economic depression did not lead to religious revival. Second, there was a significant "mushrooming of the newer and smaller religious groups, the sects" which was "perplexing to the major denominations." Third, the "somewhat precipitous decline of the evangelical liberal theology, which had been so conspicuous a part of Protestant life in the first quarter of the century," was hastened by the "lash of depression." Handy concludes that "during the period of religious and economic depression, then, the 'Protestant era' in America was brought to a close; Protestantism emerged no longer the 'national religion.'"[65]

Handy's description of the "American religious depression" has much relevance to the Disciples of Christ. First, in the years between 1926 and 1936 the Disciples of Christ recorded a loss in membership.[66] It was not a decade of revival for Disciples in terms of evangelism. Second, if the classification of the Independents as more sectarian is correct, then Handy's second observation fits well the increase in a separate sphere of religious activity for these disaffected

Beyond the Society Concept

Disciples. Third, the decline of "evangelical liberal theology" and the disillusionment with a Protestantism closely identified with American culture must have deeply affected the Disciples, who were obstreperously "Protestant" and "American." This was the period in which many Disciples became active in the Ku Klux Klan. McAllister and Tucker see this involvement as a fearful reaction to Roman Catholic immigration and other perceived threats to "old values and old ways."[67] For Disciples a comparatively liberal (that is, not Calvinistic), thoroughly American (Anglo-Saxon for many), evangelical, and militantly Protestant form of religion was one of the "old ways."

The suggestion that the religious and economic depression made a significant impact upon the Disciples of Christ is supported by William O. Paulsell's "The Disciples of Christ and the Great Depression 1929-1936." Paulsell concludes that "the impact of the Depression upon the institutional life of the brotherhood was felt in painful ways," including a decline in giving for missionary causes and the withdrawal of missionaries from the field, "ministerial unemployment and salary reductions among pastors," the inability of many congregations to repay loans from the Department of Church Erection and the difficulty of the department in "meet[ing] requests from debt ridden congregations," and the inability of benevolent homes to meet increasing needs of the elderly.[68] By December 1932 the UCMS had accumulated a deficit of $1,126,952.34. This led to greatly reduced budgets and services. It was not until 1936 that the income of the UCMS began to gain ground again.[69]

The depression years were years of organizational change for the Disciples. While the National Benevolent Association and the Board of Church Extension separated from the UCMS in 1933,[70] unification again came to the forefront in the arena of promotion. In 1931 the International Convention of Disciples of Christ directed the Commission on Budgets and Promotional Relationships to begin exploring further cooperation in promotion. The Commission appointed a Committee of Nine who drafted the plan for Unified Promotion. The board objectives of the plan were:

> The elimination of competition among the agencies which approach the local churches for funds.
> The development of a broad program of stewardship education which will stimulate in the brotherhood the sense of Christian obligation for the adequate support of our general program of missionary, educational, and benevolent work.

The objectives of the plan were to be met by the following means:

> ... The total giving of the brotherhood to all agencies participating will be ascertained, and on the basis of the receipts of each for the past five years the Budget Commission will allot each a percentage of the total receipt which is in harmony with this experience.
> ... A central office will be set up for the keeping of records and for the receiving of such offerings as churches desire to send through this channel. Any church or individual will be wholly free, however, to send offerings direct to any agency.

So that the "perfect freedom of every giver" was "safeguarded," offerings to a specific agency could be designated so as not to be "leveled up against the percentages," and "gifts for specific purposes," while "leveled up against the percentages," would be "scrupulously used" for the designated purposes. The central office of Unified Promotion pledged to "seek to represent all our great causes" but also "avoid the multitudinous appeals to which our local churches ... have been subjected in the past."[71] The International Convention approved the plan and created Unified Promotion at Des Moines in 1934. By that time it "had been approved by seven national boards, twenty-three state societies, and five colleges."[72]

In the spring of 1935 the Board of Review of Unified Promotion met for the first time in Indianapolis and decided that "Unified Promotion be set up as a corporation under the name, 'Unified Promotion, Inc., Disciples of Christ,'" and that offices for the corporation be set up at Missions Building, Indianapolis.[73] Unified Promotion was incorporated in the state of Indiana in 1935. The membership of the corporation was divided into two classes, Members and Associate Members. Only the Members were given voting privileges and their number was limited to thirty-six. Members were elected by the corporation itself for a term of three years, and candidates for membership were to be "qualified persons ... actively connected with and recommended by the ... corporations or organizations whose work is ... being promoted" by Unified Promotion.[74]

Promotion was not the only area in which the decade of the 1930s brought continued efforts at coordination to the Disciples. Whereas the aim of Unified Promotion was basically to bring harmony to the promotional and stewardship education efforts of the agencies of the Disciples, the next coordination effort focused upon program planning. As in the case of the Commission on Budgets and Promotional Relationships, the impetus for the formation of the Home and State Missions Planning Council came from within the UCMS: Willard M. Wickizer, chairman of the Society's Division of Home Missions, let the way.[75]

Beyond the Society Concept

Willard Wickizer was asked to speak to the annual meeting of the secretaries of the state missionary societies in 1936. The following year, a meeting of the state secretaries and the members of state missionary societies' boards was called. There, "it was decided to recommend to the agencies a plan of cooperative program planning."[76] At the 1938 International Convention in Denver this plan was approved and the Home and State Missions Planning Council was formed. Its membership was to be made up of representatives of the Home Missions Department of the UCMS, the executives of the participating societies, and thirty persons elected at large. At first, the Council's program planning responsibilities were divided among six primary committees. While the "programs planned did not have official status and each society was left free to determine what program plans and materials were to be used," this cooperation effort brought about "a common strategy . . . for program planning and effective materials."[77] Soon the Home and State Missions Planning Council was organized into nine standing committees: Local Church Life, Evangelism, Effective Ministry, Town and Country Church, Christian Service, Missionary Policy and Strategy, World Outreach, Urban Work, and Stewardship.[78]

Promotion and program planning unification were not the only spheres of organizational activity among Disciples in the 1930s. Another organization which came into being in this decade was the Disciples Peace Fellowship. During the years 1930 to 1935 a number of state and local peace organizations came into being among the Disciples. In 1935 the Disciples Peace Fellowship, "the first and only international Disciples peace organization," was formed. The Fellowship was "an organization independent from the international convention and all other agencies so that it could be free to speak and act without official approval." The Disciples Peace Fellowship was not Independent in the sense that it found its constituency among the conservative Disciples. "In general the *Christian Standard* has preferred to be at least moderately hostile to DPF and pacifism."[79] The Fellowship was organized on the basis of a Covenant which says, in part,

> WE DO SOLEMNLY covenant together to use our powers to the uttermost, to promote peace and to oppose war now and always.
>
> We propose to carry out this covenant for the abolition of war by fostering good will among nations, races, and classes, by opposing military preparations;
>
> By striving to build a social order which will remove the causes of war.[80]

The Disciples Peace Fellowship grew rapidly from the organizing group of seventy-five to seven hundred members within its first year. However, the activity of the Fellowship declined during the World War II years and thereafter to virtual inactivity during its second decade.[81] Structurally, the Fellowship illustrates that Disciples were continuing their historic pattern of organizing as they saw fit societies for specific purposes.

Another significant organization came into being in the days just before the United States' entry into World War II. In 1939 the International Convention authorized the appointment of a committee to explore the possibility of forming a historical society for the Disciples. Two years later the Convention approved the constitution of the Disciples of Christ Historical Society. The organization of the Historical Society followed the traditional society pattern:

> Membership is open to everybody at the rate of a dollar a year or $25 for life. Annual institution membership is available to any person designated by the institution on payment of $10 or more, according to a scale of assessments to be worked out by the executive committee.

The executive committee, of at least twelve persons, was to be elected by the membership of the Historical Society. In keeping with traditional practice the annual meeting was to be held in connection with the International Convention.[82] The Historical Society first placed its archives on campus at Culver-Stockton College in Canton, Missouri, but it was moved to Nashville, Tennessee, in 1952.[83]

The decade of the 1930s was characterized by two organizational or structural patterns among Cooperative Disciples. First, there was a pronounced effort to bring greater coordination to both promotional and programming activities. Second, however, was the persistence of the society pattern. This second trend was not only observable in the creation of new societies like the Disciples Peace Fellowship and the Disciples of Christ Historical Society but also in the withdrawal of the National Benevolent Association and the Board of Church Extension from the UCMS and the reluctance of the National Benevolent Association to ratify Unified Promotion.[84]

The organizational life of the Disciples of Christ was affected in several ways by World War II. In the late 1930s the invasion of China by the Japanese began to cause increasingly urgent appeals for relief to be brought to the Disciples, for China had been a major mission field. The International Convention appointed a Committee on Relief Appeals. When in December 1941 the United States

Beyond the Society Concept

became directly involved in the war, Disciples were faced by a new set of demands, including "repatriation of missionary families from war zones, service to Japanese people evacuated from our Pacific coast area, and service to men in the armed forces."[85] Several special structures were created to meet the conditions created by the war, including the Chaplaincy Endorsement Commission of the International Convention, a "clearing house for Disciples ministers seeking to serve as chaplains"; the Committee on War Services, which "gave assistance to Japanese-American Disciples were interned by the United States government" and which allocated funds to Disciples congregations that were in a position to develop programs for persons in the military or give aid to persons displaced by the war; and a Committee on Conscientious Objectors and a Committee on Ministerial Exemption, both "formed to aid Disciples who refused to participate in the war because of religious convictions."[86] As had been the case with the Men and Millions movement in World War I, World War II came at a time when Disciples were in the midst of a special stewardship emphasis. Nineteen forty-one was the fourth year of a Five Year Program of Advance. The fifth-year phase of the program "was revised to become an Emergency Million drive." The goals of this drive included clearing the debts of the Disciples agencies and aiding congregations feeling the ill effects of the war.[87]

The war also gave new impetus to a consideration of the global responsibilities of the Disciples of Christ. In 1943 the International Convention and the UCMS, by joint action, created a Commission on World Order as part of its Department of Social Welfare.[88] This Commission, together with the Board of Higher Education and the Association for the Promotion of Christian Unity (formerly the Council on Christian Union), sponsored a conference on The Church and the New World Mind at Drake University in 1944.[89] The more significant and lasting expression of the Disciples' enlarged global vision, however, was the founding of the Week of Compassion. Whereas many of the aforementioned war programs were aimed principally at the Disciples' own members, the Week of Compassion "was to raise funds for needs beyond the brotherhood's own program, to be distributed principally through Church World Service and the World Council of Churches."[90] The first Week of Compassion was observed on 20-27 February 1944 and has thereafter continued as part of the Disciples' program. Two other bodies came into being in 1944. One was the Commission on the Promotion of Christian Literature which was "formed for the purpose of helping to prepare citizens and Christians for a new kind of world, for postwar rehabilitation and enduring peace."[91] That same year the UCMS was directed by the International Convention to create the second new body, a Department of Laymen's Organizations.[92]

The increased organizational activity during the war years did not completely divert the Disciples from their own peculiar troubles. Independent historian James DeForest Murch identifies 1944 as the year that the *Christian Standard* virtually abandoned efforts at unifying the two wings of the Disciples. The 1944 International Convention "elected as its president an outspoken advocate of open membership," causing the "lines" between the two groups to "stiffen immediately."[93]

Among those supporting the International Convention, the year 1946 also marked two significant developments in structure. First, the International Convention opened offices in Indianapolis in September 1946 with the services of a full-time executive secretary, Gaines M. Cook.[94] The Disciples of Christ now had a definite headquarters. Perhaps equally significant was the publication in the same year of O.L. Shelton's *The Church Functioning Effectively*. Shelton was Dean of the School of Religion of Butler University in Indianapolis. The book was written at the urging of the Committee on Local Church Life of the Home and State Missions Planning Council.

The key concept in Shelton's book is that of "function." Shelton finds function, rather than a fixed pattern of organization, to be the basis of congregational structure in the New Testament. Church organization,

> with leaders responsible for various functions, is firmly rooted in the teachings of the New Testament. . . .
>
> These continuing functions of the church are the responsibility of each congregation today. In a small church, they may be performed by a simple organization; in a large church, the organization may be complex and intricate.[95]

Shelton suggests an organization in which each of several functions are designated as "departments" and assigned to committees. He divides the departments into those "for the enrichment of church life"—Membership, Education, Worship and Devotional Life, Finance and Stewardship, and Property—and those "to extend the outreach"—Evangelism, Missionary, and Education.[96] The chairpersons of the various committees form an executive board, which together with the elders and deacons, form a general board. "Widely accepted from the first, the functional approach to church program was adopted within a short time by a large number of Disciples congregations."[97]

The adoption of such an organizational pattern by many Disciples congregations further attests to the emergence of two different ecclesiological philosophies within the Disciples. Shelton's book did not claim to be a discovery

Beyond the Society Concept

of or a restoration of a primitive pattern of church organization. Rather, it was written with the assumption that Willard Wickizer expresses forthrightly in the volume's introduction:

> Some communions—the Disciples of Christ being one—have held that the pattern of local church organization is to be found in the New Testament. And it is true that the New Testament does make certain references to the organizational pattern of the early church, but it is also true that nowhere is there to be found what might be called an *organizational blueprint* which was divinely intended for use by a modern congregation with its complex program and its multiplicity of auxiliary organizations.[98]

With the creation of a permanently staffed office for their International Convention and the widespread adoption of "functional church organization," the Disciples were moving beyond the concept of being just a gathering of individuals and their societies. The various activities and organizations of the World War II years had strengthened this direction of development.

Another experience which moved a segment of Disciples in the direction of unified effort was the 1947 to 1950 Crusade for a Christian World. The goals of the Crusade were to increase membership, form new congregations, recruit ministers, expand missions, and raise "millions of dollars over and above regular offerings." While not completely successful, "the Crusade was experienced as a tremendous victory."[99] One of the ideas which came out of the Crusade was that of planning Disciples' programs for a decade at a time.[100] Therefore, on the heels of the Crusade was launched the Long Range Program.[101]

Meeting in San Francisco in 1948, the International Convention of Disciples of Christ again called for a study on more effective cooperation among the agencies. The next year, the Convention authorized the creation of a Council of Agencies which met for the first time in Hiram, Ohio, from June 27 to July 1, 1950.[102] The Council of Agencies—the "Agencies" being the state societies, national agencies, and the Board of Higher Education's member institutions—served

> . . . as a clearinghouse among the agencies for clearance of impingements or overlapping of work and long-range planning in brotherhood life. It . . . proved itself so effective in this regard that the International Convention changed its bylaws in 1952 to require

all member agencies of the Convention to belong to the Council of Agencies.[103]

The first task of the Council of Agencies was the development of the Long Range Program for the decade of the fifties.[104] The plan included program emphases for each year and the goal of doubled giving for outreach causes in the entire decade.[105]

In 1949 an additional effort in the direction of program coordination was made when the National Church Program Coordinating Council was formed. It began to function in 1950.[106] The purpose of this Council was to "coordinate program and materials as they are being planned so there is neither duplication nor competition in program approaches to the local church."[107] The National Church Program Coordinating Council was made up of representatives of the Home Missions Planning Council, the Curriculum Committee, Unified Promotion, the Committee on Local Church Program of the UCMS, the Christian Board of Publication, National Christian Missionary Convention, National Layman's Advisory Commission, Commission on World Order, and the National Association of State Secretaries.[108]

Another coordinating council that came into being in the early fifties was the Curriculum and Program Council. Formed by the UCMS and the Christian Board of Publication in 1953, this Council's purpose was to coordinate and evaluate programs and materials for Christian education. A biennial Christian Education Assembly, which included the thirty-member Council, the professors of religious education at Disciples colleges and seminaries, and forty other members, was to contribute "information and opinion" into "the curriculum-building process."[109]

By 1953, then, the Disciples who were in fellowship with the International Convention and its agencies had developed a unified approach to promotion (Unified Promotion), coordination in program planning (Home and State Missions Planning Council and the National Church Program Coordinating Council), coordination in curriculum and education (Curriculum and Program Council and the Christian Education Assembly), and a single clearinghouse body for all related agencies (Council of Agencies) with responsibility for long-range planning (Long-Range Program). In addition, the International Convention had a full-time staff and permanent headquarters and the local congregations were organizing along "functional" lines.

It was out of one of the structures created after World War II that the concrete beginnings of Restructure came. At the Council of Agencies meeting for the biennium 1954-56 a Committee on Future Work was appointed under

Beyond the Society Concept

the chairmanship of A. Dale Fiers. When this committee reported to the Council of Agencies in 1956, one of its recommendations was "that the Interim Committee [of the Council of Agencies] appoint a permanent sub-committee on Brotherhood Organization and Inter-agency Relationships."[110] A consultation of this sub-committee, chaired by Wilbur H. Cramblet, at the Chicago Divinity House in 1957[111] has been called "the most crucial step toward restructure."[112]

In 1958, a Conference on Unification was held in Indianapolis which was attended by 250 persons. The aim of the Conference was to work toward "organizational and promotional unification at the state level."[113] This was followed in 1959 by the publication of a *Manual on Unification*, in which "guidelines were established for the unification of missionary societies, women's organizations, departments of religious education, and other such agencies so that a unified program might be presented to the congregations and one state, provincial, or area office could be maintained."[114] Also during 1958, the Council of Agencies sponsored a series of Listening Conferences, a summary of the findings of which was presented at the 1953 meeting of the Council at Culver-Stockton College.[115] At this meeting, Willard Wickizer presented a paper, "Ideas for Brotherhood Restructure," which concluded:

> Of this I am sure, it is high time our brotherhood take a look at its organized life in its totality and restructure it according to a basic plan. For too long we have been willing to add patch on patch, never moving according to a carefully worked out master plan. I believe the mood of our people would support such an undertaking at this time.[116]

After this meeting, the Council of Agencies brought the matter of restructure to the attention of the Board of Directors of the International Convention. On October 15, 1958, the Committee on Brotherhood Structure was appointed. This committee was to conduct research to determine the scope of the restructure task and to determine the basis for representation on a future Commission on Brotherhood Structure.[117] The two basic decisions made by this Committee were that the "leadership in any program of restructure" ought to be "centered in the International Convention itself as the voice of all the churches"; and that "thorough cooperation between the churches and the agencies" would be necessary "to create a total program for the church."[118]

In 1959 the Board of Directors of the International Convention reported to the Convention their intention of recommending the creation of a Commission on Brotherhood Structure. The following year the Board of Directors brought the report of their Committee on Brotherhood Structure to the attention of the International Convention. This report included the rationale for restructure, recommendations as to its scope, its ways and means, and the financial support of its proposed Commission. The report was accepted and the Board of Directors empowered to begin implementation of the recommendations contained therein. The Board of Directors appointed a Central Committee which met in 1961 and began preparing nominations for a Commission on Brotherhood Restructure of approximately 120 members.[119]

Restructure, then, began concretely in the late 1950s in the wake of several years of vigorous organizational activity by Disciples. In addition to the concrete beginnings of Restructure, three developments of note occurred in the late fifties. First, in 1957 the International Convention of Disciples of Christ changed its name to the International Convention of Christian Churches (Disciples of Christ). This is symbolic of the evolution of Disciples structure beyond the society concept. Although the Convention was still not truly representative of the churches in the sense of being a delegate body, it was clearly moving further away from understanding itself as a mass meeting of individuals. The second development was the publication, in 1955, of Vernon M. Newland's *Directory of the Ministry of the Undenominational Fellowship of Christian Churches and Churches of Christ*.[120] This was yet another signal that the Cooperatives and Independents were formalizing their status as two separate bodies (before Restructure). The third development was the trend in the direction of a more formally representative structure at the state level of Disciples organizations.

In 1957 only seven states had delegate conventions. Eleven states had mass-meeting type organizations with Committees on Recommendations. Seven states had mass meetings with some kind of "protective clauses," such as the requirement of church membership for voting privileges or the referral of controversial matters to another body. However, thirteen states functioned with a mass-meeting structure. By 1962, state delegate conventions had doubled to fourteen, and only seven states were functioning as mass-meeting conventions.[121]

The years between 1917 and the formal restructuring of the Disciples of Christ were years of almost constant organizational evolution. Two world wars, a religious depression, and an economic depression contributed to the trend toward coordination and unification by one group of Disciples and the increasing disaffection among another group, which in turn created its own structures. But by 1960 the society concept was no longer persuasive to the leaders of the Cooperative Disciples. They were ready to become a church.[122]

---

1. Fiers, "Structure—Past, Present, and Future," 148.
2. Ibid.
3. Lair, *Christian Churches and Their Work*, 148.
4. DeGroot, *Disciple Thought*, 138.
5. Willcockson, "Our Conventions through a Century," 614.
6. Mayes, "Restructure in the Light of Structure," 50.
7. Willcockson, "Our Conventions through a Century," 614.
8. Ibid.
9. McAllister and Tucker, *Journey in Faith*, 341.
10. Ibid.
11. Willcockson, "Our Conventions through a Century," 614.
12. McAllister and Tucker, *Journey in Faith*, 341.
13. "The New Constitution," *Christian-Evangelist* 54 (8 November 1917):1214, 1230.
14. Lair, *Christian Churches and Their Work*, 133.
15. Corey, *Attack and Controversy*, 45.
16. McAllister and Tucker, *Journey in Faith*, 342.
17. Ibid., 342-43; Robert L. Jordan, *Two Races in One Fellowship* (Detroit: United Christian Church, 1944), 63-64; Brenda M. Cardwell and William K. Fox, Sr., *Journey Toward Wholeness: A History of Black Disciples of Christ in the Mission of the Christian Church*, vol. 1: *From Convention to Convocation: No Longer 'Objects of' Mission But 'Partners In' the Work (1700-1988)* (n.p.: National Convocation of the Christian Church [Disciples of Christ], 1990), 28-29.
18. David A. Vargas, "A Historical Background of the National Hispanic and Bilingual Fellowship," translated by Luis E. Ferrer, *Discipliana* 46 (3: Fall 1986):38-39.
19. Mayes, "Restructure in the Light of Structure," 55.
20. Ibid., 58.
21. Dee James Atwood, "The Impact of World War I on the Agencies of the Disciples of Christ" (Ph.D. dissertation, Vanderbilt University, 1978), 156.
22. Ibid., 148-156.
23. McAllister and Tucker, *Journey in Faith*, 336.
24. Atwood, "Impact of World War I," 153, 156-62.
25. Crain, *Development of Social Ideas among Disciples*, 71.
26. William R. Warren, *The Life and Labors of Archibald McLean* (St. Louis: Bethany Press, 1923), 313.
27. "Ready for the Launching," *Christian Standard* 54 (16 August 1919):1133.

28. "Proposed United Christian Missionary Society," *Christian Standard* 54 (16 August 1919):1133.

29. Ibid.

30. "Ready for the Launching," 1133.

31. Crain, *Development of Social Ideas among Disciples*, 71.

32. "Ready for the Launching," 1133.

33. Corey, *Attack and Controversy*, 61.

34. "To the Rescue of the Restoration Movement," *Christian Standard* 54 (26 July 1919):1045.

35. Tucker, *J. H. Garrison*, 208.

36. "The Debate on the Merger," *Christian-Evangelist* 56 (23 October 1919):1108, quoted in Tucker, *J. H. Garrison*, 209.

37. Winfred E. Garrison, *Heritage and Destiny: An American Religious Movement Looks Ahead* (St. Louis: Bethany Press, 1961), 111.

38. Corey, in *Attack and Controversy*, writes that on the mission field "the main emphasis has been on grouping together the people who are followers of Christ as opposed to the great non-Christian population surrounding them. However, no explanations of this kind seemed to satisfy the *Christian Standard*, which adhered to its literal point, trying, if possible, to win the issue" (76).

39. Crain, *Development of Social Ideas among Disciples*, 72.

40. Tucker, *J. H. Garrison*, 209; Corey, *Attack and Controversy*, 60-101; McAllister and Tucker, *Journey in Faith*, 381-82.

41. Tucker, *J. H. Garrison*, 209.

42. "Broadcasting the Story of the Convention of Disciples of Christ," *Christian-Evangelist* 59 (7 September 1922):1144, quoted in Tucker, *J. H. Garrison*, 209.

43. Tucker, *J. H. Garrison*, 210.

44. Corey, *Attack and Controversy*, 84-85, 89, 88.

45. *Second Annual Report of the United Christian Missionary Society* (St. Louis: United Christian Missionary Society, 1922), 251, quoted in Corey, *Attack and Controversy*, 88.

46. *Facts About the Visit of John T. Brown to Some of the Mission Fields and Answers to His Statements in the Christian Standard* (St. Louis: Executive Committee of the United Christian Missionary Society, 1924), 13-14, quoted in Corey, *Attack and Controversy*, 92-93.

47. "To the Rescue of the Restoration Movement," 1045.

48. W. E. Garrison, *Heritage and Destiny*, 111.

49. "Why We Can Not Support the U.C.M.S.," *Christian Standard* 57 (16 December 1922):318. Two recent accounts of the open membership controversy from sharply different angles of vision are Mark G. Toulouse, "Practical Concern and Theological Neglect: The UCMS and the Open Membership Controversy," in *A Case Study of Mainstream Protestantism*, ed. Williams, 194-235 and Webb, *In Search of Christian Unity*, 287-315.

50. Robert O. Fife, "The North American Christian Convention: 1927-1977," *Discipliana* 37 (Summer 1977):19, 20, 29, 19.

51. Murch, *Adventuring for Christ*, 70, 72-78.

52. McAllister and Tucker, *Journey in Faith*, 397.

53. For Information to the Executive Committee, memorandum, United Christian Missionary Society File, Disciples of Christ Historical Society, Nashville, Tennessee.

54. Ibid.

55. W. E. Garrison, *Religion Follows the Frontier*, 296.

56. Ibid.

57. Ibid., 297.

58. Fife, "North American Christian Convention," 20.

59. Thomas Madron, Hart Nelson, and Ratha Yokley, "Rural-Urban Differences in Religiosity," *Rural Sociology* 36 (September 1971):394.

60. U. S. Bureau of the Census, *Summary and General Tables* [1916], 339-41.

61. U. S., Department of Commerce, Bureau of the Census, *Religious Bodies: 1926*, vol. 1, *Summary and Detailed Tables* (Washington, D.C.: Government Printing Office, 1930), 384, 390, 394, 407, 437, 445, 453, 458-59, 511, 531.

62. Marty, *Righteous Empire*, 218.

63. Robert T. Handy, *The American Religious Depression: 1925-1935*, Facet Books Historical Series, ed. Richard C. Wolf, no. 9 (American Church) (Philadelphia: Fortress Press, 1968).

64. Ibid., 4-10.

65. Ibid., 14, 15, 21-22.

66. U.S., Department of Commerce, Bureau of the Census, *Religious Bodies: 1936*, vol. 2, pt. 1, *Denominations A to J* (Washington, D.C.: Government Printing Office, 1941), 536.

67. McAllister and Tucker, *Journey in Faith*, 356-58.

68. William O. Paulsell, "The Disciples of Christ and the Great Depression 1929-1936" (Ph.D. dissertation, Vanderbilt University, 1965), 292-93.

69. McAllister and Tucker, *Journey in Faith*, 389.

70. Crain, *Development of Social Ideas among Disciples*, 72.

71. "Council Votes Approval of Unified Promotion Plan," *Christian-Evangelist* 72 (14 March 1935):356-57.
72. DeGroot and Garrison, *The Disciples of Christ*, 508.
73. "Budget and Review Boards in Meeting," *Christian-Evangelist* 72 (2 May 1935):582.
74. Articles of Incorporation of Unified Promotion, Inc., Disciples of Christ, 1-3, Unified Promotion File, Disciples of Christ Historical Society, Nashville, Tennessee.
75. Crain, *Development of Social Ideas among Disciples*, 317.
76. Ibid.
77. Lair, *Christian Churches and Their Work*, 155.
78. DeGroot and Garrison, *The Disciples of Christ*, 504.
79. Mark A. May, "Disciples Peace Fellowship: Historical Formation and the First Twenty Years, 1935-55," *Discipliana* 40 (Summer 1980):22-24.
80. "The Covenant of the Disciples Peace Fellowship Adopted at San Antonio National Convention, October 18, 1935," *Christian-Evangelist* 74 (16 April 1936):501, quoted in May, "Disciples Peace Fellowship," 24.
81. May, "Disciples Peace Fellowship," 23, 25-26.
82. "Disciples Historical Society Organizes and Starts Job," *Christian-Evangelist* 79 (15 May 1941):591.
83. McAllister and Tucker, *Journey in Faith*, 400; see also, James M. Seale, *Forward from the Past: The First Fifty Years of the Disciples of Christ Historical Society* (Nashville: Disciples of Christ Historical Society, 1991).
84. "Ratifications of Unified Promotion," *Christian-Evangelist* 72 (14 March 1935):357.
85. Crain, *Development of Social Ideas among Disciples*, 155-56.
86. McAllister and Tucker, *Journey in Faith*, 406-407.
87. Ibid., 407.
88. Crain, *Development of Social Ideas among Disciples*, 145.
89. Ibid., 146; McAllister and Tucker, *Journey in Faith*, 408.
90. Crain, *Development of Social Ideas among Disciples*, 157.
91. McAllister and Tucker, *Journey in Faith*, 408-409.
92. Lair, *Christian Churches and Their Work*, 192.
93. Murch, *Christians Only*, 277.
94. McAllister and Tucker, *Journey in Faith*, 413-14.
95. O. L. Shelton, *The Church Functioning Effectively* (St. Louis: Christian Board of Publication, 1946), 8, 10, 23.
96. Ibid., 38, 39-40.
97. McAllister and Tucker, *Journey in Faith*, 413.

98. Willard M. Wickizer, Introduction to *Church Functioning Effectively*, by Shelton, 7.

99. Kenneth L. Teegarden, *We Call Ourselves Disciples* (St. Louis: Bethany Press, 1975), 23.

100. McAllister and Tucker, *Journey in Faith*, 413.

101. Teegarden, *We Call Ourselves Disciples*, 23.

102. "Agencies Look to the Future," editorial, *Christian-Evangelist* 88 (26 July 1950):719.

103. Spencer F. Austin, "Our Channels of Service," in *Primer for New Disciples*, ed. Samuel F. Pugh (St. Louis: Bethany Press, 1963), 125-26.

104. McAllister and Tucker, *Journey in Faith*, 416.

105. Teegarden, *We Call Ourselves Disciples*, 23.

106. McAllister and Tucker, *Journey in Faith*, 416.

107. Austin, "Our Channels of Service," 126.

108. National Church Program Co-ordinating Council, Information for Use in Orientation Conferences (1960), 2, Restructure File, Disciples of Christ Historical Society, Nashville, Tennessee.

109. Lair, *Christian Churches and Their Work*, 237-38.

110. Minutes of the Council of Agencies, 1956, quoted in Loren E. Lair, *The Christian Church (Disciples of Christ) and Its Future* (St. Louis: Bethany Press), 1971, 27.

111. McAllister and Tucker, *Journey in Faith*, 420.

112. Lair, *Christian Church (Disciples of Christ)*, 29.

113. Ibid., 32.

114. McAllister and Tucker, *Journey in Faith*, 420.

115. Lair, *Christian Church (Disciples of Christ)*, 34.

116. Wickizer, "Ideas for Brotherhood Restructure," 124.

117. Mayes, "Restructure in the Light of Structure," 75.

118. McAllister and Tucker, *Journey in Faith*, 421.

119. "Concerning Brotherhood Restructure: Report of the Board of Directors of the International Convention," Report no. 30 to the 1960 Assembly, Louisville, Kentucky, in *Reports and Resolutions in Regard to Brotherhood Restructure: Approved by Assemblies of the International Convention of Christian Churches (Disciples of Christ)* (Indianapolis: International Convention of Christian Churches [Disciples of Christ], n.d.), 2-8.

120. McAllister and Tucker, *Journey in Faith*, 385-86.

121. DeGroot, *Disciple Thought*, 141-42.

122. "Concerning Brotherhood Restructure: Report of the Board of Directors" [1960], 4-5.

CHAPTER VII

AN OVERVIEW OF RESTRUCTURE

The first three chapters of this study traced the evolution of an ideology in the Campbell-Stone movement. This ideology was centered on four basic ideals: <u>restoration, union, liberty, and mission.</u> Tensions existing within the Campbell-Stone movement from its first generation were caused both by the varied origins of the movement and by differences of opinion among the movement's founders. But it was in the second generation of the movement that the divergence in the interpretation of the movement's four basic values became pronounced. This divergence was compounded by social and particularly sectional differences which contributed to the first major schism in the Campbell-Stone movement, a schism which resulted in the identification of the Churches of Christ as separate from the Disciples of Christ.

In the twentieth century a second schism began to emerge. The dividing wedge in this case was the ideological differences between a conservative party for whom the movement's four ideals centered in a strict restorationism and a progressive party which had begun to soften the exclusivistic aspects of the movement's ideology and seek means of cooperation with the historic churches. This tendency among the progressives was made apparent by increasing ecumenical activity by Disciples in the twentieth century. In the 1950s and 1960s, both the writings of the Panel of Scholars and the participation of Disciples in the Consultation on Church Union underscored the fact that restoration as a method of seeking Christian union had been supplanted among a significant group of Disciples by ecumenism.

The fourth through sixth chapters focused upon structural developments that paralleled the aforementioned ideological developments. Again in the case of structure, divisive tendencies existed in the Campbell-Stone movement from its first generation. The movement's founders, particularly Alexander Campbell, underwent considerable change as to their structural convictions. However, one concept did come to dominate the polity of the Disciples of Christ. That concept was the society. Despite efforts to create a different kind of polity on several occasions, the extracongregational life of the Disciples continued to be expressed by societies of individuals well into the twentieth century. Between 1875 and 1917 a great many societies with a variety of functions were created by the Disciples. However, it was also during this period that the multiplication of societies, the end of isolation of Disciples leaders in terms of theological education, participation in broadly Protestant foreign missions and temperance movements, and social changes brought about by urbanization combined to produce change in this society polity.

The first change in the society polity was the creation of the International Convention of Disciples of Christ, which included a delegate body—the Convention's Committee on Recommendations. Also significant was the trend toward unification of the societies. This trend was manifested in the creation of the United Christian Missionary Society, the Commission on Budgets and Promotional Relationships, Unified Promotion, and the Home and State Missions Planning Council. This trend was resisted by conservative Disciples, who created alternative structures which were designed to preserve both an exclusivistic interpretation of restorationism and mission (that is, opposition to open membership) and an atomistic interpretation of liberty (that is, opposition to the idea of *the* Society [UCMS] rather than societies).

The creation of a set of alternative educational, missionary, and conventional structures by the conservatives by the end of the 1920s manifested the existence of the second schism in the Campbell-Stone movement. This schism produced the groups informally known as Independents and Cooperatives. Throughout the 1940s and 1950s the Cooperatives continued to create structures designed to unify or coordinate the work of the societies. These structures included the Council of Agencies, the National Church Program Coordinating Council, the Curriculum and Program Council, and the Christian Education Assembly. It was out of the Council of Agencies that the beginnings of Restructure came.

The remainder of this study will focus upon the ideological dimension of Restructure in terms of the movement's four basic ideals. The aim of this work is not to detail the complex organizational history of Restructure, but rather to describe the culmination of a long ideological and structural evolution in the Restructure process. In order to do this the major structures formed in Restructure will be briefly described and the major ideological parties that emerged in Restructure will be identified.

There was considerable continuity in the several bodies that were brought into being during the process of creating a Commission on Brotherhood Restructure. The Committee on Brotherhood Structure, which was appointed by the Board of Directors of the International Convention in 1958, was composed of eleven regular and two ex officio members. This was the committee that initially defined the restructure task and whose report to the International Convention in 1960 really began the process of Restructure at that level.[1] The successor of the Committee on Brotherhood Structure, in terms of carrying forward the task it had set forth, was the Commission itself. Of the thirteen members (regular and ex officio) of the Committee on Brotherhood Structure, eleven were named to the Commission on Brotherhood Restructure.[2] However, the Commission on Brotherhood Restructure was a large body (125 members at its inception in 1962).[3] The nomination of the Commission had been entrusted to a committee which the Board of Directors of the International Convention appointed in 1961—the Central Committee of the Commission on Brotherhood Restructure.[4]

The Central Committee of the Commission was largely composed of religious professionals. When originally formed the Committee had eighteen members.[5] Thirteen of the eighteen were ministers.[6] Of the remaining five members, one was the second vice-president of the International Convention; another was a pastor's wife and president of the board of directors of Unified Promotion; a third was the president of a Disciples of Christ college; a fourth was the chairman of the board of directors of the Christian Board of Publication; and the fifth was on the boards of trustees of the National Benevolent Association and the Disciples of Christ Historical Society. The Central Committee was not only primarily clerical rather than lay; it was also heavily laden with ministers who were involved in extralocal Disciples organizations. Of the thirteen ministers on the Committee, only four were local pastors. Among the other nine, two were state secretaries, four were staff members of national level Disciples agencies, and three were educators.[7] The composition of the Central Committee changed somewhat during Restructure, but these characteristics were retained and even strengthened. By 1965 there were twenty-seven members on the Central Committee. Of the twenty-seven, twenty-three were ministers. Thirteen of the members were staff members (one retired) of national level Disciples agencies; four were educators at institutions related to the Disciples Board of Higher Education; three were state secretaries; and four were pastors of local congregations.[8] Four of the original five lay members of the Central Committee remained, all of whom had national level agency ties other than their membership on the Central Committee. Therefore, not only did the original impetus for Restructure come out of the extralocal agencies (specifically the Council of Agencies), but the process remained largely in the hands of those with extralocal agency ties.

Earlier it was suggested that the diversification of national agencies, the end of isolation of Disciples ministers in terms of their theological education, the change to a more interdenominationally cooperative approach to missions, and urbanization each influenced the structural history of the Campbell-Stone movement. In light of this suggestion, the characteristics of the Central Committee of the Commission on Brotherhood Restructure in terms of national agency involvement, theological education, ecumenical participation, and urbanism become significant. The national agency involvement of the members of the Central Committee has been established. In terms of theological education, no fewer than nine of the thirteen ministers on the original Central Committee received at least part of their graduate or theological education at non-Disciples institutions.[9] No fewer than sixteen of the twenty-three ministers on the expanded 1965 Central Committee received at least part of their graduate or theological education at non-Disciples institutions. The University of Chicago, Yale, and Union Theological Seminary were particularly well-attended by the members of this group.[10]

Ecumenical interest and participation might be measured, in part, by direct, active participation in the National Council of Churches, in the World Council of Churches, or on the boards, committees, commissions, or departments of the Disciples' own Council on Christian Unity. Of the original eighteen Central Committee members, at least twelve were or had been active in the National Council, four in the World Council, and nine in the Council on Christian Unity.[11] Of the twenty-seven members of the enlarged Central Committee, at least twenty-two were or had been active in the National Council, nine in the World Council, and fifteen in the Council on Christian Unity.[12]

In terms of urbanism, thirteen of the eighteen members of the original Central Committee were from cities with populations of more than 250,000, and all eighteen were from cities of more than 25,000. Of the twenty-seven members of the later Committee, twenty-two were from cities of more than 250,000, and all but one of the remaining five lived in cities of 25,000 or more.[13] Thus, in terms of agency involvement, ecumenical outlook in education and council involvement, and urban residence, the members of the Central Committee reflected the characteristics that had influenced the Cooperative Disciples' organizational development since before the turn of the century.

When the actual Commission on Brotherhood Restructure was formed, its composition reflected to some degree that of the Central Committee. The Central Committee reported in 1962:

> The Central Committee has served as a nominating committee to the Board of Directors for the selection of a representative and responsible Commission.
> Among the criteria of qualifications to serve on the Commission were the following: 1) ability to give the necessary time; 2) depth of interest and constructive attitude toward the Brotherhood; 3) capacity to approach problems of objectivity, e.g., with an open mind, an irenic spirit; 4) a person who has the respect of other people in the state; 5) ability to work with others; 6) competence in one or more of the following areas—churchmanship, biblical thought, theology, church

history, organization and administration, current problems and issues of the social order, the church in modern culture, legal experience, ability to interpret.

The following categories were kept in mind as all selections were made: geography—state and area, laymen, laywomen, ministers, theological professors, administrators, agency representatives and members-at-large with exceptional experience. The present 125-member Commission represents 34 lay people and 91 ministers; 17 women and 108 men; 30 churches that may be classified as small (500 or less) and 95 that are large.[14]

The Commission was heavily skewed in the directions of being clerical rather than lay, male rather than female, and representing large congregations rather than small congregations. Although the Committee asserted that congregations having five hundred or fewer members "may be classified as small," in actuality the *average* size of Disciples congregations at this time was 219 members.[15] The perspective of the Commission would be theologically educated and sophisticated, oriented toward the urban or large congregation, and thoroughly Cooperative. Of the Commission's original 125 members, nineteen were from Indianapolis, nine of whom were on the Central Committee (which in 1962 had twenty-four members).[16]

Granville T. Walker, minister of the 3,543-member University Christian Church in Forth Worth, Texas, was elected to chair both the Central Committee and the full Commission on Brotherhood Restructure.[17] Walker had been a pastor of Disciples churches, had chaired the undergraduate Bible department of Texas Christian University, and been president of the International Convention. He was a Ph.D. graduate of Yale and the author of *Preaching in the Thought of Alexander Campbell*.[18] When the office of the Commission on Brotherhood Restructure first opened in February 1961, George Earle Owen was appointed administrative secretary.[19] Owen's services were made available to the Commission by the UCMS, in which Owen was executive chair of one of the Society's three divisions.[20]

By 1963, the Central Committee of the Commission on Brotherhood Restructure reported that three groups were functioning: the full Commission (around 125 members), the smaller Central Committee (which had expanded to twenty-five members).[21] In addition, the voluntary service of George Earle Owen gave way to the appointment of A. Dale Fiers as part-time administrative secretary of the Commission.[22]

A. Dale Fiers was, at that time, the president of the UCMS.[23] Fiers was a graduate of Bethany College and Yale Divinity School. He served as the pastor of various Disciples congregations in Ohio from 1929 until he became president of the UCMS—a position he held from 1951 to 1964. Fiers was also active in the National and World Councils of Churches and was a Disciples delegate to the Consultation on Church Union (COCU) beginning in 1962.[24] Fiers left his position with the Commission to become the executive secretary of the International Convention in 1964. Shortly thereafter, Kenneth L. Teegarden was called upon to become the administrative secretary of the Commission on Brotherhood Restructure.[25] It was under Teegarden's administrative leadership that the process of Restructure was brought to completion. He has been called the "architect" of Restructure.[26]

Kenneth Teegarden was born and reared in Oklahoma and began his undergraduate studies at Oklahoma State University in 1938.[27] His intention at that time was to become a lawyer and his studies were concentrated in American and world history. Teegarden brought to the Restructure process a "sense of constitutional responsibility" that was in part influenced by this background. Another factor from Teegarden's early life that he believed made an impact upon his approach to Restructure was the atmosphere of "frontier life" and "populism" which he sensed while growing up in Oklahoma. Teegarden had been a regular participant in a Disciples congregation from a very early age.[28] Teegarden completed his undergraduate studies at Phillips University (a Disciples college in Enid, Oklahoma) and also earned an M.A. degree there. Thereafter he earned the B.D. degree from Brite Divinity School of Texas Christian University (a Disciples institution in Forth Worth). After seminary Teegarden held several pastorates in Oklahoma, Texas, and Arkansas.[29] He was active in the Board of Higher Education, Unified Promotion, and the UCMS, and served on the general board of the National Council of Churches.[30]

At the time he was made administrative secretary of the Commission on Brotherhood Restructure, Teegarden was serving as executive secretary of the Arkansas Christian Missionary Society.[31] In this capacity, as a state secretary, Teegarden had already been named to the Commission on Brotherhood Restructure. Once in the position of administrative secretary of the Commission, Teegarden undertook to read "everything that Alexander Campbell ever wrote on church organization." According to Teegarden, this was the "second strongest influence" (after that of his general background) on his approach to Restructure.[32]

From 1962 through 1967 the full Commission on Brotherhood Restructure met annually. The Central Committee met more frequently and was "the most responsible entity" for actually drafting the Commission's proposals. The Executive Committee also met more frequently and was "an administrative group that prepared agendas."[33] By 1965 the Executive Committee was composed of the following persons in addition to Granville Walker, A. Dale Fiers, and Kenneth Teegarden: Myron C. Cole, Gaines M. Cook, Howard E. Dentler, Stephen J. England, George Earle Owen, and Willard M. Wickizer.[34]

Myron C. Cole was born in Abilene, Kansas, and reared in Glendale, California. He was a 1931 graduate of Chapman College (a Disciples institution) and had undertaken graduate study at the University of Chicago, George Williams College, and Yale. He had held pastorates in California, Ohio, Oregon, and Indiana. He was active in the Council on Christian Unity of the Disciples of Christ, served as a Disciples representative to the National Council of Churches and had chaired the 1957 Program Committee of the International Convention.[35]

Gaines M. Cook was born and reared in LeRoy, Illinois. He was educated at Eureka College (a Disciples college in Eureka, Illinois), from which he earned the A.B. degree in 1921, and Yale, from which he earned the B.D. degree in 1925. He was the pastor of several congregations in Illinois and one in New York. He was on the board of trustees of The College of the Bible, chairman of the Home and State Missions Planning Council, and president of the National Association of State Secretaries. Cook held several positions as a member of the general board of the National Council of Churches, and was also a delegate to the first and second assemblies of the World Council of Churches.[36] In 1946 Cook left his position as state secretary in Ohio to become the first full-time executive secretary of the International Convention, in which position he remained until 1964.[37]

Howard E. Dentler was born in Chicago. He did undergraduate work in economics at Stetson University (Southern Baptist) in Deland, Florida, and received his B.D. degree from The College of the Bible. He was pastor of Central Christian Church in Jacksonville, Florida, from 1957 to 1962.[38] In 1961 Dentler became the assistant to the executive secretary of the International Convention. In that position he also served as the editor of the Disciples' *Year Book*.[39]

Stephen J. England was the dean of the Graduate Seminary of Phillips University in Enid, Oklahoma. By 1966 England had been on the faculty at Phillips for forty-one years.[40] He had studied at Colorado College, Phillips University, Princeton Theological Seminary, the University of Chicago, the University of Michigan, and received the Ph.D. degree from Yale.[41] He served as the chairman of the Disciples' Board of Higher Education. He was active in the Faith and Order Commission of the World Council of Churches and was on the advisory board for the Revised Standard Version of the Bible. In 1966 England was the president of the Disciples' International Convention.[42]

George Earle Owen was a native of Virginia. He was a graduate of Bethany College (B.A.), the University of Chicago (M.A.), Union Theological Seminary (B.D.), and Columbia University (Ed.D.). Owen held four pastorates in Pennsylvania, Virginia, and New York. He was a news correspondent for the *Christian* and the *Christian Century*. In 1948 he attended the first assembly of the World Council of Churches. By 1966 Owen had been associated with the UCMS in many capacities in the United States and abroad.[43] He was the executive chairman of the Division of General Departments of the UCMS when he became the first voluntary administrative secretary of the Commission on Brotherhood Restructure.[44]

Willard M. Wickizer had been the chairman of the Committee on Brotherhood Structure.[45] It was he who had presented the paper, "Ideas for Brotherhood Restructure" at the 1958 meeting of the Council of Agencies.[46] Wickizer was a B.A. graduate of the University of Oklahoma and had earned an M.R.E. (Master of Religious Education) degree from Boston University. He served congregations in Oklahoma, Kansas, Iowa, and Missouri, and was once the chairman of the board of the Missouri Christian Missionary Society. However, most of his career was with the UCMS. It was as chairman of the Division of Home Missions of the UCMS that Wickizer helped to organize the Home and State Missions Planning Council.[47] He served for twenty-two years as the administrative secretary of this body. Wickizer was the administrative secretary of the National Church Program Coordinating Council from 1950 through the time of his membership in the Commission on Brotherhood Restructure, and was the chairman of the Council of Agencies from 1960 to 1962. Wickizer also served at one time as vice-president of the National Council of Churches.[48]

These biographical sketches demonstrate that the patterns already apparent in the Commission on Brotherhood Restructure and in the Central Committee are even more pronounced in the Executive Committee. All of the members of the Executive Committee were clergy who were experienced in the national level of the organized life of the Disciples. Seven of the nine members had received part of their graduate theological education at non-Disciples institutions (five of them had studied at Yale). All but two members of the Executive Committee were active in the National Council of Churches.[49] Seven of the nine were from cities with populations of over 250,000 (five were from Indianapolis).

Overview of Restructure

In addition to the Executive and Central Committees of the Commission on Brotherhood Restructure, there was a structure created by the Commission itself to carry out its task—a set of nine Special Task Committees:

1. SPECIAL TASK COMMITTEE on Revision of the Basic Documents dealing with *Dynamics of Restructure, The Nature of the Restructured Brotherhood We Seek* and *Basic Assumptions*.
2. . . . on Continuing Theological Evaluation of the Developments and Recommendations which result from the Restructure process.
3. . . . on the Program Structures of the Brotherhood and the Relationships of the National and State Program Planning Bodies.
4. . . . on the Promotional Structures and Relationships in the Brotherhood.
5. . . . on the Structure of the Local Church.
6. . . . on the Ecumenical Relationship of the Brotherhood.
7. . . . on Restructure Participation Meetings.
8. . . . on The Nature and Authority of the International Convention.
9. . . . on the Ministry.[50]

The work of these task committees was "the first major influence" on the *Provisional Design of the Christian Church (Disciples of Christ)*.[51] These task committees were authorized by the full Commission in its 1963 annual meeting in Chicago, and were brought into being by the Central Committee during the 1963-64 year.[52] The task committees were composed not only of members of the Commission but also of "persons of special competence" who were drawn "from the Brotherhood-at-large."[53] Not everyone on the Commission was assigned to a task committee.[54] The task committees were chaired by (in the order in which the committees are listed above): W. B. Blakemore, Ronald E. Osborn, James A. Moak, Spencer P. Austin, Jo M. Riley, Virgil A. Sly, Harrell A. Rea, Leslie R. Smith, and Paul S. Stauffer.[55]

W. B. Blakemore was born in 1912 in Perth, Australia. He was the son of a Disciples minister. He grew up in St. Louis and attended the Union Avenue Christian Church there during the years that the UCMS had its headquarters in St. Louis. In 1933 he graduated from Washington University with a B. S. in engineering. Blakemore went on to the Divinity School of the University of Chicago from which he graduated with M.A. (1937), B.D. (1938), and Ph.D. (1941) degrees. After ordination in 1941 Blakemore began teaching at the University of Chicago, and after 1945 he was the dean of the Disciples Divinity

House there. He became active in the Council of Agencies, the Board of Higher Education, the Council on Christian Unity, the Disciples of Christ Historical Society, the National Evangelistic Association, the Home and State Missions Planning Council, and the National and World Councils of Churches. He edited the *Scroll*, the publication of the Campbell Institute. He was also the general editor of the *Panel of Scholars Reports*.[56] Blakemore himself contributed to the *Reports* "The Issue of Polity for Disciples Today," which sets forth a view of polity very similar to that adopted by the Disciples during Restructure. Blakemore was the inaugural lecturer of the Forrest F. Reed Lectures of the Disciples of Christ Historical Society. Based on his experience as "a delegate-observer in the last session of the Second Vatican Council," Blakemore lectured on "how their dialogues with the Reformed churches, the world and Rome are leading the Christian Churches to new discoveries about the nature of the church."[57] Blakemore headed the Special Task Committee on the Revision of the Basic Documents, in which capacity he "made a large contribution to the wording of the reports which came from the commission, especially to the ... preamble to the Provisional Design."[58]

Ronald E. Osborn chaired the Special Task Committee on Continuing Theological Evaluation. The major influence on Osborn's background may be stated in his own words. "No debt equals that which I owe my father, G. Edwin Osborn. In my youth he was my pastor, in college and seminary my teacher, in all the years of my ministry until his death the most congenial of comrades."[59] Ronald Osborn was educated at Phillips University (A.B., M.A., and B.D.) and at the University of Oregon (Ph.D). He served in several pastorates and as editor-at-large of the *Christian Century*. In the 1960s he was dean, vice-president, and professor of church history at Christian Theological Seminary in Indianapolis.[60] Osborn was a member of the Board of Higher Education and the board of trustees of the Disciples of Christ Historical Society.[61] He was also very active in the World Council of Churches, and was a delegate to COCU beginning in 1962.[62] Osborn edited the first volume of the *Panel of Scholars Reports*, and contributed to the *Reports* "A Theology of Denominations and Principles for Brotherhood Restructure," "One Holy Catholic and Apostolic Church: The Continuing Witness of Disciples of Christ," "Dogmatically Absolute, Historically Relative: Conditioned Emphases in the History of Disciples of Christ," and "Crisis and Reformation: A Preface to Volume I."[63] In this preface he offered a forthright and systematic refutation of the restoration emphasis in the traditional Disciples "plea."[64] Osborn's influence on the work of the Commission on Brotherhood Restructure was a key factor in giving the process of Restructure a new direction.[65] When Osborn delivered his three lectures

Overview of Restructure

to the Commission in 1964,[66] "at that moment, the decision was made to switch from an association of churches to the Christian Church (Disciples of Christ)."[67]

Ronald Osborn was a controversial figure during Restructure because of his forthrightness in denouncing restorationism and his heavy involvement in the ecumenical movement. Critics of Disciples ecumenism and Restructure found ammunition in Osborn's 1965 book, *A Church for These Times*, in which Osborn wrote sympathetically about the "possibilities in episcopacy."[68]

James A Moak, who chaired the Special Task Committee on the Program Structures of the Brotherhood, was the state secretary of the Kentucky Association of Christian Churches.[69] He was a graduate of Transylvania College and The College of the Bible.[70] Before becoming the state secretary in Kentucky in 1957, Moak had served several congregations in Kentucky as pastor and had been the president of the Unified Program of the Christian Churches of Kentucky and the pastoral evangelist of the Mississippi Christian Churches. He had been on the advisory boards of several Disciples educational institutions and active in the Council of Agencies and Home and State Missions Planning Council.[71]

Spencer Austin chaired the Special Task Committee on Promotional Structures. Austin was born in Oklahoma. He earned A.B. and B. D. degrees from Phillips University in Enid, Oklahoma. In 1957 Austin became the executive secretary of Unified Promotion. For eleven years prior to assuming that position he was on the staff of the UCMS, "first as Director of Evangelism and then as chairman of the Division of General Services."[72] As director of Unified Promotion, Austin participated in the Council of Agencies and in other "interagency commissions and councils of the brotherhood." Austin was also active in the ecumenical movement—he was a member of the assembly of the National Council of Churches and served on the executive committee of Church World Service.[73]

Jo M. Riley, who chaired the Special Task Committee on the Structure of the Local Church, was reared and educated in Kentucky. He graduated from Transylvania College and The College of the Bible. During seminary Riley served congregations in Kentucky. After serving as a Navy chaplain in World War II, Riley had pastorates in Kentucky, Indiana, and North Carolina. He did additional study at Union Theological Seminary and Christian Theological Seminary. He was on the executive committees of the Council on Christian Unity and the Board of Higher Education.[74]

Virgil A. Sly headed the Special Task Committee on Ecumenical Relationships. Sly was a graduate of Cotner College, a Disciples institution in Lincoln, Nebraska. He joined the staff of the UCMS in 1927. In 1950, Sly became the chairman of the Division of World Mission. He had served under five presidents of the UCMS when he became the sixth in 1964. Sly had been a member of the board of directors of Unified Promotion since its formation. He was active in the Council of Agencies and served the Council on Christian Unity as director of the Department of Ecumenical Services. He chaired the Program Committee of the International Convention in 1962.[75]

Harrell A. Rea chaired the Special Task Committee on Listening Conferences (later named "Restructure Participation Meetings").[76] He was a graduate of both the undergraduate college and the seminary of Texas Christian University. He began his ministerial career as an education director and was subsequently the pastor of several congregations in Texas. In 1954 and 1955 Rea was the director of Church Development of the Texas Board of Christian Churches. After another pastorate he returned to administration as the executive secretary of the Christian Church Commission of the Greater Kansas City Area. Rea was active in the Home and State Missions Planning Council, for whom he chaired the Urban Committee in the early 1960s.[77]

The Special Task Committee on the Nature and Authority of the International Convention was chaired by Leslie R. Smith. Smith was a graduate of Cotner College and Yale Divinity School. He undertook additional graduate study at the Divinity School of the University of Chicago. In 1963 Smith was the senior minister of Central Christian Church in Lexington, Kentucky, immediate past president of the International Convention, chairman of the life and work committee of the board of trustees of the UCMS, on the board of curators of Transylvania College, and a member of the Board of Higher Education. Smith was a Disciples representative to the Central Committee of the World Council of Churches in 1958.[78]

The Special Task Committee on the Ministry was chaired by Paul S. Stauffer. Stauffer was born in Norwood, Ohio. He did his undergraduate work at Transylvania College and his seminary studies at The College of the Bible. He did additional graduate study at the University of Chicago and Union Theological Seminary. Stauffer served the Union Avenue Christian Church in St. Louis as associate minister and served several pastorates in Missouri and Kentucky. Active in extralocal Disciples organizations, Stauffer "served on many boards and committees," including seminary boards. Beginning in 1964, he was the chairman of the board of directors of the Council on Christian Unity. Stauffer was active in the National and World Councils of Churches and was a Disciples representative to COCU beginning in 1962.[79]

As a group those who chaired the special task committees conform generally to the patterns which characterized the Commission on Brotherhood Restructure,

Overview of Restructure

the Central Committee, and the Executive committee. They were all male, all clergy; all of them were either staff or volunteer members of national Disciples agencies; the majority of them received at least part of their graduate education at non-Disciples institutions; the majority were active in the World Council of Churches; and all of them resided in cities with populations of more than fifty thousand.[80]

The Special Task Committee on the Nature and Authority of the International Convention had proposed a "General Association of Christian Churches." However, in 1964 a basic shift occurred in the Restructure process (a shift associated with Ronald Osborn's lectures on the Church) when the Commission on Brotherhood Restructure rejected the proposal for a general association in favor of the idea of creating the Christian Church (Disciples of Christ). A new task committee was created and charged with the responsibility of writing a "design" for the Christian Church (Disciples of Christ). This committee, which first met in July 1964, had sixteen members "plus the Executive Committee of the commission serving in an ex officio capacity."[81] Of the sixteen regular members, thirteen were ministers;[82] twelve were employed by extralocal Disciples institutions or agencies (six were on the staffs of national level agencies, four were state secretaries, and two were educators at a Disciples seminary); two were pastors of local congregations; and two were laymen.[83] The congregations of the two members who were local pastors each had more than fifteen hundred members. The majority of the sixteen were involved in the National or World Councils of Churches.[84] Chairing the new task committee was W. A. Welsh.[85]

W. A. Welsh was a native of Fort Worth, Texas. He was an undergraduate and seminary alumnus of Texas Christian University, where he also taught. He served several pastorates in Texas before coming to the thirty-eight-hundred-member East Dallas Christian Church in 1949. In 1964, when he was named chairman of the Special Task Committee on Nature and Design, he was the president of the International Convention and had been named the tenth president of Lexington Theological Seminary (The College of the Bible).[86] He was also active in the National Council of Churches.[87]

There was a strong link between the organizations entrusted with the Restructure process and the organizations that had evolved among Cooperative Disciples by the mid-twentieth century. Additionally, the ecumenical involvement of many of the leaders of Restructure suggests a link between the ideology of the leaders of Restructure and the ideology that had evolved among Cooperative Disciples. Ecumenical involvement was not a product of Restructure among Disciples; it existed before, during, and after Restructure. In light of the composition of the Commission and its major committees, Loren Lair's statement that "the Commission on Restructure was not packed. It was not loaded with staff personnel,"[88] would be difficult to support. In some senses, the Commission was "packed." However, this does not mean that the process of Restructure was self-serving to its leaders and detrimental to the denomination at large. After all, it was principally the extralocal, organized, cooperative life of the Disciples that was being restructured. For that reason the process was most appropriately accomplished by those who were involved in that organized life. Those are precisely the persons with whom the responsible bodies were "packed." The impact of Restructure upon the denomination as a whole may be seen, in part, by examining the structures resulting from Restructure.

Not surprisingly, the structures that resulted from Restructure resembled, more than anything else, those that had evolved during the history of cooperative work among the Disciples of Christ. The continuity of leadership that prevailed into Restructure paralleled an organizational continuity that also persisted throughout Restructure and beyond it. This fact is reflected in the following statement in the *1969 Year Book*: "The general committee and commission structure of the International Convention has been carried over for the time being into the Christian Church."[89] If the beginning of the formal process of Restructure is identified with the creation of the Committee on Brotherhood Structure in 1958, then 1957 may be said to be immediately "pre-Restructure." Similarly, if Restructure may be said to have been formally completed with the adoption of the *Provisional Design for the Christian Church (Disciples of Christ)* at Kansas City, Missouri, in 1968, then 1969 may be said to be immediately "post-Restructure." The organizational continuity that persisted throughout Restructure may be seen by comparing the structures of the Disciples of Christ in these two years (see Table). The pattern of continuity is much more evident than the fact of change in these organizations.

The immediate result of Restructure was not so much a change in the organizational shape of the Disciples as it was a change in the organizational language of the Disciples. That language reflected a process that had been going on for a long time—the process of the Campbell-Stone movement's becoming, in fact, a denomination. Because the Disciples of Christ had begun, in part, as a Christian unity movement, they were reluctant to admit that they had become still another separate denomination. One solution was to claim that the Campbell-Stone movement was not another denomination, but, in fact, *the* Church. This option has been chosen by some in the Churches of Christ.[90] A second alternative was to retain ecclesiological language that denied a denominational status to a body that was, by any objective standard, a separate and identifiable religious body. This second alternative has been visible among

Overview of Restructure 197

those Independents who wish to call their group "the undenominational fellowship of Christian Churches and Churches of Christ."[91]

A third alternative was that chosen by the Cooperative Disciples. It was the alternative that flowed logically out of the fifty years of increasing organizational development and coordination as a denomination. It was also the alternative that conformed to the recognition that other Christian bodies, the historic churches, were legitimate partners in the mission of the Church universal. That alternative was to admit to and embrace denominational status and to adopt churchly organizational language.

As the composition of the main Restructuring leadership shows, Restructure was carried out largely by those who were committed to those organizations that had arisen among Cooperative Disciples. They did not wish to scuttle those organizations, but to give those organizations—and the congregations that supported them, and which they were designed to serve—a greater sense of their relatedness. Well before Ronald Osborn presented the lectures that have been credited with moving the Restructure process "toward the Christian Church,"[92] the committee on Brotherhood Structure presented a rationale for Restructure which said, in part:

> Much of the problem that the Disciples of Christ have had with organization stems from the fact that . . . we have had almost no theology of *Church* beyond the local congregation. . . .
>
> A further factor in the problem has been that the Disciples of Christ did not set out to be a separate religious body. They were to be a movement within Protestantism and . . . were fearful that the building up of a general organizational life would cast them in the role of being just another communion. And yet as time passed and the union of all Christendom did not take place and they were forced to continue as a separate group an increasing number of Disciples . . . have felt that they must become corporately involved . . . in all the . . . activities in which other church bodies are engaged.
>
> . . . During the past half century there has come to the Disciples of Christ a growing sense of maturity. An increasing number of our people have come to feel that no matter what we started out to be we are in deed and in fact a separate religious body and as such we should act in a responsible fashion but that our present organizational structure keeps us from a full expression of our maturity. Furthermore the conviction has come to us that the *Church* is something more than the sum total of local congregations, that it has a very real and

vital total entity that should be reflected in its corporate structure. These changing concepts have already had a profound effect on our organized life.[93]

An expression of the corporateness, the totality, the reality of an entity that came to be called the Christian Church (Disciples of Christ) was the principal act of Restructure. However, this expression of the corporate life of Disciples was not confused with the Church universal. As Osborn put it:

> What then is the character of our corporate life? It is something far more than a convention, far more than a policy of cooperation, far more than an association of churches. It is the church, as surely as any congregation is the church. It is not yet the whole church, but it is the church.[94]

This, then, was the fundamental change brought about by Restructure. The Christian Church (Disciples of Christ) would no longer seek to deny the reality of its denominational existence. It would not style itself "undenominational." Nor would it claim to be the Church universal. Nor would it continue to deny its churchly character behind a series of euphemisms of its own tradition's device: society for extracongregational denominational organization, brotherhood for the entire denomination, secretary or evangelist for those engaged in state and national ministries.

The document that contained the new ecclesiological language was originally adopted as *A Provisional Design for the Christian Church (Disciples of Christ)*. The polity that was embodied in the *Design* is best summarized in the third paragraph of its Preamble:

> Within the universal body of Christ, the Christian Church (Disciples of Christ) manifests itself organizationally in free and voluntary relationships at congregational, regional, and general levels. Each manifestation, with reference to the function for which it is uniquely responsible, is characterized by its integrity, self-government, authority, rights and responsibilities.[95]

Thus, the *Design* constituted the Christian Church (Disciples of Christ) as a single entity within the Church universal. That single entity was composed of local, regional, and general "manifestations" that were already largely in existence before Restructure, but which would now be understood as part of

TABLE:

CORRESPONDENCE OF 1957 DISCIPLES OF CHRIST STRUCTURES
TO THOSE OF 1969[96]

DISCIPLES STRUCTURES, 1957	DISCIPLES STRUCTURES, 1969
International Convention of Disciples of Christ (Assembly)	General Assembly of the Christian Church (Disciples of Christ)
Committee on Recommendations	General Board
Nominating Committee	General Nominating Committee
Officers (of the Convention)	Officers (of the Assembly)
Board of Directors	Administrative Committee
Convention Office (staff)	General Office (staff)
Department of Public Relations	Office of Interpretation
COMMITTEES:	COMMITTEES:
	Credentials
	Reference and Counsel
Fraternal Relations	
Necrology	
Program and Arrangements	Assembly Program and Arrangements
Time and Place	Assembly Time and Place
Selective Service Status of Ministerial Students	Selective Service Status of Ministerial Students
Week of Compassion	Week of Compassion
Year Book Publication	*Year Book* Publication
Relief Appeals	

	Reconciliation
World Call	*World Call* Publication
All Canada	All Canada
COMMISSIONS:	COMMISSIONS:
Chaplaincy Endorsement	Chaplaincy Endorsement
Promotion of Christian Literature	Christian Literature
Brotherhood Finance	Brotherhood Finance
Budgets and Promotional Relationships	
	Cooperative Policy and Practice
INTERAGENCY BODIES:	INTERAGENCY BODIES:
Curriculum and Program Council	Curriculum and Program Council
Home and State Missions Planning Council	Home and State Missions Planning Council
National Church Program Coordinating Council	National Church Program Coordinating Council
Council of Agencies	
COOPERATING ORGANIZATIONS:	ADMINISTRATIVE UNITS:
Brazil Christian Mission	
Board of Church Extension	Board of Church Extension
Board of Higher Education	Board of Higher Education
Christian Board of Publication	Christian Board of Publication
Christian Foundation	Christian Church Foundation

Christmount Christian Assembly, Inc.	Christmount Christian Assembly, Inc.
Council on Christian Unity	Council on Christian Unity
Disciples of Christ Historical Society	Disciples of Christ Historical Society
	Disciples Peace Fellowship
European Evangelistic Society	European Evangelistic Society
National Association of State Secretaries	Conference of State and Area Secretaries and Board Chairmen
National Benevolent Association	National Benevolent Association
National City Christian Church Corporation	National City Christian Church Corporation
National Evangelistic Association	National Evangelistic Association
Pension Fund	Pension Fund
UCMS	UCMS
Unified Promotion	Unified Promotion
State Organizations	Regions
National Christian Missionary Convention	National Convocation of Trustees for the National Christian Missionary Convention

a single entity. Thus, the "cooperating organizations" of 1957 became the "administrative units" of 1969. The earlier language implied separateness; the later language implied unity. The International Convention of Disciples of Christ—renamed the International Convention of Christian Churches (Disciples of Christ) late in 1957—gave way to the General Assembly of the Christian Church (Disciples of Christ). Again, the earlier language (convention of church*es*) emphasized the separateness of the congregations. The new gathering was to be called the assembly of *a* church. However, the change in the national gathering was more than a change in nomenclature. After several unsuccessful attempts during the history of the Disciples of Christ, the denomination was finally to have a proportionately representative body:[97]

> All members of the Christian Church who register for the General Assembly shall have all privileges of the Assembly except that voting privileges shall be limited to the following: (a) Voting representatives from congregations. Each congregation of the Christian Church shall be entitled to have two voting representatives, plus one additional voting representative for each 500 participating members or major fraction thereof over the first 500. These voting representatives from congregations shall be in addition to persons holding the office of ordained minister.
>
> (b) Voting representatives from regions. Each region shall be entitled to have one voting representative for each 3,000 participating members or major fraction thereof within the region. Each region shall have a minimum of three voting representatives. These voting representatives from regions shall be in addition to persons holding the office of ordained minister. The voting representatives from each region shall include both men and women.
>
> (c) The ordained ministers who have ministerial standing in the Christian Church in accordance with the policies established by the General Assembly. . . .
>
> (d) Members of the Christian Church not otherwise voting members who are the chief administrative officers of institutions and general boards which are recognized by the General Assembly.
>
> (e) Members of the General Board not otherwise voting members.[98]

This representative body was designed to have the final authority within the Christian Church (Disciples of Christ). The General Assembly would receive all items of business from the General board and act upon them in the Assembly's biennial meeting. Provision was also made within the *Design* for the submission of business on an emergency basis directly to the General Assembly through the Committee on Reference and Counsel.[99]

The General Assembly was designed to be a broadly representative body. Ideally, it would represent congregations, regions, and institutions of the Christian Church (Disciples of Christ) on a largely proportionate basis. In light of this

Overview of Restructure

fact, it may be said that the leaders of Restructure did not conspire to take control of the Christian Church (Disciples of Christ). Rather, they created a structure, the General Assembly, which would place the final authority in the hands of a broadly representative body. Whether or not the congregations, regions, and institutions of the Disciples of Christ take advantage of the opportunity to participate in the General Assembly, the *Design* does provide that opportunity. Despite the fact that the Commission on Brotherhood Restructure, and especially the Central, Executive, and Task Committees were led by persons with national and regional level interests, the *Design* did not structurally centralize authority.

The General Board created during Restructure was secondary to the General Assembly in two ways: first, it only recommended action to the General Assembly; and second, the Board was elected from the General Assembly—half from the regions on a proportionate basis, the other half from the Assembly at large. The *Design* stipulated that one-third to one-half of the General board be ministers.[100] The General Board would be without doubt an influential body; but its influence was, by the *Design*, subordinate to the authority of the General Assembly.

The *Design* also provided for an Administrative Committee, three-quarters of whom were to be drawn from the General Board. In addition, the officers of the Christian Church were ex officio members of the Administrative Committee. The officers of the Christian Church included the volunteer officers of the General Assembly—a moderator and first and second vice-moderators. The moderator, whose term of office was two years, presided at the General Assembly. The other officers of the Christian Church—the general minister and president, secretary, and treasurer—were salaried. The term of office of the general minister and president was six years. The Administrative Committee, which was the program planning, implementation, grievance, and promotional body, included both staff and volunteers, and was the liaison between the professional administrative personnel of the Christian Church (Disciples of Christ) and the larger, more representative bodies. The Administrative Committee, like the General Board, was to be at least one-half lay in composition.[101]

Perhaps the clearest indicator that Restructure did not really place power in the hands of an oligarchic structure is the language used in the paragraphs which set forth the rights and responsibilities of congregations.

> Among the rights recognized and safeguarded to congregations are the right: to manage their affairs under the Lordship of Jesus Christ; to adopt or retain their names and charters or constitutions and bylaws; *to determine in faithfulness to the gospel their practice with*

respect to the basis of membership; to own, control and incumber their property; to organize for carrying out the mission and witness of the church; to establish their budgets and financial policies; to call their ministers; and to participate through voting representatives in forming the corporate judgment of the Christian Church. . . .

While congregations are responsive to the needs of general and regional programs established with the participation of the congregations' representatives in the general and regional assemblies, all financial support of the general and regional programs of the Christian Church by congregations and individuals is voluntary.[102] (Italics mine.)

The rights of individual congregations, even when it came to the long-contested question of open membership, were preserved in the *Design*. Equally, the *Design* made clear that the regional and general manifestations of the Christian Church (Disciples of Christ) intended no encroachment on the property rights of congregations. This is significant because allegations of intended encroachments upon the property rights of congregations were a prominent part of the controversy surrounding Restructure.[103]

Restructure exhibited a pattern of continuity. The principal bodies that were entrusted with the Restructure process were dominated by leaders who were experienced in the state and national organizational life of the Disciples. The structures created resembled nothing so much as the structures that had evolved among Cooperative Disciples during the generation that preceded the formal process of Restructure. The *Provisional Design* provided for a General Assembly which would be empowered to take final action upon the recommendations originating from the church's other bodies. This Assembly was established on a broadly representative basis. The rights of the individual congregation were carefully safeguarded in the *Design*. Participation in and financial support of the regional and general manifestations of the Christian Church (Disciples of Christ) was strictly voluntary. The moral suasion of the general and regional manifestations and the congregations' sense of covenant with the larger bodies, rather than any formal authority, was to hold the Christian Church (Disciples of Christ) together.[104]

The actual organizational shape of the Disciples of Christ did not change in a revolutionary way in the process of Restructure. The organizations of the Disciples and that which bound them together remained intact. What changed more dramatically was the ecclesiological language of the Disciples. This language was brought up to date with the ideology that had evolved among Cooperative

Disciples. Because Restructure represented more a change in self-description and self-understanding than a change in structure, the controversy that accompanied Restructure was largely ideological. Debate related to Restructure swirled around the most cherished values of the Campbell-Stone heritage. Alternative interpretations of faithfulness to the Campbell-Stone movement's ideals were articulated especially clearly by four identifiable groups during the Restructure process. It is to those groups that this study now turns.

---

1. "Concerning Brotherhood Restructure: Report of the Board of Directors" [1960], 2-8.
2. "Members of the Commission on Brotherhood Restructure," *Mid-Stream* 2 (December 1962):100-105.
3. "[Report of the] Central Committee of the Commission on Brotherhood Restructure," Report no. 29 to the 1962 Assembly, Los Angeles, Calif., in *Reports and Resolutions*, 10.
4. "Concerning Brotherhood Restructure: Report of the Board of Directors of the International Convention," Report no. 30 to the 1961 Assembly, Kansas City, Mo., in *Reports and Resolutions*, 8.
5. Ibid.
6. *1962 Year Book (July 1, 1961-June 30, 1962) of the Christian Churches (Disciples of Christ)* (Indianapolis: International Convention of Christian Churches [Disciples of Christ], 1962), 343-449 passim.
7. Ibid., 8, 84-149 passim; "Mrs. Forrest L. (Dorothy) Richeson: Biographical Data," "John Rogers: Biographical Data," Biographical Files, "Mrs. Forrest L. Richeson" and "John Rogers," Disciples of Christ Historical Society, Nashville, Tennessee. "State secretaries" were the chief executives of the Disciples state missionary organizations.
8. Commission on Brotherhood Restructure, *The Direction in Brotherhood Restructure* (Indianapolis: International Convention of Christian Churches [Disciples of Christ] n.d.), 4; *1965 Year Book (July 1, 1964-June 30, 1965) of the Christian Churches (Disciples of Christ)* (Indianapolis: International Convention of Christian Churches [Disciples of Christ], 1965), 9-10, 39, 42, 47, 73, 79, 82, 137, 151-52, 213. The four who were local pastors served congregations averaging 1,890 in membership—nearly eight times the size of the average Disciples congregation, which was 237 members at that time (*1965 Year Book*, S26, S154, S220, S292, S342). All four pastors were involved in Disciples agencies at the national level in addition to their membership on the Commission on Brotherhood Restructure (*1965 Year Book*, 10, 41, 83).

9. "Biographical Information Concerning: Spencer P. Austin," "Clarence E. Lemmon: Biographical Data," "Biographical Information Concerning: Lester B. Rickman," "Harlie L. Smith: Biographical Data," "Biographical Information: Dr. Joseph Martin Smith," "Biographical Information: Willard M. Wickizer, Sr.," Biographical Files, "Spencer P. Austin," "Clarence E. Lemmon," "Lester B. Rickman," "Harlie L. Smith," "Joseph M. Smith," and "Willard M. Wickizer," Disciples of Christ Historical Society, Nashville, Tennessee; Granville T. Walker, *The Greatest of These* ... (St. Louis: Bethany Press, 1963) jacket; Beazley, ed., *Interpretative Examination*, 407, 410.

10. Ibid.: "Biographical Data: Dr. Myron C. (Clifford) Cole," "Biographical Data: Dr. Gaines M. Cook," "Edward S. Moreland: Biographical Data," "Forrest L. Richeson: Biographical Data," Biographical Files, "Myron C. Cole," "Gaines M. Cook," "Edward S. Moreland," and "Forrest L. Richeson," Disciples of Christ Historical Society, Nashville, Tennessee; Stephen J. England, *The One Baptism* (St. Louis: Bethany Press, 1960), jacket; Beazley, ed., *Interpretative Examination*, 406, 413.

11. *1957 Year Book (July 1, 1956-June 30, 1957) of Christian Churches (Disciples of Christ)* (Indianapolis: International Convention of Christian Churches [Disciples of Christ], 1957), 280, 286; *1962 Year Book*, 127-30, 313-328, 336.

12. *1957 Year Book*, 279, 286; *1962 Year Book*, 128, 315-328; *1965 Year Book*, 82-83, 256-277; Beazley, ed., *Interpretative Examination*, 413; England, *One Baptism*, jacket. The number of persons directly involved in the National and World Councils is particularly significant in light of the fact that the structure of the Councils themselves limited the number of persons who could be directly involved from any one denomination (*1965 Year Book*, 313).

13. "Members of the Commission," 100-105; *1962 Year Book*, 104, 344; Commission on Brotherhood Restructure, *Direction in Restructure*, 4; U.S., Department of Commerce, Bureau of the Census, *County and City Data Book, 1962: A Statistical Abstract Supplement* (Washington, D.C.: Government Printing Office, 1962), 583-610.

14. "[Report of the] Central Committee" [1962], 10.

15. *1962 Year Book*, 823.

16. "Members of the Commission," 100-105.

17. *1962 Year Book*, 775; "Concerning Brotherhood Restructure: Report of the Board of Directors" [1961], 9.

18. Walker, *Greatest of These* ... , jacket.

19. "Concerning Brotherhood Restructure: Report of the Board of Directors" [1961], 9.

20. *1962 Year Book*, 214.

21. "[Report of the] Central Committee" [1962], 10-11; Commission on Brotherhood Restructure, *Direction in Restructure*, 4.
22. "Report of the Commission on Brotherhood Restructure," Report no. 31 to the 1963 Assembly, Miami Beach, Fla., in *Reports and Resolutions*, 11-12.
23. *1962 Year Book*, 212.
24. Beazley, ed., *Interpretative Examination*, 410.
25. McAllister and Tucker, *Journey in Faith*, 441.
26. Short, interview.
27. "Kenneth LeRoy Teegarden," biographical information sheet, Biographical File, "Kenneth L. Teegarden," Disciples of Christ Historical Society, Nashville, Tennessee.
28. Teegarden, interview.
29. "Kenneth LeRoy Teegarden," biographical sheet.
30. *1962 Year Book*, 86, 182, 323.
31. "Kenneth LeRoy Teegarden," biographical sheet.
32. Teegarden, interview.
33. Ibid.
34. Commission on Brotherhood Restructure, *Direction in Restructure*, 4. Leslie R. Smith and Robert W. Burns had served on the Executive Committee earlier (George G. Beazley, Jr., "Editorial," *Mid-Stream* 3 [September 1963]:5).
35. "Biographical Data: Dr. Myron C. (Clifford) Cole."
36. "Biographical Data: Dr. Gaines M. Cook."
37. McAllister and Tucker, *Journey in Faith*, 413-14.
38. Beazley, ed., *Interpretative Examination*, 408.
39. *1962 Year Book*, 8, 1.
40. Barry K. Robinson, "Meet the President," *Christian* 104 (27 February 1966):265.
41. England, *One Baptism*, jacket.
42. Robinson, "Meet the President," 264-65; England, *One Baptism*, jacket.
43. "Biographical Information: Dr. George Earle Owen," Biographical File, "George Earle Owen," Disciples of Christ Historical Society, Nashville, Tennessee.
44. "Concerning Brotherhood Restructure: Report of the Board of Directors" [1961], 9.
45. "Concerning Brotherhood Restructure: Report of the Board of Directors" [1960], 3.
46. Blakemore, gen. ed., *Panel of Scholars Reports*, 3:112, editor's note.
47. "Biographical Information: Willard M. Wickizer, Sr."; Crain, *Development of Social Ideas Among Disciples*, 317.

48. "Biographical Information: Willard M. Wickizer, Sr."

49. *1962 Year Book*, 316, 317, 323; *1965 Year Book*, 258, 259, 263, 267.

50. A. Dale Fiers, "Report to the Commission on Brotherhood Restructure: June 29-July 1, 1964, Louisville, Kentucky," *Mid-Stream* 4 (Fall 1964):14-15.

51. Lair, *Christian Church (Disciples of Christ)*, 74.

52. Granville T. Walker, "State of Brotherhood Restructure: A Report Submitted to the Commission on Brotherhood Restructure, Louisville, Kentucky, June 29, 1964," *Mid-Stream* 5 (Fall 1964):6.

53. Fiers, "Report to the Commission," 14.

54. Teegarden, interview.

55. "Minutes of the General and Business Proceedings of the Commission on Brotherhood Restructure, July 1-4, 1963, Pick-Congress Hotel, Chicago, Illinois," *Mid-Stream* 3 (September 1963):12-13.

56. Ronald E. Osborn, "'Intelligence in Ministry': The Vocation of Wm. Barnett Blakemore," *Discipliana* 42 (Fall 1982):35-38.

57. "Blakemore Sees Hope in Dialogue: Dean of Disciples Divinity House, Chicago, Delivers First Forrest Reed Lectures," *Christian* 103 (5 December 1965):1556.

58. Osborn, "'Intelligence in Ministry,'" 38.

59. Ronald E. Osborn, *In Christ's Place: Christian Ministry in Today's World* (St. Louis: Bethany Press, 1967), 10.

60. Osborn, *In Christ's Place*, jacket.

61. *1965 Year Book*, 41, 89.

62. Beazley, ed., *Interpretative Examination*, 413.

63. Blakemore, gen. ed., *Panel of Scholars Reports*, vols. 1, 2, 3.

64. Osborn, "Crisis and Reformation," 25-26.

65. Teegarden, interview.

66. Ronald E. Osborn, "The Church of Christ on Earth," "The Nature of the Church," "The Building of the Church," *Mid-Stream* 4 (Fall 1964):32-77.

67. Teegarden, interview.

68. Ronald E. Osborn, *A Church for These Times* (New York: Abingdon Press, 1965), 140-41.

69. *1962 Year Book*, 289.

70. "Moak Resigns as General Minister," *Kentucky Christian* 75 (September 1980):1.

71. "Biographical Information: James A. Moak," Biographical File, "James A. Moak," Disciples of Christ Historical Society, Nashville, Tennessee.

72. "Biographical Information Concerning: Spencer P. Austin."

73. *1962 Year Book*, 122; "Biographical Information Concerning: Spencer P. Austin."

74. C. E. Lemmon, ed., *Preaching on New Testament Themes: Sermons by Active Pastors of Present-Day Christian Churches (Disciples of Christ)* (St. Louis: Bethany Press, 1964), 25.

75. "Biographical Information: Dr. Virgil A. Sly," Biographical File, "Virgil A. Sly," Disciples of Christ Historical Society, Nashville, Tennessee.

76. Fiers, "Report to the Commission," 15.

77. "Harrell Allen Rea," biographical information sheet, Biographical File, "Harrell Allen Rea," Disciples of Christ Historical Society, Nashville, Tennessee.

78. "Leslie R. Smith: Biographical Data," Biographical File, "Leslie R. Smith," Disciples of Christ Historical Society, Nashville, Tennessee.

79. Beazley, ed., *Interpretative Examination*, 416-17.

80. Commission on Brotherhood Restructure, *Direction in Restructure*, 4; U. S. Bureau of the Census, *County and City Data Book, 1962*, 587-95.

81. Lair, *Christian Church (Disciples of Christ)*, 67-70, 82, 83.

82. *1965 Year Book*, M5-M97.

83. Lair, *Christian Church (Disciples of Christ)*, 83.

84. *1965 Year Book*, 263-67, 277, S286, S314.

85. Lair, *Christian Church (Disciples of Christ)*, 83.

86. W. A. Welsh, *Villains on White Horses: Sermons on Passages from Paul* (St. Louis: Bethany Press, 1964), jacket.

87. *1962 Year Book*, 324.

88. Lair, *Christian Church (Disciples of Christ)*, 47.

89. "[Report of the] General Office, Christian Church (Disciples of Christ)." Report no. 1 to the 1969 General Assembly, Seattle, Washington, by A. Dale Fiers, General Minister and President, in *1969 Year Book and Directory (July 1, 1968-June 30, 1969) of the Christian Church (Disciples of Christ)* (Indianapolis: Christian Church [Disciples of Christ], 1969).

90. Harrell, "Peculiar People," 35-36.

91. Howard E. Short, Foreword to McAllister and Tucker, *Journey in Faith*, 6.

92. Ronald E. Osborn, *Restructure . . . Toward the Christian Church (Disciples of Christ): Intention, Essence, Constitution* (St. Louis: Christian Board of Publication, 1964).

93. "Concerning Brotherhood Restructure: Report of the Board of Directors" [1960], 4-5.

94. Osborn, *Toward the Christian Church*, 54.

95. "A Provisional Design for the Christian Church (Disciples of Christ)," in *1969 Year Book*, 17-29, 18.

96. *1957 Year Book*, 6, 224; "A Provisional Design for the Christian Church (Disciples of Christ)," in *1969 Year Book*, 18, 20-22, 25; "[Report of the] General Office" [1969], by Fiers, in *1969 Year Book*, 39-40; *1969 Year Book*, M6-M28; "[Report of the] Division of Homeland Ministries of the United Christian Missionary Society," Report no. 18, in *Business Docket of the General Assembly, Christian Church (Disciples of Christ), Cincinnati, Ohio, October 26-31, 1973* (Indianapolis: General Office of the Christian Church [Disciples of Christ], 1973), 89; McAllister and Tucker, *Journey in Faith*, 399. "General Office" is listed as an "administrative unit" (*1969 Year Book*, M6). All Canada and *World Call* in the 1957 column are listed under "Cooperating Organizations" (*1957 Year Book*, 6). "Regions" are listed as "Manifestations" rather than "administrative units" ("Provisional Design," 18). The "National Convocation of Trustees" is listed with the committees and commissions rather than "administrative units" (*1969 Year Book*, M9).

97. The adoption of a delegate assembly was actually a two-step process. In 1966 the International Convention amended its bylaws "to provide for a delegate assembly." Only two assemblies, at St. Louis in 1967 and Kansas City in 1968, were held under this interim measure. After the adoption of the Provisional Design in 1968 the annual International convention assemblies gave way to the biennial General Assemblies of he Christian Church (Disciples of Christ) ("A Proposal to Amend the By-Laws of the International Convention of Christian Churches (Disciples of Christ) to Provide for a Delegate Assembly." Report no. 34 to the 1964 Assembly, Detroit, Mich., in *Reports and Resolutions*, 21-23; McAllister and Tucker, *Journey in Faith*, 441-43).

98. "Provisional Design," 19.
99. Ibid., 20.
100. Ibid., 20.
101. Ibid., 21-22.
102. Ibid., 28.
103. Teegarden, *We Call Ourselves Disciples*, 24-25.
104. Ibid., 69-73.

CHAPTER VIII

FOUR IDEOLOGICAL OPTIONS IN RESTRUCTURE

During the process of Restructure at least four identifiable groups emerged with the aim of articulating a possible direction for the process in terms of the Campbell-Stone movement's ideals. These groups differed as to the shape they wished Restructure to take and each attempted to make an impact on that process. Each group formed organizations and produced and distributed literature to the congregations of the Disciples of Christ that were in fellowship with the International Convention.

The first group is composed of those who were given the task of Restructure. This is the group whose leadership was described in chapter seven. The ideological perspective of this first group is presented in the publications of the Commission on Brotherhood Restructure, its committees, and the closely related structures of Cooperative Disciples life.

The second group was the Disciples for Mission and Renewal. According to Ronald Osborn, this was "a group of radical activists" who began to "press for a more secular theology and for a commitment to the social programs of the New Left."[1] The main leader of this group was Charles Bayer. Bayer was a member of the Commission on Brotherhood Restructure. His group has been characterized as a form of "loyal opposition" to Restructure. However, this group for the most part supported Restructure and only wished it had gone further.[2]

A third group that articulated a point of view on Restructure was the Atlanta Declaration group that emerged in 1966. The Atlanta Declaration group was made up of individuals with strongly Cooperative commitments.[3] It included a number of distinguished ministers who related to congregations that had been supporting Cooperative causes. This made them more serious contenders than the Independents for making an impact on Restructure. This group held to an ecclesiology that was steeped in traditional Disciples antiecclesiasticism and sought to "preserve personal and congregational freedom by limiting Restructure to the agencies."[4]

The main leader of the Atlanta group was Robert W. Burns, a former president of the International Convention and a member of the Commission on Brotherhood Restructure. The Atlanta group has also been styled the "loyal opposition" to Restructure.[5] This group produced its own documents about Restructure and also distributed the writings of "old-line liberals,"[6] such as A. T. DeGroot and W. E. Garrison. Ironically, though these liberals had sharp differences with the Independents on other issues, their libertarian ecclesiologies had much in common. The dissent of the Atlanta group and its supporters "caused mild alarm within the Commission [on Restructure] and altered the climate in which it discussed theological issues."[7]

The fourth group is that representing the Independent point of view. This perspective was interjected into the discussions on Restructure by the Committee for the Preservation of the Brotherhood. Although this Committee's principal leader claims that the Committee's composition was originally equally divided between Cooperatives and Independents, the Independent character of the Committee for the Preservation of the Brotherhood is made clear in the identity of its main propagandist, James DeForest Murch.[8] This fourth group did not represent a major constituency within the Cooperative Disciples community. Rather, this group was part of a separate communion, with a fifty-year-old tradition of criticism of the organizations of Cooperative Disciples.[9] However, the Committee for the Preservation of the Brotherhood made its point of view known to the congregations that were Cooperative through mass mailings and in that way affected Restructure.[10]

It was from among the ideological alternatives articulated by these four groups that the Disciples of Christ had to choose in Restructure. The basic ideology of the Disciples of Christ was traditionally cast in terms of the four ideals of restoration, union, liberty, and mission. Therefore, the leaders of Restructure addressed each of these ideals as the process unfolded. Unquestionably, one of the most important theological voices in the Restructure process was that of Ronald Osborn. Osborn recalls having "dared to propose" at the first meeting of the Commission that restorationism would not be an adequate methodology for Restructure. That restoration "was no longer tenable in the light of current understanding of the New Testament"[11] had been one of the conclusions of the Panel of Scholars (see chapter three). Kenneth Teegarden, administrative secretary of the Commission on Brotherhood Restructure from 1965 to the completion of the Commission's work, has estimated that 100 of the 130 members of the Commission read the *Reports* of the Panel of Scholars, which provided "the theological and sociological underpinnings for the process" of Restructure.[12]

Three members of the Commission on Restructure had themselves contributed to the Panel of Scholars' repudiation of restorationism. In the *Reports*, Ronald Osborn had written, "Restorationism has been rejected or redefined beyond recognition by Disciple scholarship (e.g., as found in the faculties of accredited seminaries), and the notion that the New Testament is a constitution for the church is repudiated by biblical scholars generally."[13] A second contributor to the Panel of Scholars *Reports* who was also a member of the Commission

Ideological Options in Restructure

was Ralph G. Wilburn. He had concluded that since "the restoration idea is basically a false concept.... it would seem wise to abandon the use of the term altogether."[14] A third person common to the Panel of Scholars and the Commission on Brotherhood Restructure also served on the commission's Central Committee and chaired the Task Committee on Basic Documents.[15] This was W. B. Blakemore. Blakemore concurred with his colleagues Osborn and Wilburn: "Whatever the historic significance for Disciples of 'restorationism,' it is not our tradition."[16]

The Commission on Brotherhood Restructure incorporated the conception of restorationism that had been expressed in the writings of the Panel of Scholars into its own documents. That is, restorationism was honored as part of the past tradition of the Disciples of Christ but it was not to be the method by which new structures were to be created. Rather than restructuring along lines provided by a notion of restoration, the Commission saw its task as being "guided by principles which characterize the wholeness of Christ's church." Seven such principles were articulated by the Commission:

I. The Brotherhood Seeks Structures Rooted in Christ's Ministry Made Known through Scripture . . .
II. The Brotherhood Seeks Structures that are Comprehensive in Ministry and in Mission . . .
III. The Brotherhood Seeks Structures by which Congregations May Fulfill their Ministries . . .
IV. The Brotherhood Seeks Structures that are Responsibly Inter-Related . . .
V. The Brotherhood Seeks Structures that Manifest both Unity and Diversity . . .
VI. The Brotherhood Seeks to be Ecumenical . . .
VII. The Brotherhood Seeks Faithful in Stewardship

In terms of the four traditional values of the Campbell-Stone movement, the principles which guided the Commission on Brotherhood Restructure carried forward a heavy emphasis on unity and mission. This emphasis was sometimes stated in terms of ecumenicity and ministry. Although the first principle refers to the rooting of structure in Scripture, this is not understood in restorationist terms.[17]

The repudiation of the restoration ideal must be understood in the light of the commitment of the leaders of Restructure to the Campbell-Stone movement's other ideals. Restoration was understood as a *method* by which the movement hoped to achieve the union of the Church universal and the evangelization of the world. Thus, the unity and the mission of the Church had priority over the particular method by which they were pursued. Therefore, if restorationism appeared to be a hindrance rather than a viable method to achieve the Church's penultimate and ultimate goals, it was to be abandoned.

The Cooperative Disciples had participated in the ecumenical movement and this, rather than restorationism, seemed to be the more promising contemporary method of seeking the goal of Christian union. So the Commission encouraged Disciples to continue "wholehearted participation in the ecumenical movement."[18] The Commission not only showed its commitment to Christian unity as sought in the ecumenical movement, but also pointed to the relationship between unity and mission, or ministry. "The Christian Churches (Disciples of Christ) should continue with other bodies vital conversations and negotiations looking toward larger unions which may more fully manifest the unity given us in Christ and be more fruitful for the ministry of Christ's church in the world."[19]

Virgil Sly also emphasized the linkage between mission and unity in his 1963 paper for the Commission and called attention to the primacy of mission:

> Although mission and unity had their origins at about the same time ... and ... advanced together in close contact during the past one hundred and fifty years, the fact is the creative impulse and demand for unity has largely arisen from Christian mission. . . .
> ... Through all the multitudinous, multiform and varied threads of the cloth of Christian unity there is one common thread that glows like gold in the pattern of the warp. At virtually every point these threads trace their origin within the enterprise of Christian mission.[20]

An important part of the background of Sly's statement was the theologizing on mission that had undergirded the UCMS's 1959 "Strategy of World Mission" and which the UCMS and the Council on Christian Unity had sponsored through their Commission on the Theology of Mission. These theological reflections were neither complete nor widely known as Restructure progressed. But mission leaders such as Sly had come to clarity on the conviction that mission is one mission and that it belongs fundamentally to God.[21]

The ideals of unity and mission, then, were strongly affirmed in the process of Restructure and seen as linked together. Since the restoration idea was seen as an encumbrance to the pursuit of unity and mission it was not a major principle in Restructure in the eyes of the Commission's leadership.

Ideological Options in Restructure

The fourth traditional ideal of the Campbell-Stone movement is that of liberty. Liberty was neither as enthusiastically affirmed as unity and mission nor so clearly abandoned as restoration. The best summary of the position of the leaders of Restructure on the issue of liberty, or freedom, is that they advocated "freedom with responsibility."[22]

By the 1964 assembly of the International Convention, several "trends and directions for developing a design" had been accepted that attempted to embody responsible freedom. These included the affirmation "that each manifestation of the church shall have freedom and responsibility to exercise its appropriate functions under its natural authority . . . and to respond appropriately at its level to the Lordship of Jesus Christ."[23]

Like the concept of restoration, the concept of liberty as originally held by members of the Campbell-Stone movement had to be qualified. The character of the qualification placed upon the traditional concept of liberty was an emphasis upon responsibility that grew out of an understanding of the missionary and ecumenical nature of the Church.

> The nature of the Church derives from its task. This task is now, and has always been, the effective communication of the good news of the love of God in Christ Jesus . . .
>
> The Church is ecumenical. . . . The deeper reality and nature of the Church are found in its ecumenicity rather than in its fragmented, local nature. The nature of the local Church, the universal Church in a particular place, is seen in its congregational freedom and responsibility. . . . We find ourselves in 1964 unwilling to continue the compromise between the concept of the wholeness of the Church which is ours historically and the practice (begun in 1849) of fragmentation resulting from individual rather than corporate responsibility. It is to secure greater freedom to act responsibly that we come to restructure.[24]

In addition to linking the idea of responsibility with that of freedom, the leaders of Restructure recognized that another issue, that of authority, was closely related to freedom and responsibility.[25] W. B. Blakemore's three lectures to the 1965 meeting of the Commission on Brotherhood Restructure were on "Freedom, Authority, and Responsibility in the Church." Blakemore's lecture on "Authority" noted: "It is precisely when we have identified the right authority that we have freedom in the church. But it must be the right authority—Christian conscience—and Christian conscience is always full of responsibility."[26]

Ronald Osborn points out that one place that the Restructure leaders expressed their conviction as to the authority of Jesus Christ in the Church was in their refusal to use the phrase "the autonomy of the congregation" in the *Provisional Design for the Christian Church (Disciples of Christ)*. "Freedom, yes! Autonomy, no! For Jesus Christ is Lord both of the disciple and the church. And Christian freedom is found in joyful commitment to Christ and to the will of God."[27] This was the concept of freedom, authority, and responsibility that was adopted in the *Provisional Design*. The *Design* very carefully identified the "rights recognized and safeguarded to congregations." But it also stressed the lordship of Christ and spoke of "the responsibilities by which congregations voluntarily demonstrate their mutual concern for the mission and witness of the whole church."[28]

The commitments of the leaders of Restructure relative to the historic values of the Campbell-Stone movement are perhaps best summarized in the language of the *Provisional Design*, the fruit of their labors in Restructure. The Preamble states, in part,

> Within the universal body of Christ, the Christian Church (Disciples of Christ) manifests itself organizationally in free and voluntary relationships. . . .
> In order that the Christian Church through free and voluntary relationships may faithfully express the ministry of Christ made known in scripture, may provide comprehensiveness in witness, mission, and service, . . . may assure both unity and diversity, and may advance responsible ecumenical relationships, as a response to God's covenant, we commit ourselves to one another in adopting this provisional design for the Christian Church.

The leaders of Restructure, then, advocated a version of the historic values of the Campbell-Stone movement that emphasized the unity (universality, wholeness, ecumenicity) and mission (ministry, witness, service) of the Church. They recognized that structures must be adapted, rather than "restored": "The nature of the church, given by Christ, remains constant; . . . yet in faithfulness to its mission it continues to adapt its structures to the needs and patterns of a changing world." They affirmed that the authority of Jesus Christ added a dimension of responsibility to the freedom and voluntaryism that characterized their tradition: "All dominion in the church belongs to Jesus Christ, its Lord and head, and any exercise of authority in the church on earth stands under his judgment."[29] It was this adaptation of the movement's traditional values that was adopted

Ideological Options in Restructure

and accepted by the main body of Cooperative Disciples who became the Christian Church (Disciples of Christ).[30]

The second group that articulated an ideological option during Restructure eventually organized as the Disciples for Mission and Renewal under the leadership of Charles H. Bayer. This group was made up of "a significant number of younger ministers and laypersons" who were "disturbed" by the organizational emphasis of Restructure and "wanted to emphasize the mission of the church and its renewal. For several years a publication known as *Bread and Wine* was issued and distributed [by Disciples for Mission and Renewal] to members and to persons attending the General Assembly."[31]

The Disciples for Mission and Renewal have been called a "loyal opposition," but they are better characterized as "disappointed proponents" of Restructure. That is, they advocated a more thorough restructuring of the Disciples of Christ than that which occurred. This position is clearly stated in an article from the 1968 issue of *Bread and Wine*, "The Mountain Has Labored":

> But at least the mouse has been born alive....
>   All right—we support Restructure, but what has really changed? We have adopted an interim procedure with provisional machinery. Who knows how long it will be until these provisional plans are changed and we find some fresh new approach to denominational life? What the provisional design does, essentially, is to change some names.

The article goes on to say that some "redesigning" that was "long overdue" was to occur, but expresses its author's disappointment that

> the sacrosanct Congregation is still a law unto itself (autonomous). The design is full of euphemisms for autonomy like "free and voluntary" and "by mutual consent." From the very beginning, when there were some suggestions that "autonomy was a dead issue", we have backed off and most of the public relations materials produced by the Brotherhood tried to say, "Look, your darn congregation is safer than ever. We can't touch it, won't touch it, and don't want to touch it." We are not at all sure that for any part of the church to consider that it is a [sic] "a law unto itself" is a responsible Biblical position....
>   ... Many of us hoped that Restructure could have produced something exciting and fresh. We had a unique opportunity to say a new word on behalf of the American church. What we said was

something pedestrian and tired. Why two thousand churches should want to withdraw from the Brotherhood over what was in the *Provisional Design* boggles the mind.

Even so, we support what little Restructure has done. It may make the next steps easier. It may give us a little better way of moving where we ought to be, and for that we are thankful.[32]

This is the language of disappointed hopes rather than opposition.

The leader of the Disciples for Mission and Renewal, Charles H. Bayer, was pastor of the University Disciples of Christ Church at Chicago. Bayer had previously been pastor of the First Christian Church at Alexandria, Virginia. He had received both his undergraduate and seminary education at Phillips University. Bayer was active in the organized life of Cooperative Disciples and in interdenominational councils of churches.[33] He was also a member of the Commission on Brotherhood Restructure.[34]

The source of Bayer's disappointment in the process of Restructure may be seen in a paper that he presented to the Commission on Brotherhood Restructure in July 1963, "The Church's Need for Renewal and the Spiritual Vitality of the Brotherhood." Bayer wrote of the "desire for a more efficient, smoother running, more productive denominational organization" that underlay Restructure, but insisted that "a philosophy of salvation by promotional engineering" would not address the denomination's need. What was needed was "vitality, relevance, a sense of the essence of the church, a discovery of the nature of the church, and a recovery of the mission of the Christian."

Bayer listed some of the problems that reorganization would not solve in the life of the Disciples. These included the problem of "internal division" between the Independents and the Cooperatives, the divisions in the Church generally, competition within the denomination, unrest in the ministry, and the "irrelevance of the institutional church." In contrast, Bayer wrote of "renewal" as "the work of the Holy Spirit, by which the church is hearing the Gospel, coming under the judgment of its Lord, being shattered and re-formed." This renewal would include the church's "rethinking of its message and its mission; the recovery of its revolutionary role in society [and] the breaking down of its destructive identification with the worst in society."[35]

Bayer's emphasis, and the emphasis of the Disciples for Mission and Renewal, was upon a concept of renewal that would move the Disciples toward "a more secular theology and ... commitment to the social program of the New Left."[36] This agenda is suggested in the "Basic Affirmations" articulated by the group in 1967:

Ideological Options in Restructure

1. We affirm that the Christian Gospel is announced so that the *world* might be renewed.
2. We affirm that God speaks through secular structures as well as through religious structures.
3. We affirm that the church is an agency through which God is calling the world into wholeness, and that the shape of her structure does matter.
4. We affirm that importance of action by the individual Christian as he works either within or without traditional church structures.
5. We affirm that the fundamental, theological, and liturgical task is to put the Christian affirmation in terms modern secular man can hear.
6. We affirm that the Lord of the World calls institutions, sacred and secular, to radical reformation so that justice and humanization might become incarnate in the social fabric.[37]

These affirmations contain an emphasis upon "wholeness" and upon mission that give them some contact with the perspective of the leaders of Restructure. Additionally, the leaders of the Restructure did use the language of reformation and renewal. However, there is an emphasis upon the "secular" which is present in the affirmations of the Disciples for Mission and Renewal which does not characterize the mainstream of the Restructure process.

Clearly, Bayer's group represented a constituency within the Disciples of Christ who were ready for a more radical departure from the traditional emphases of the Campbell-Stone movement than that which was represented by Restructure. "The Mountain Has Labored" is basically a criticism of the pattern of continuity which existed between the restructured Christian Church (Disciples of Christ) and the Cooperative structures which had preceded it.[38] Bayer's paper before the Commission shows what his stance was relative to the traditional values of the Campbell-Stone movement. First of all, restoration was supplanted by renewal as the way in which structures are thought to arise within the Church:

> Renewal does not suggest that there ought to be no church structures.... As we hear the voice of Christ, as we open ourselves to the Spirit of God, are shattered and renewed, there will come from the grave where we have laid away our reliance on the institution, a new being. Organization will develop. There will be bones and muscle as well as heart, but structure will flow out of meaning. Organization will develop to serve purpose and essence.

Bayer agrees with the leadership of Restructure that restoration as the method of seeking Christian union has given way to participation in the ecumenical movement. He writes of the "frustration" of Disciples in this arena:

> Our contribution of outstanding personalities in the inter-church movement is without equal in this nation, but as a denomination we don't quite seem to fit in. Part of the reasons for the calling of this commission was a sense that we have got to become a more solid, responsible body if anybody is ever going to be able to negotiate seriously with us.[39]

The commitment to the ecumenical movement is clearly present in this statement. Also present is the suggestion that "responsibility" needs to take the place of "amorphous, gelatinous congregationalism" in order for the ecumenical "frustration" to end. Thus Bayer seems to share not only the perspective on restoration that characterized the leaders of Restructure, but also their commitment to the ecumenical movement and reservations this commitment had created about the traditional understanding of liberty that had characterized the Campbell-Stone movement.

The traditional value upon which Bayer disagrees with the leaders of Restructure is that of mission. As the "Basic Affirmations of Disciples for Mission and Renewal" show, Bayer's group conceived of their mission—their "fundamental, theological, and liturgical task"—as putting "the Christian affirmation in terms modern secular" humanity could comprehend.[40] This "secular theology" is not a major dimension of the *Design* which came out of Restructure.

In terms of the traditional values of the Campbell-Stone movement, the Bayer group basically stood with the leaders of Restructure in their disavowal of the restoration idea, commitment to the ecumenical movement, and desire to qualify the liberty ideal with a sense of responsibility. The Disciples of Mission and Renewal believed that the process of Restructure had failed to effectively attach responsibility to freedom, and, in fact, believed that little change had been accomplished with Restructure.[41] This group differed most with the leaders of Restructure in their concept of mission.

Another group which articulated an ideological perspective distinguishable from that of the leaders of Restructure was the Atlanta Declaration Committee. This group was begun by Laurence V. Kirkpatrick, the general secretary of the World Convention of Churches of Christ. This organization "serve[d] the Brotherhood of Christian Churches, Churches of Christ, and Disciples of Christ Churches."[42] The World Convention normally met at five-year intervals for

Ideological Options in Restructure 221

the purpose of fellowship and inspiration. It was supported by both Independent and Cooperative Disciples.[43] Kirkpatrick was a native of Oklahoma and was educated at Phillips University (B.A.), Yale (B.D.), and Columbia University (Ph.D.). He served in several pastorates before joining the staff of the World Council of Christian Education in 1959. In 1961 Kirkpatrick was a consultant of the third assembly of the World Council of Churches in New Delhi, India. He was a member of the board of directors of the Board of Church Extension and the board of the graduate seminary of Phillips University.[44] It was Kirkpatrick who convened the Atlanta Declaration Committee, who made the initial contacts and got it started, but it was Robert W. Burns who "did most of the work after it got organized."[45]

It is Burns's name that is most closely associated with the Atlanta Declaration Committee.[46] The group got its name from the fact that Burns agreed to let the group that Kirkpatrick had convened meet at the Peachtree Christian Church in Atlanta, Georgia, where Burns was pastor. Later, Burns became the secretary of the Atlanta Declaration Committee and the editor of its documents.[47]

Burns had been the minister of the Peachtree Christian Church since 1930. Prior to becoming pastor there he had been the minister of Disciples congregations in Iowa and Missouri. Burns's background was strongly Disciples of Christ. His father was Walter Scott Burns. Robert was reared in the famous Union Avenue Christian Church in St. Louis. He attended Drake University, completed his B.A. degree at Washington University in St. Louis, and earned his B.D. degree from Eden Theological Seminary. Burns served as the parliamentarian of the International Convention of Disciples of Christ throughout the 1950s. In 1962-63 he was president of the International Convention.[48] Burns was a member of the Commission on Brotherhood Restructure and the Commission's Central Committee.[49]

The Atlanta Declaration Committee was convened and principally led by persons who were active, Cooperative Disciples. Burns himself had been strongly in favor of Restructure in the beginning.[50] What changed Burns's mind about Restructure and the crucial issue in his later opposition to it was his conviction that the real purpose of Restructure was to prepare the Disciples of Christ for participation in a merger along the lines being discussed in the Consultation on Church Union (COCU).[51] The perception that Restructure was connected to COCU is strongly reflected in the literature that was produced and distributed by the Atlanta Declaration Committee.[52] In addition to Robert Burns, historian A. T. DeGroot and Frank N. Gardner (professor of Christian thought at Drake University and a member of the Panel of Scholars) wrote for the Atlanta group.[53] Both DeGroot and Gardner focused much of their criticism upon COCU and the kind of ecclesiology it might eventually advocate.[54]

The original document of the Atlanta Declaration Committee was issued on May 4, 1967. It was authorized by a "Progress Committee" chaired by another well-known Disciple, George C. Stuart. Stuart had received his undergraduate and seminary education at Texas Christian University. He had served congregations in Texas, Tennessee, Illinois, Michigan, and Florida. He had been a member of the Disciples delegation to the World Council of Churches in 1954. In 1957, he joined the faculty of Christian Theological Seminary, where he remained for four years as head of the department of preaching.[55] Stuart had written several works for publication and, along with Burns, DeGroot and Gardner, wrote for the Atlanta group.[56]

One of the documents that Stuart wrote, *The Wrong Fork*, took its name from W. E. Garrison's 1964 Address, *A Fork in the Road*. Stuart's work included "Thoughts on Restructure" by W E. Garrison. Although Garrison was not a member of the Atlanta Declaration Committee, his views on Restructure were in agreement with those of the group's chairman.[57] Thus, the Atlanta Declaration Committee could claim the sympathy of one of the "deans" of Disciples of Christ historians, W. E. Garrison, and could claim the other, A. T. DeGroot, as a member. The "well-known ministers" who comprised most of the membership of the Atlanta group[58] also included a member of the Panel of Scholars (Gardner) and a former Disciples seminary professor (Stuart). Both DeGroot and Garrison tie this group to the "old-line liberals."[59]

What was the character of the opposition of this "loyal," "well-known," and, in part, "liberal" group to Restructure? That question may be answered in terms of the four traditional ideals of the Campbell-Stone movement.

First of all, the Atlanta group differed from the leaders of Restructure in their evaluation of the validity of the principle of restoration. Whereas the characteristic understanding of the restoration ideal among the leaders of Restructure was that it had been part of an honored past but had to be abandoned, the characteristic understanding among the Atlanta group, according to Robert W. Burns, was the affirmation of "the restoration principle interpreted in a nonlegalistic way." Burns identified the position of the Atlanta Declaration Committee as being between that of the leaders of Restructure who had substituted ecumenism for restoration and the Independents who were "legalistic restorationists." To Burns, restoration meant

> getting back to original, authentic, apostolic Christianity. Now, notice the words I used. I did not use the word "primitive." Original,

Ideological Options in Restructure

authentic, apostolic Christianity. Getting back to what Christianity was when it came fresh from the hands of Christ himself.

This position is differentiated by Burns from that of the Independents: "It's ... whether you're trying to restore the *best* of the spiritual values in the New Testament or whether you're trying to restore the mechanical forms."[60]

In 1964 Burns was invited to speak at Milligan College, an Independent college in Tennessee.[61] He was asked to speak on the topic, "Restoration: Where Do We Go from Here in Conventions and Agencies." Burns wrote to "all 131 of our [Cooperative Disciples] agency presidents, as well as to the executive heads of our state or county conventions." Burns received about eighty responses which he pulled together as the basis of his lecture. On the idea of restoration, Burns concluded:

> By restoration we mean that the church ought to teach now what Christ and the apostles taught as recorded in the New Testament. By restoration we mean that the church ought to expect now of her members what Christ and the apostles expected of the early Christians as revealed in the New Testament. By restoration we mean that Christ is Lord of all the Church and His will for us today may be known as we search the scriptures to discover the mind of Christ and His apostles on the issues they faced then and seek to understand what is the will of God for us today based on the will of God made known in Christ.[62]

Burns also addressed the issue of Restoration by Restructure. He called Restructure "the means by which we hope to restore the radiance of the apostolic church." In looking at the history of the restoration in the origins of the Campbell-Stone movement, Burns added, "In restoration by restructure we are expressing an understanding of the scriptural teaching about the church which was precious to our founding fathers." Burns also reported that some of his respondents had rejected the restoration idea, but added: "I emphasize that these who reject the restoration idea are a small minority among the persons with whom I have worked ... closely for over forty years."[63]

Another member of the Atlanta Declaration Committee who had made clear his views on restoration was A. T. DeGroot: In his 1960 *Restoration Principle*, DeGroot advocated restoration "defined in essentially spiritual terms" as opposed to "legalistic primitivism or restorationism" which he believed had "stunted the spiritual development and limited the growth of scores . . . of movements of this kind."[64]

Within the Atlanta Declaration Committee, then, there was a continued commitment to the ideal of restoration. There was disagreement on the one hand with the ideal's abandonment such as had been suggested in the *Panel of Scholars Reports* and by the methodology of the Commission on Brotherhood Restructure.[65] On the other hand, the Atlanta group did not advocate a "legalistic" restorationism such as that of the Independents, but a "spiritualized" version of the ideal.

It was on the issue of Christian unity that the Atlanta Declaration Committee differed most sharply with what they believed to be the position of the leaders of Restructure. Burns affirms that his main objection to Restructure was *not* an objection to the polity reflected in the *Provisional Design*, but to the relationship he perceived between Restructure and COCU. Burns believed that "the national officers had outrageously deceived the Brotherhood by saying there was no connection."[66] In the *Atlanta Declaration of Convictions and Concerns: With Commentary Authorized by the Atlanta Progress Committee*, the statement is made:

> It is time for candor in recognizing that Restructure is intimately related to the efforts of some to carry our Brotherhood into the proposed Church Union. At the Dallas convention a letter from George Beazley, Executive Secretary of the Council on Christian Unity, was read into the record. It reads, "If you want to hasten Church Union, push Restructure, because that way the local congregations will not have to vote on union. Otherwise, we would have to vote congregation by congregation on a proposed union." And it should be remembered that all area and national properties of *the* Christian Church could be taken over by the Church Union by a majority vote of the General Assembly.
>
> Alarming also is the attempt to discard any consensus of our people as the basis for Brotherhood action. Again, Mr. Beazley writes, "We are in the stage of trying to find some way in which a church truly catholic, truly evangelical, and truly reformed can be constituted. At the present state, opinions of people, whether conservative or liberal, are beside the point. You cannot establish a church simply by consensus."[67]

Ideological Options in Restructure

Burns and the others in the Atlanta Declaration Committee were concerned by the "connectionalism" that they saw as characterizing both the *Provisional Design* and COCU.[68]

The terms in which the Atlanta Declaration Committee understood the ideal of Christian unity were similar to those in which they understood the ideal of restoration. Their attitude toward COCU was clearly negative.[69] However, this was not opposition to the principle of unity. The Atlanta Declaration Committee drew a distinction between "institutional union" and "unity in faith."

> The unification of all our church life and mission under one correlated control may appear to be the answer to all our Brotherhood problems, but we believe such a result to be only wishful thinking. Institutional oneness has been attempted over and over again since the early days of the church, and never with success.... *Spiritual unity binds us together in a fellowship that transcends organizational ties.*[70]

Thus, the Atlanta group affirmed a "spiritual" understanding of unity which they contrasted to the more visible form of unity represented by COCU in much the same way that they supported a "spiritual" interpretation of restoration. Frank Gardner, while recognizing that the Disciples had "long advocated a 'plea for unity,'" suggested that "it is a debatable question as to whether 'Christian unity' and 'Church Union' are synonymous [*sic*] terms." Gardner saw as contrary to the traditions of the Disciples of Christ the acceptance by COCU of: creeds, the office of bishop, the baptism of both believers and infants, and the idea that only ordained persons should preside at the Lord's Supper.[71]

Burns believed that members of the Commission had attempted to distort history by suggesting that lay elders, who traditionally celebrated the Lord's Supper in Disciples churches, were actually ordained.[72] Ronald Osborn confirms that the "theologians and ecumenists" in the Commission did attempt, unsuccessfully, to have the office of elder included in the order of ministry in the *Design*. He also agrees with Burns that the motivation for so doing derived from their participation in COCU.[73] Burns recalled that he challenged the notion that there was a tradition of ordaining elders among Disciples of Christ and called for a "straw vote" on whether or not the practice was familiar to the members of the Commission. According to Burns, only a "pitiful little handful" of the members expressed familiarity with the practice.[74]

The fact that a considerable portion of the writings of the Atlanta group focused upon COCU reflects the group's underlying concern that the leaders of Restructure were committed to a merger along the lines of COCU but were not admitting this to the denomination as a whole.[75] For example, in the writings of A. T. DeGroot much of the focus was upon the notion of the historic episcopacy, in apostolic succession. DeGroot contrasted the lineage of the episcopal tradition with that of the "Free Church," in which tradition he included the Disciples of Christ.[76]

In terms of traditional Campbell-Stone ideals, the main issue with respect to COCU was that it seemed to be developing in the direction of a polity that violated the Disciples ideal of freedom.[77] The Atlanta group's adherence to the ideal of liberty so conditioned their commitment to the ideal of unity that they opposed both COCU, for being unity at the expense of liberty, and Restructure for being tied to COCU.[78]

In addition to opposing COCU, the Atlanta Declaration Committee touched upon the basic issue of unity in their expression of concern for the "internal" unity of the Campbell-Stone movement: "We hope to continue our relations with all disciples, including those in the Christian Church (Disciples of Christ), those who cooperate outside the present International Convention, and all others who belong to the Campbell-Stone movement."[79] The Atlanta group apparently regarded the attainment of greater unity within the Campbell-Stone movement as an integral part of a wider witness on the issue of Christian unity. Despite the fact that the division between Independents and Cooperatives was largely a reality, the continuation of a loosely defined structure would continue to permit a nominal unity between these groups. By maintaining this nominal unity, the Disciples of Christ could demonstrate that "unity with diversity is possible."[80]

Although W. E. Garrison was not a member of the Atlanta Declaration Committee, his "Thoughts on Restructure" were distributed by the Committee. The Committee also quoted approvingly from his *Fork in the Road* address.[81] In this address, Garrison expressed his hopes for the continuation of the nominal "internal" unity between Independents and Cooperatives. Garrison saw the maintenance of a loosely defined structure which would permit a range of divergent opinions to be embodied within it as not only the "right fork" for Disciples but also as "a microcosm of the United church."[82]

Common to the thought of Garrison, DeGroot, and Burns was the notion that the Campbell-Stone movement had something distinctive to offer in the quest for Christian unity.[83] To Garrison it was being "a pilot project for the united church." DeGroot described the Disciples' contribution in terms of "the restoration principle."[84] Burns believed that "the greatest gift we can give to the ecumenical movement today is a really free church."[85]

Ideological Options in Restructure

In a sense, Garrison, DeGroot, and Burns seemed to support *both* the ecumenical movement *and* a version of the "restoration plea." But by 1963 an emerging Disciples leadership saw *either* participation in a wider ecumenical movement as a partner with other Christian communities *or* the continued insistence upon the "restoration plea" as the basis for Christian unity as clear alternatives.[86] The Panel of Scholars and the Commission on Brotherhood Restructure, for the most part, came to advocate the former.[87] In the final analysis the Atlanta Declaration Committee "spiritualized" the "restoration plea," but they still were committed to it.[88]

Less clear than their stand on restoration, union, and liberty is the Atlanta Declaration Committee's conception of the character of the Church's mission. The members of the committee were concerned over evangelism. This concern was expressed in their reporting of a loss of membership experienced by Disciples during a period of population growth in the United States.[89] The Church's mission was tied, in the thought of the Atlanta group, to their principal concern—freedom. DeGroot claimed that the free churches had "stimulated and led in the creative upsurge" of global mission. Further, he believed that it had been "democratic idealism" that had given "success to the popular, people's churches in North America."[90]

DeGroot linked freedom of polity with success in missions. But the "mission" of the Campbell-Stone movement, according to the Atlanta group, was the maintenance "of a voluntary, free-consent cooperative Brotherhood"—a "free church" rather than a denomination.[91] The Atlanta group saw the mission of that "Brotherhood" in terms of expressing greater unity within the Campbell-Stone movement and "ever widening" their "free fellowship."[92]

The differences between the understanding of the Atlanta Declaration Committee and that of the leaders of Restructure relative to the traditional values of the Campbell-Stone movement touch each of the four ideals. The leaders of Restructure basically jettisoned restoration, while the Atlanta group "spiritualized" it. The leaders of Restructure stated their commitment to the ecumenical movement, while the Atlanta group opposed the ecumenical movement's expression in COCU and sought mainly "internal" and possibly "microcosmic" Christian unity. The leaders of Restructure sought to qualify liberty with an enhanced commitment to responsibility, while the Atlanta group exalted the value of liberty. The leaders of Restructure understood the mission of the church in ecumenical terms, while the Atlanta group understood the mission of the Campbell-Stone movement to be, properly, the maintenance of "the free traditions of the Restoration Movement."[93] The Atlanta Declaration Committee differed even more sharply with the Disciples for Mission and Renewal. The continuation of the autonomy of the local congregation that was so sharply criticized by the Disciples for Mission and Renewal was one of the major emphases of the Atlanta Declaration Committee.[94] The Atlanta group's Restoration Movement-centered concept of mission contrasted sharply with the Renewal group's "secular" concept of mission. While the Disciples for Mission and Renewal were calling for a unity based on the "wholeness" of the *world*, the Atlanta group even had reservations about the wholeness of the Church—if it compromised freedom.

The Atlanta Declaration Committee did oppose Restructure, but it was a "loyal opposition." It was an opposition that came from within the ranks of Cooperative Disciples.[95] The Atlanta Declaration Committee encouraged congregations to stay with the restructuring Christian Church (Disciples of Christ).[96] And, for the most part, the members of the Committee itself stayed with the Christian Church (Disciples of Christ). Although the members of the Atlanta group were concerned about maintaining ties with the Independents, they were not themselves in the Independent community.[97]

The fourth group that articulated an ideological alternative to Disciples of Christ during the Restructure process were Independent Disciples. The Independent point of view on Restructure was mainly articulated by James DeForest Murch.[98] Murch had taken a leadership role in the development of a literature, in a channel for the support of missions, of a national convention, and of educational institutions which were designed to be alternatives to those of the Cooperative Disciples.[99] Murch was also a leader in the formation of the National Association of Evangelicals, a group designed to be an alternative to the National Council of Churches.[100] Murch's Independent affiliation extended as far back as the actual division between Cooperative and Independent Disciples.[101]

The organization of an Independent group for the purpose of making an impact upon Restructure occurred in a city that had long been known as a center of Independent strength. Canton, Ohio, was the home of the largest church of Disciples at the time of the creation of the North American Christian Convention. Its pastor, P. H. Welshimer, was the chairman of the committee that formed the North American Christian Convention.[102] It was at a series of meetings at that same church, First Christian Church, Canton, that James DeForest Murch proposed that a group be organized to oppose Restructure. From these meetings Murch returned to his home in Washington, D.C. and wrote *Freedom or Restructure?*. B. D. Phillips agreed to underwrite the cost of having this pamphlet sent to every church in the "whole Brotherhood." Later, a Committee for the Preservation of the Brotherhood was formed under whose name the pamphlet and several other documents were eventually distributed throughout the Disciples of Christ. In addition to Murch, the committee consisted of B. D. Phillips, Sherill Storey, Mildred Welshimer Phillips, Dean E. Walker, Murhl Rogers, Rolland Ehrman, and Harold Davis.[103] Storey and Rogers were Independent ministers.[104] Dean E. Walker was the president of Milligan college.[105] Rolland Ehrman was the vice-president of the T. W. Phillips Gas and Oil Company, an attorney, and "deeply involved in the development of Emmanuel School of Religion,"[106] which was begun by the faculty of Milligan College.[107]

Benjamin Dwight Phillips, who provided the financial means to distribute what James DeForest Murch wrote on Restructure, was the central figure around whom much of the committee revolved. He was the chairman of the committee, and his wife, Mildred (daughter of P. H. Welshimer), and son-in-law and business associate, Rolland Ehrman, were also members.[108] B. D. Phillips was the son of Thomas W. Phillips—"oil producer, congressman, religious writer, and philanthropist."[109] Thomas W. Phillips was one of the original underwriters of the *Christian Standard*[110] and was the author of *The Church of Christ, by a Layman*. He was a major contributor not only to Phillips University, but to most of the educational, missionary, and benevolent organizations of the Disciples of Christ.[111] B. D. Phillips succeeded his father in the leadership of the "industrial holdings of the family"[112] and continued the financial support of Disciples of Christ causes.

Phillips University, Hiram College, Culver-Stockton College, Bethany College, and the Disciples of Christ Historical Society were prominent examples of Disciples of Christ institutions which received substantial financial contributions from the Phillips family under B. D.'s leadership. However, in the 1960s Phillips began to have misgivings about the direction that some of the historically Disciples-related colleges were going. Specifically, he saw that the "Restoration Plea" was not being emphasized at these institutions. Gradually he withdrew his support from the colleges related to the Cooperative Disciples and concentrated upon those of the Independent camp. The Bible colleges of the Independents reflected Phillips's own educational philosophy.[113] The older Disciples of Christ colleges were becoming liberal arts colleges.

B. D. Phillips's reaction to the findings of the Panel of Scholars indicates that he was deeply dissatisfied with the ideological evolution that had taken place among the leaders of Cooperative Disciples thought.[114] His personal doctrinal views were those which by the time of Restructure were characteristic of the Independents.

The attacks of the Committee for the Preservation of the Brotherhood upon Restructure came in basically four salvos relatively early in the Restructure process. Murch's first pamphlet, *Freedom or Restructure?* circulated early in 1964.[115] Phillips financed the sending of four copies to every congregation listed in the *Year Book of the Christian Churches (Disciples of Christ)*. The pamphlet was issued anonymously.[116] About the same time, Dean E. Walker circulated a pamphlet, *The Tradition of Christ*.[117] The second salvo came early in 1965 in the form of another anonymous pamphlet written by Murch and financed by Phillips. This time the title was *The Truth about Restructure*.[118] The third wave came in the form of *Restructure Reports* which were first issued by the Committee for the Preservation of the Brotherhood in late 1965.[119] The fourth salvo was Phillips's sending out of one thousand copies of Murch's book, *The Free Church*, to "key churches free of charge."[120] This and another *Restructure Report* came out in 1966.[121] The Independent Disciples' opposition to Restructure emerged well before the "loyal opposition" of the Atlanta Declaration Committee.[122]

The basic thesis of *Freedom or Restructure* is stated in its opening paragraphs. Allegedly speaking for the "two million of us" who "have some relationship with the International Convention," Murch writes:

> The freedom of our local churches has been a long-standing, deeply-cherished and zealously-guarded characteristic of our fellowship. Our Supreme Head is Jesus Christ. Our doctrine and discipline are to be found in the New Testament and the New Testament alone. Our local churches are free to conduct their own affairs without extracongregational interference. . . .
>
> Now this freedom is being challenged by the International Convention's plan to "Restructure the Brotherhood."
>
> The International Convention . . . is moving to become a full-fledged denomination with centralized ecclesiastical authority. . . .
>
> State and regional conventions are being reorganized as arms of the central denominational machine. . . .
>
> Local churches are being deprived of their rights.

The pamphlet's author sees Restructure as part of a "general design which has been well-known to an inner circle of Convention leadership for perhaps twenty years." The Commission is viewed as "not at all representative," and "as an additional safeguard that the intentions and goals of the 'palace guard' will be achieved," the "actual work of the Commission" would be accomplished by

Ideological Options in Restructure

an even smaller and less representative group—the Central and Executive Committees. The pamphlet identifies changes that Restructure would purportedly bring to the conventions, agencies, congregations, and ecumenical activities of the Disciples of Christ.[123] These changes are expressed mainly in terms of moving toward a "centralized denominational body which can control all phases of church work, all church properties and endowments and can speak officially for the whole brotherhood." This "centralized denominational body" would have "full legal authority to represent the Disciples . . . in all relationships with other denominations, even to effecting merger . . . with an ecumenical World Church in which all traces of our distinctive testimony as a people would be lost forever."

The pamphlet hits hardest on two issues: the potential loss of church property by local congregations and the potential of Restructure as a step in the direction of "ecumenicity and merger." An essentially local concept of church and an unconcealed hostility to the ecumenical movement pervade the pamphlet.[124] The pamphlet was designed to appeal to local congregations' fears of losing their property and their distinctive identity.[125] These same emphases were carried forward in *The Truth about Restructure*.

The Truth about Restructure focused upon the Commission on Brotherhood Restructure's "The Nature of the Structure Our Brotherhood Seeks." The only purpose of the Commission's document, according to the pamphlet, is the creation of a "denomination with strong centralized authority" such as had been described in the previous pamphlet. In *The Truth about Restructure* Murch contrasts the polity that he sees in Restructure with that which he believes to be the pattern of the New Testament.

> The churches planted by the Apostles were distinctly local institutions. Nothing like a national church or an area church having jurisdiction over many congregations . . . appears in the New Testament. . . . The kind of structure and unity being currently proposed by the advocates of Restructure originated in later church history (A.D. 100 to 400) and was without benefit of Apostolic teaching or example. It had a humanly devised centralized episcopal structure, supplanting local self-governing churches and eventuated finally in the ecclesiastical organization known as the Roman Catholic Church.

Murch saw the Commission on Brotherhood Restructure as being committed to bringing every function, congregation, and agency of the Disciples of Christ "into subjection to their humanly structured Super-Church."[126] The assumptions of restorationism are clearly the basis of *The Truth about Restructure*. The idea that the New Testament contains a single pattern of church polity, an anti-Roman Catholicism rooted in an understanding of history which identifies the Roman Catholic Church with the loss of the pattern, a radically local conception of the church, and a stress on the assumed unique insight and importance of the writer's own particular religious communion are all present in the pamphlet.[127]

Further, Murch states his conception of the diametrical opposition of ecumenism and restorationism. He comments on prior unity efforts by the Disciples of Christ: "Every consultation and negotiation is marked by some kind of compromise or surrender of the distinctive position of the Restoration Movement." Murch states the issue, as he sees it, most clearly in a contrast he draws between "our present and historic practice," in which "the unity of all Christians is sought through . . . restoration," and the "proposed practice under Restructure," in which "Christian unity is sought through . . . the creation of an Ecumenical World Church."[128]

That Restructure was, in fact, the "strategy for merger" and that the way to prevent this "strategy" was to preserve "local church autonomy" continued to be the basic thesis of the documents of the Committee for the Preservation of the Brotherhood.[129] The pamphlets even included legal advice on how congregations could secure "locally autonomous" status in the eyes of the law.[130]

In terms of the traditional emphases of the Campbell-Stone movement, the Committee for the Preservation of the Brotherhood was oriented strongly toward the ideals of restoration and liberty. Their understanding of unity and mission was conditioned by their commitment to these first two values. Dean E. Walker summed up the Independent view well:

> The point . . . is that Christ did live and die and rise from the dead; that He did ascend to the Father; and that He did bring with Him a people of God, to whom He gave an order for recognition and nurture; and that these gifts are the norms and the constants in the subsequent history of the Church. The restoration of the Church's possession of this tradition of Christ and its obligation to exemplify this restoration is not only valid, it is the only ground of truly ecumenical unity and the only hope for the conversion of the world.[131]

Ideological Options in Restructure

In Walker's view, then, restoration is *the* basis for unity and mission. Murch concurs that Christian unity and Christian mission are only to be supported in connection with restoration:

> Christian missions, in the traditional sense of a program to send out missionaries to preach and teach the Gospel and establish churches "after the New Testament pattern", is gradually being abandoned. In its place has come something called "ecumenical mission" for which there is, as yet, no clear definition. *Missionaries* are being replaced by *fraternal workers* and the number of them is gradually diminishing. Mission properties are being transferred from the Disciples to foreign church bodies related to the World Council of Churches.[132]

In addition to its commitment to the principle of Christian unity only "through the restoration of the New Testament church,"[133] the Committee expressed its concern for the "internal" unity of the Campbell-Stone movement:

> We see the movement of Restructure of the Brotherhood as divisive. We believe that its advocates, if they achieve their aims, will be responsible for a disgraceful "church split" of enormous proportions. *We want to preserve the brotherhood.*[134]

Restoration was also the basis for liberty, according to Walker, in that "structurally, the return to the tradition of Christ restores only the Christian congregation," which in turn "allows liberty in methods of cooperation."[135] Murch advances the same point of view in the negative terms of opposition to the "centralized authority" for which no pattern "appears in the New Testament."

The Committee for the Preservation of the Brotherhood, then, represented an ideology which upheld a conservative restorationism. That is, it continued to advocate the notion that the New Testament contained a pattern of church structure. It regarded this single New Testament pattern as including, at minimum, "local congregational autonomy."[136] The Committee therefore rejected the ecumenical movement on the basis of that movement's not being predicated on restorationist assumptions with an attendant commitment to liberty.[137] Rather, this Independent group concerned itself with "internal" unity among branches of the Campbell-Stone movement. For similar reasons, "ecumenical missions" were opposed. Mission, like unity, was seen in exclusively restorationist terms.

The Committee for the Preservation of the Brotherhood articulated an option that contrasted most sharply with that of the Disciples for Mission and Renewal. It also bore little resemblance to the positions of the leaders of Restructure. Among Cooperatives, only the Atlanta Declaration Committee had sounded some of the same themes as the Independents. In contrast to all the Cooperative groups, the Committee for the Preservation of the Brotherhood advocated a pattern (not "spiritualized") restorationism. Although the Atlanta group was more doctrinally liberal, the Committee for the Preservation's concepts of mission and ecclesiastical/structural liberty bore some resemblance to those of the Atlanta group. The Independents' concepts of liberty and mission were opposed to both the "secular" emphasis of the Disciples for Mission and Renewal and the cooperative ecumenism of the Restructure leaders. The Committee for the Preservation's attitude of hostility to the ecumenical movement and to Cooperative Disciples life in general was different from the more focused fears of the Atlanta group on some forms of ecumenism and from the Atlanta group's history of Cooperative support. Of course, the Independents' hostility to ecumenism stood in even sharper contrast to the Restructure leaders.

Although the members of the Committee for the Preservation of the Brotherhood articulated the ideological perspective of Independents on Restructure, they were not the only Independents to make an impact on the process. According to Kenneth L. Teegarden, the loss of nearly 400,000 members that is reflected in the 1970 (as opposed to the 1960) Disciples *Year Book* was mainly due to "a successful campaign by 'independent' leaders to get congregations to withdraw their names from the official *Year Book* listing." Letters that were sent to congregations claimed that, as a result of changes brought about by Restructure,[138] congregations should remove their names from the *Year Book* or "lose their property and the right to call their own pastors."[139]

Considering the emphasis that both the Committee for the Preservation of the Brotherhood and the Atlanta Declaration Committee had placed upon presumed threats to congregational freedom in Restructure, it is understandable that some congregations withdrew. However, Teegarden explains that "the major portion of the 2000-plus congregations that had their names removed were thorough-going independent churches and had been carried out of historical tradition." Because of congregational freedom, "unreporting and marginal churches" had remained in the *Year Book*—their names could only be removed by their own action.[140] An irony in this entire development is that, in spite of all the talk about Restructure's being divisive, the restructured Christian Church (Disciples of Christ) enacted no device by which to exclude congregations. The "division" came totally on the basis of the voluntary withdrawal by congregations

Ideological Options in Restructure

of their names from the *Year Book*. Furthermore, the very "threatened" freedoms which were alleged to be the basis of the withdrawal were explicitly guaranteed in the *Design*.[141]

Of course, there were those who had wished to deny the existence of this second division. The concern for "internal" unity was one of the themes common to the Independents and the Atlanta Declaration Committee.[142] There were, no doubt, some congregations that were ideologically Independent but that maintained ties with the International Convention of Christian Churches (Disciples of Christ).[143] However, the congregations that withdrew that had actual ties with the Convention were relatively few. This fact is exhibited in two ways. First, most congregations that withdrew had not been sending reports to the *Year Book*. Second, most congregations that withdrew had been sending little or no financial support to the Cooperative causes of the Disciples of Christ. In commenting upon a listing of the congregations that were deleted from the *Year Book* during the late 1960s, Kenneth Teegarden pointed out that "in many cases" the most recent report received was twenty to forty years old. In addition, "nearly two-thirds of the outreach funds given to the Disciples" had been given by only forty of the nearly twenty-six hundred withdrawing congregations.[144] Thus the "division" was more *formally* than *actually* associated with Restructure.

Four distinct ideological positions were articulated during the process of Restructure. These may be summarized in terms of the four traditional ideals of the Campbell-Stone movement.

The leaders of Restructure emphasized the mission and the unity of the Church. Concepts of "wholeness" and "witness and service" are prominent in the *Design* produced by the leaders of Restructure.[145] Restoration was not a major influence on the *Design*.[146] The leaders of Restructure wished to qualify their communion's historic commitment to liberty with notions of "responsibility" and "covenantal relationship."[147] However, a continued commitment to liberty is evidenced in the representative structure of the General Assembly of the Christian Church (Disciples of Christ) and in the assurances written into the *Design* relative to the "free and voluntary" character of the interrelations in the Christian Church (Disciples of Christ).[148] The position articulated by the leaders of Restructure was accepted by the majority of the assembled representatives of the Christian Church (Disciples of Christ).[149]

The second ideological alternative was articulated by the Disciples for Mission and Renewal. This group exhibited no commitment to the principle of restoration. They were committed to the ideal of Christian unity and identified that ideal with ecumenical participation.[150] This group also was disappointed in the continued commitment to liberty manifested in the restructured church.[151]

Finally, the Disciples for Mission and Renewal pressed for a more "secular" (world-centered rather than church-centered) conception of the church's mission than that exhibited by any of the other three groups.

The ideological option offered by the Atlanta Declaration Committee included a "spiritualized" form of restorationism. The dominating commitment in this group was to liberty. The Atlanta group included some who were not hostile to the ecumenical movement, but who nonetheless believed that the unity and the mission to which the Disciples of Christ were committed had to be limited to forms that were compatible with freedom.

The Independents interjected into Restructure (through the Committee for the Preservation of Brotherhood) an undiminished commitment to the conception of restoration that was most strongly linked to a radical and localistic interpretation of congregational liberty. This primary commitment to restoration and liberty dictated the terms in which they understood both unity and mission. Unity and mission were supported only in terms exclusive to the Campbell-Stone movement.

These were the ideological alternatives placed before the Cooperative Disciples during the process of Restructure. With the adoption of the *Provisional Design* the alternative articulated by the leaders of Restructure was affirmed. The challenge then became living according to that expression of the movement's historic ideals.

---

1. Ronald E. Osborn, "Theological Issues in the Restructure of the Christian Church (Disciples of Christ): A Not Unbiased Memoir," *Mid-Stream* 19 (July 1980):278.

2. McAllister and Tucker, *Journey in Faith*, 446; Teegarden, interview; Charles Bayer, private interview, Lexington, Kentucky, 12 September 1990.

3. Robert W. Burns, letter to Dr. A. Dale Fiers, 21 July 1967, Atlanta Declaration Group File, Disciples of Christ Historical Society, Nashville, Tennessee.

4. Osborn, "Theological Issues in Restructure," 277.

5. Burns, letter to Fiers, 21 July 1967.

6. *Where Are We Going in Restructure?* (Atlanta: Atlanta Declaration Committee, 1580 Peachtree St. NW, [ca. 1967]), 5; George C. Stuart, *The Wrong Fork* (Atlanta: Atlanta Declaration Committee, 1580 Peachtree St. NW, [ca 1967]), 3-4.

7. Osborn, "Theological Issues in Restructure," 277-78.

8. Murch, *Adventuring for Christ*, 288-89.

Ideological Options in Restructure

9. Ibid.; Corey, *Attack and Controversy*; McAllister and Tucker, *Journey in Faith*, 444.
10. McAllister and Tucker, *Journey in Faith*, 444.
11. Osborn, "Theological Issues in Restructure," 282.
12. Teegarden, interview.
13. Osborn, "Crisis and Reformation," 26.
14. "Members of the Commission," 105; Wilburn, "Critique of the Restoration Principle," 241-42.
15. "Members of the Commission," 100; Lair, *Christian Church (Disciples of Christ)*, 67.
16. Blakemore, "Where Thought and Action Meet," 17.
17. Commission on Brotherhood Restructure, "The Nature of the Structure Our Brotherhood Seeks (Revised)," *Mid-Stream* 4 (Fall 1964):24-27.
18. Commission on Brotherhood Restructure, "Nature of the Structure," 27.
19. Ibid.
20. Virgil A. Sly, "The Importance of Brotherhood Restructure as Seen from an Ecumenical Perspective," *Mid-Stream* 3 (September 1963):60-62.
21. Toulouse, *Joined in Discipleship*, 185-91.
22. Granville T. Walker, "In Restructure Disciples Seek: Freedom with Responsibility," *World Call* 44 (May 1962):25.
23. Commission on Brotherhood Restructure, *Direction in Restructure*, 10.
24. Lester G. McAllister and Ronald E. Osborn, "Freedom through Restructure," *Commission's Inter-Comm*, 13 April 1964, 7-8. The *Commission's Inter-Comm* was a newsletter issued quarterly to members of the Commission by the Office of the Commission on Brotherhood Restructure in Indianapolis.
25. Ibid., 8.
26. W. B. Blakemore, "The Three Lectures, 'Freedom, Authority, and Responsibility in the Church,'" *Mid-Stream* (Fall 1965):55-56.
27. Osborn, "Theological Issues in Restructure," 299.
28. "Provisional Design," 18, 28.
29. Ibid., 18.
30. McAllister and Tucker, *Journey in Faith*, 446; Murch, *Adventuring for Christ*, 286.
31. McAllister and Tucker, *Journey in Faith*, 446.
32. "The Mountain Has Labored," *Bread and Wine*, 28 September 1968, 1.

33. McAllister and Tucker, *Journey in Faith*, 446; "Charles H. Bayer: Biographical Data," Biographical File, "Charles H. Bayer," Disciples of Christ Historical Society, Nashville, Tennessee.

34. "Members of the Commission," 100.

35. Charles H. Bayer, "The Church's Need for Renewal and the Spiritual Vitality of the Brotherhood: A Paper Presented to the Commission on Restructure, July, 1963," *Mid-Stream* 3 (September 1963):168-68, 169-72, 167.

36. Osborn, "Theological Issues in Restructure," 278.

37. Disciples for Mission and Renewal, Minutes of the Steering Committee, Chicago, 24-25 November 1967. (Mimeographed.)

38. "Mountain Has Labored," 1.

39. Bayer, "Need for Renewal," 177, 169.

40. Disciples for Mission and Renewal, Minutes.

41. "Mountain Has Labored," 1.

42. "Biographical Sketch of Dr. Laurence V. Kirkpatrick," Biographical File, "Laurence V. Kirkpatrick," Disciples of Christ Historical Society, Nashville, Tennessee.

43. McAllister and Tucker, *Journey in Faith*, 392.

44. "Biographical Sketch of Dr. Laurence V. Kirkpatrick."

45. Burns, interview.

46. McAllister and Tucker, *Journey in Faith*, 445; Lair, *Christian Church (Disciples of Christ)*, 94; Murch, *Adventuring for Christ*, 291.

47. Burns, interview; Atlanta Declaration Committee, *A Reaffirmation of Convictions and Concerns* ([Atlanta]: Atlanta Declaration Committee, 1968), 8.

48. "Dr. Robert W. Burns, President & Senior Counselor, Christian Church Counseling, Inc.: Biographical Sketch, December 1, 1978," (mimeographed, Personal Files of Robert W. Burns, Atlanta, Georgia.

49. "Members of the Commission," 100.

50. Robert W. Burns, "The Validity of Restructure: [Address to] Southern Christian Convention, Tupelo, Mississippi, April 14, 1966," Restructure File, Disciples of Christ Historical Society, Nashville, Tennessee.

51. Burns, interview.

52. Atlanta Declaration Committee, *Reaffirmation of Convictions and Concerns*, 3-4; *Atlanta Declaration of Convictions and Concerns: With Commentary Authorized by the Atlanta Progress Committee* (Atlanta: [Atlanta Declaration Committee], 1580 Peachtree St. NW, [ca. 1967]), 10-11; Barrett J. Whiteley, *Statements of Intent: "Connectionalism" and "COCU" in "A Provisional Design*

for the Christian Church (Disciples of Christ)" (Revised) ([Atlanta: Atlanta Declaration Committee], 1967).

53. *Where Are We Going in Restructure*, 5.

54. Frank N. Gardner, *March 21, 1968 [Letter to] the Reverend Dr. Robert W. Burns*, (Atlanta: [Atlanta Declaration Committee], 1580 Peachtree St., NW, [ca. 1968]); Alfred T. DeGroot, *Extra Ecclesiam Nulla Salus (or, Restructure Problems)* Fort Worth: By the Author, 1968).

55. "George C. Stuart: Biographical Data," Biographical File, "George C. Stuart," Disciples of Christ Historical Society, Nashville, Tennessee; Stuart, *Wrong Fork*, 1.

56. "George C. Stuart: Biographical Data"; *Where Are We Going in Restructure*, 5.

57. Stuart, *Wrong Fork*, 1, 3-4.

58. Osborn, "Theological Issues in Restructure," 277.

59. Stuart, *Wrong Fork*, 3-4; *Where Are We Going in Restructure*, 5.

60. Burns, interview.

61. Robert W. Burns, "Restoration: Where Do We Go from Here in Conventions and Agencies: A Message by Robert W. Burns, pastor of the Peachtree Christian Church, Atlanta, Georgia, August 19, 1964, at the Week of the Ministry, Milligan College, Tennessee," Atlanta Declaration Group File, Disciples of Christ Historical Society, Nashville, Tennessee, 1; McAllister and Tucker, *Journey in Faith*, 383.

62. Burns, "Restoration," 1, 3.

63. Ibid., 5, 11.

64. DeGroot, *Restoration Principle*, 7-8.

65. Osborn, "Crisis and Reformation," 26; Wilburn, "Critique of the Restoration Principle," 241; Blakemore, "Where Thought and Action Meet," 17; Commission on Brotherhood Restructure, "Nature of the Structure," 24; Osborn, "Theological Issues in Restructure," 282.

66. Burns, interview.

67. *Atlanta Declaration of Convictions and Concerns: With Commentary*, 10-11.

68. Burns, interview.

69. Burns, interview; Gardner, *[Letter to] The Reverend Dr. Robert W. Burns*; Whiteley, *Statements of Intent*.

70. *Where Are We Going in Restructure*, 1-4.

71. Gardner, *[Letter to] the Reverend Dr. Robert W. Burns*, 1-3.

72. Burns, interview.

73. Osborn, "Theological Issues in Restructure," 301-304.

74. Burns, interview.
75. Ibid.
76. Alfred T. DeGroot, *Episcopacy, In Succession* (Fort Worth: By the Author, n.d.), 3-25, 13-14.
77. Burns, interview.
78. Ibid.
79. Atlanta Declaration Committee, *Reaffirmation of Convictions and Concerns*, 4, 2.
80. Robert W. Burns, *The Whole Armor of God: An Address by Robert W. Burns, President, International Convention of Christian Churches (Disciples of Christ) at the Opening of the Assembly, October 11, 1963, Miami Beach, Florida, U.S.A.* (Atlanta: n.p., 1963), 14.
81. Stuart, *Wrong Fork*, 1.
82. Ibid; Winfred E. Garrison, *A Fork in the Road: A Penetrating Analysis of Decisions Facing Disciples* (Indianapolis: Pension Fund of Christian Churches, 1964), 6-11.
83. DeGroot, *Restoration Principle*, 171-75; W. E. Garrison, *Fork in the Road*, 11; Burns, *Whole Armor of God*, 14.
84. DeGroot, *Restoration Principle*, 134-35, 169-85.
85. Burns, *Whole Armor of God*, 14.
86. Osborn, "Crisis in Reformation," 25-26.
87. Ibid., 26; Wilburn, "Critique of the Restoration Principle," 248; Commission on Brotherhood Restructure, "Nature of the Structure," 27.
88. Burns, interview.
89. Atlanta Declaration Committee, *Reaffirmation of Convictions and Concerns*, 4-5.
90. DeGroot, *Episcopacy, In Succession*, 14.
91. *Atlanta Declaration of Convictions and Concerns: With Commentary*, 4-5; *Where Are We Going in Restructure*, 4.
92. *Atlanta Declaration of Convictions and Concerns: With Commentary*, 5; Burns, *Whole Armor of God*, 14; *Where Are We Going in Restructure*, 4.
93. *Atlanta Declaration of Convictions and Concerns; With Commentary*, 4.
94. Atlanta Declaration committee, *Reaffirmation of Convictions and Concerns*, 6-7; "Mountain Has Labored," 1.
95. Burns, interview.
96. Atlanta Declaration Committee, *Reaffirmation of Convictions and Concerns*, 6-7.
97. Burns, interview.

Ideological Options in Restructure 241

98. Murch, *Adventuring for Christ*, 292.
99. Murch, *Christians Only*, jacket.
100. James DeForest Murch, *Cooperation without Compromise: A History of the National Association of Evangelicals* (Grand Rapids, Michigan: Wm. B. Eerdmans Publishing Co., 1956), 32-47.
101. Murch, *Christians Only*, jacket.
102. Garrett, *Stone-Campbell Movement*, 637.
103. James DeForest Murch, *B. D. Phillips: Life and Letters* (Louisville: Standard Printing Co., 1969), 168-69.
104. *1969 Directory of the Ministry of the Undenominational Fellowship of Christian Churches and Churches of Christ* (Springfield, Illinois: Specialized Christian Services, 1969), 133, 136.
105. Dean Everest Walker, *The Tradition of Christ* (Milligan College, Tennessee: Milligan College Press, n.d.), 2.
106. "In Memoriam—Rolland L. Ehrman," *Envoy: Emmanuel School of Religion* 5 (June 1973):5.
107. Murch, *Adventuring for Christ*, 320.
108. Murch, *B. D Phillips*, 168-171.
109. Lewis A. Foster, "B. D. Phillips," in *B. D. Phillips*, by Murch, 243.
110. McAllister and Tucker, *Journey in Faith*, 217-18.
111. Murch, *B. D. Phillips*, 14, 13.
112. Foster, "B. D. Phillips," 243.
113. Murch, *B. D. Phillips*, 101-16, 117-50, 183-99, 99-100.
114. B. D. Phillips, letter to Dr. Bill L. Barnes, Director of Development, Christian Theological Seminary, November 1963, quoted in Murch, *B. D. Phillips*, 137-38.
115. McAllister and Tucker, *Journey in Faith*, 444; A. Dale Fiers, "From the Commission Office," *Commission's Inter-Comm*, 13 April 1964, 1.
116. McAllister and Tucker, *Journey in Faith*, 444.
117. [Granville] Walker, "State of Brotherhood Restructure," 10.
118. Stephen J. England, letter to Friends, 13 May 1965, Restructure File, Disciples of Christ Historical Society, Nashville, Tennessee; Murch, *B. D. Phillips*, 169; McAllister and Tucker, *Journey in Faith*, 144.
119. Kenneth L. Teegarden, letter to Members of the Commission on Brotherhood Restructure, 15 October 1965, Restructure File, Disciples of Christ Historical Society, Nashville, Tennessee.
120. Murch, *B. D. Phillips*, 171.
121. Murch, *Free Church*, ii; *Restructure Report*, September 1966.
122. McAllister and Tucker, *Journey in Faith*, 445.

123. Committee for the Preservation of the Brotherhood [James DeForest Murch], *Freedom or Restructure? An Open Letter to Christian Churches and Churches of Christ* (Indianapolis: Committee for the Preservation of the Brotherhood, P. O. Box 1471, [1964], 1-2, 9, 7-8, 10-23.

124. Ibid., 11-12, 20-23, 21.

125. Ibid., 19-20.

126. Committee for the Preservation of the Brotherhood [James DeForest Murch], *The Truth about Restructure: A Second Open Letter to Christian Churches and Churches of Christ* (Indianapolis: Committee for the Preservation of the Brotherhood, P. O. Box 1471, [1965]), 3, 4-7.

127. Ibid., 4-5, 18; Wilburn, "Critique of the Restoration Principle," 231-32.

128. Committee for the Preservation of the Brotherhood [Murch], *Truth about Restructure*, 11-12, 18, 23.

129. Committee for the Preservation of the Brotherhood [Murch], *Freedom or Restructure*, 21, 24; Committee for the Preservation of the Brotherhood [Murch], *Truth about Restructure*, 23-24; "Legal Advice to Our Free Churches." *Restructure Report*, September 1965, 3-4; "Restructure: The Strategy for Merger," *Restructure Report*, September 1966, 1.

130. "Good Legal Advice," *Restructure Report*, September 1966, 4.

131. Dean Walker, *Tradition of Christ*, 18-19.

132. Committee for the Preservation of the Brotherhood [Murch], *Freedom or Restructure*, 13.

133. Committee for the Preservation of the Brotherhood [Murch], *Truth about Restructure*, 23.

134. "Questions and Answers," *Restructure Report*, September 1965, 4.

135. Dean Walker, *Tradition of Christ*, 9, 11.

136. Committee for the Preservation of the Brotherhood [Murch], *Truth about Restructure*, 4-5, 23.

137. Ibid., 12, 18; Murch, *Free Church*, 120-30.

138. Teegarden, *We Call Ourselves Disciples*, 24-25.

139. Teegarden, personal letter.

140. Ibid.

141. "Provisional Design," 28.

142. "Questions and Answers," 4; Atlanta Declaration Committee, *Reaffirmation of Convictions and Concerns*, 4-5.

143. Garrett, *Stone-Campbell Movement*, 717.

144. Teegarden, personal letter.

145. "Provisional Design," 18.

146. Osborn, "Theological Issues in Restructure," 282.

147. "Concerning Brotherhood Restructure: Report of the Board of Directors" (1960), 4-5.
148. "Provisional Design," 18.
149. McAllister and Tucker, *Journey in Faith*, 446; Murch, *Adventuring for Christ*, 299.
150. Bayer, "Need for Renewal," 169.
151. "Mountain Has Labored," 1.

CONCLUSION

Restructure must be understood ideologically as well as structurally. The Campbell-Stone movement has had four interlocking ideals: the *restoration* of the New Testament Church, characterized by both *unity* and *liberty*, and empowered by that unity and liberty to *evangelize* the world. The evangelization of the world was the ultimate value to which restoration and unity were instrumental. For the most part, Disciples have believed, hoped, and even insisted that liberty would characterize the united Church. But the mission of the Church for the evangelization of the world and not liberty for its own sake has been the ultimate value. Even unity was "that the world might believe."

As the Campbell-Stone movement attempted to embody this basic ideology, tensions became apparent in the first generation. The four basic ideals of the movement were not new. Each of them had a complex history in the history of the Church universal. The Campbell-Stone movement also had a complex network of roots.[1] This compounded the difficulty of the movement's embodying its ideals in a unified and consistent way. The four founders of the Campbell-Stone movement exacerbated the disintegrative forces that were rooted in the movement's complex origins by their own inconsistencies, changes, and disagreements. Alexander Campbell and Barton W. Stone disagreed on the nature of the Church at the level of its fundamental constitutive principle. Thomas and Alexander Campbell differed both in temperament and, at times, in their understanding of the character of the movement. Both Alexander Campbell and Walter Scott as they matured seem to have changed their opinions on extracongregational structures.

In the second generation of the Campbell-Stone movement the fellowship was strained by the death of Alexander Campbell and the participation of its members in the Civil War. During the years 1866 to 1906, the theology of the Campbell-Stone movement was dominated by a "scholasticism" which emphasized a "legalistic restorationism."[2] During this same period, the society concept came to dominate the polity of the movement. The second generation was also the time during which the first major division in the Campbell-Stone movement evolved. The division created the Churches of Christ, a conservative restorationist group located largely in the South. The remainder of the Campbell-Stone movement was largely in the upper Midwest and contained some progressive elements.[3]

The basic divergence in the movement in the interpretation of the four fundamental ideals may be seen in the utterances of four editors of the movement's second generation: Isaac Errett, James H. Garrison, David Lipscomb, and J. W. McGarvey. Isaac Errett may have been the last editorial leader to emphasize equally all four of the classic ideals of the Campbell-Stone movement. With James H. Garrison the weight of emphasis began to shift in the direction of unity and mission. On the other hand, David Lipscomb and J. W. McGarvey severely circumscribed the ideals of liberty, union, and mission by emphasizing a conservative restorationism.

Simultaneous with the ideological divergence among editorial leaders of the Campbell-Stone movement was the elaboration of the society concept of polity into a range of organizations which were designed to serve the missionary, benevolent, church-building, and ministerial relief needs of the movement. Therefore, the Campbell-Stone movement was growing both ideologically and structurally beyond the strictures of the "scholastic" generation.

Before the first division within the Campbell-Stone movement had been officially recognized, a second division had begun to evolve. The second division was essentially the completion of the first in that it came along the same ideological lines that had characterized the first. In the second case the regional factor was not important, but the division was, again, between conservative restorationists and those whose emphasis had begun to center on the union and missional values of the movement. The second division may be said to have begun about 1900 with the emergence of the *Christian Standard* as the journalistic representative of the remaining conservative restorationists within the Disciples. Like the division between the Churches of Christ and the Disciples of Christ, the division between Independent and Cooperative Disciples underwent a long evolution. From 1900 to 1971 the division became increasingly apparent. The date of this second division has been variously identified as 1927, 1944, 1955, and 1971.[4] It was clearly a *process* rather than an *event*.

For the members of the Campbell-Stone movement who ultimately became the Christian Church (Disciples of Christ), the changes in basic ideology and emphases were clearly tied to a *coming out of isolation*. This process was especially important in three areas. First, there was a gradual decrease in the isolation of the leaders of this wing of the movement in terms of their theological education. Second, the Cooperative Disciples increasingly participated in the world missions movement of American Protestantism. Third, there was a coming out of isolation on the part of the early Disciples ecumenists, such as Peter Ainslie, in their participation in the nascent ecumenical movement. This emergence from isolation was well underway by the first two decades of the twentieth century. For the remainder of the twentieth century to date the Cooperative Disciples who became the Christian Church (Disciples of Christ) have thought and acted in increasingly ecumenical terms. In a sense, the opposition to Restructure was the last stand of a Disciples exclusivism which could not accept the ecumenical assumptions of the Christian Church (Disciples of Christ).

Evidence that the opponents of Restructure were really opponents of ecumenism, particularly as ecumenism was embodied in COCU, is overwhelming. Both the Committee for the Preservation of the Brotherhood and the Atlanta Declaration Group regarded Restructure as inextricably tied to COCU. In that perception they were both correct and incorrect. They were incorrect in assuming that Restructure was entirely motivated by the desire to deliver the Disciples of Christ into a merger. There were plenty of Restructure proponents who were at most minimally interested in the ecumenical movement.[5] There was probably sufficient impetus for Restructure on strictly organizational grounds. Additionally, the ecumenists on the Commission on Brotherhood Restructure lost some significant battles during the process. Finally, the Christian Church (Disciples of Christ) adopted in its 1973 General Assembly a "cumbersome decision-making process in terms of union."[6] Therefore, one could quite legitimately conclude, as has Ronald Osborn, that "Restructure seems neither to have hastened or impeded progress toward church union."[7] But there is also a sense in which the critics of Restructure were correct in linking Restructure with ecumenism. Although Restructure was not connected to COCU in any direct "conspiratorial" way, the opponents of Restructure perhaps sensed the kind of relationship which Paul Crow describes among Restructure, the "missional question," and the "unity question." Pointing to the fact that generally those people who had misgivings about Restructure are the same ones who have questioned the "missionary strategy" of the Christian Church (Disciples of Christ) and the church's ecumenical involvements, Crow sees a relationship between this linkage and the basic question of "how you view the church, and how you view the church's relationship to the world, and where God is in all this."[8]

An obvious distinction among those who articulated ideological options during Restructure relates to the restoration method of attaining Christian unity. Among the Independents, restorationism was still affirmed in its pattern form. Among the Atlanta Declaration Group, restorationism had been softened a bit, "spiritualized," but was still present. In contrast, Restructure provided the language in which many Cooperative Disciples of Christ could finally make clear to themselves and to the Church universal that they no longer claimed to be a "restoration movement" with *the* solution to the problem of creating Christian unity, but would henceforth seek to be an ecumenically oriented "church." Restructure gave formal expression to the change of *methodology* in seeking Christian unity and the change in self-understanding.

The division between Cooperatives and Independents is related chiefly to divergence on this very issue: whether the Disciples should be a "restoration movement" or an ecumenically oriented "church." To whatever extent Restructure is linked to this division, the linkage is at the point of the same issue. The Cooperative Disciples chose to come out of isolation. The Independents self-consciously resisted coming out of isolation. This is especially apparent in the character of the Independent colleges.[9]

In sum, the opposition and advocacy of Restructure, and any division which is associated with Restructure, are primarily explainable in ideological terms. Specifically, Restructure opponents in both the Independent and Atlanta Declaration groups clung to some version of restorationism and resisted the implication that the other ideals of the Campbell-Stone movement could be pursued in any other terms. Conversely, the proponents of Restructure in both the Restructure leadership and the Disciples for Mission and Renewal wished to pursue the missional and union ideals of their heritage in the context of the ecumenical movement as one denomination among many.

Although the understanding of Church is not explicitly one of the four ideals of the Campbell-Stone movement, it underlies them all. That is, the Church is, according to the four ideals, something to be restored, unified, structured in a free way, and extended to embrace all the world. In practice, however, the liberty ideal led to the embrace of a society concept of polity which denied the churchly character of all structures beyond the local congregation. This concept fitted well with the restorationist insistence that the Campbell-Stone movement was a restoration *movement* and *not* a *church*. This, however, was a "pious subterfuge."[10]

An unbiased observer not versed in Campbell-Stone euphemisms would have recognized the extracongregational structures—the societies—of the movement after 1849 as analogous to the structures of other denominations.[11] An important development in Restructure was a decisive shift in Disciples ecclesiological self-understanding—the shift away from the society concept. To be sure, much of the organizational apparatus which had grown up among the Disciples under the society polity would persist. But with the adoption of the *Provisional Design*, membership or participation in one or more of the societies was no longer the mode by which individuals became part of the extralocal life of the Disciples. Rather, "as a member of the whole body of Christ, every person who is or shall become a member of a recognized congregation of the Christian Church thereby holds membership in the Christian Church in his region and in the Christian Church in the United States and Canada."[12] Restructure,

Conclusion

then, ended the "pious subterfuge" of denying the churchly or denominational character of the Christian Church (Disciples of Christ).

Just as Restructure represented the culmination of an ideological evolution among the Disciples of Christ, specifically an ideological evolution accompanied by a coming out of isolation, so also was Restructure the culmination of a structural evolution. Tensions in the structural traditions of the Campbell-Stone movement paralleled the tensions in the movement's basic ideology. The first step toward the establishment of a national polity had involved the embrace of the society concept that Alexander Campbell did not fully endorse. The mature Campbell (after 1830) clearly advocated a representative structure for the Disciples of Christ. Repeated efforts to create such a structure failed. The Louisville Plan was the most spectacular failure, but others followed. However, the Disciples of Christ were pushed into creating structures by their desires to accomplish certain tasks. The first of these was mission. One form of the "pious subterfuge" in which Disciples engaged for a time was to call anything that was not a congregation a missionary society. Disciples state and national cooperative efforts were organized along this line. After 1917, though, the missionary societies and the other societies that had grown up among the Disciples began to make moves toward unification and coordination. This development clearly pressed the Disciples beyond the point, organizationally, where the old "subterfuge" fit. One could hardly argue that the coordination and planning bodies that were created in the 1920s through the 1950s were simply missionary societies presided over by evangelists.[13] In fact, the Christian Church (Disciples of Christ) had developed a structure which contained most of the bodies in the restructured church well before Restructure occurred.

Restructure was characterized more by continuity of structure than change in structure. That is not to say that it was a trivial process. It may have been misnamed. Restructure helped Cooperative Disciples articulate a very significant change in self-understanding and ideological emphasis. Even during the process, Ronald Osborn suggested that it might have been misnamed:

> No little fear has been expressed throughout the brotherhood—among "cooperatives" as well as among "independents"—concerning the work of this Commission. The term *restructure* is doubtless to blame. It carries overtones of demolition. . . .
> None of us, I trust, intends anything like that. But it may just be that our title, Commission on Brotherhood Restructure, has suggested to some such a frightful prospect with regard to our present life and procedures. I realize full well that it is too late to change

our name, and I am not proposing that we do so. However, it is not mere whimsy that prompts me to ask, what if we have been called the Commission on Brotherhood Edification?[14]

The initial organizational shape of the Christian Church (Disciples of Christ) bore such a striking resemblance to that of the International Convention of Christian Churches (Disciples of Christ) and its cooperating organizations that it is clear that "demolition" was not the aim of the Commission.

If actual structural change is separated from a change in ecclesiological language and self-understanding, then one structural change stands out as significant in Restructure. That is the creation of a proportionately representative General Assembly.[15] The great irony in Restructure is that the most significant structural change that occurred was in the direction of greater rather than less representative democracy. Otherwise, a pattern of continuity prevailed. Restructure was ultimately much less of a departure from the traditions of the Disciples of Christ than its opponents apparently believed it would be.[16]

The representative General Assembly was the most visible structure resulting from Restructure, and the constituting of the Christian Church (Disciples of Christ) was the most significant ecclesiological development. However, two additional significant ecclesiological developments were the recovery from the first generation of the Campbell-Stone movement of the emphases on the lordship of Jesus Christ and the concept of covenant. A key ecclesiological paragraph in the *Provisional Design* reads:

> Within the universal body of Christ, the Christian Church (Disciples of Christ) manifests itself organizationally in free and voluntary relationships at congregational, regional, and general levels. Each manifestation, with reference to the function for which it is uniquely responsible, is characterized by its integrity, self-government, authority, rights and responsibilities.... The Christian Church confesses Jesus Christ as Lord and constantly seeks in all its actions to be obedient to his authority.[17]

Thus the *Design* contains language which makes clear that the authority that exists within the Christian Church (Disciples of Christ) is not coercive, but "is the persuasive authority of truth and goodness at work among a people covenanted to do the will of God."[18] The Christian Church (Disciples of Christ) is "a church in which relationships are 'free and voluntary' but under the absolute rule of Christ"—a "democratic monarchy."[19]

Conclusion

Organization which is "free and voluntary" and "under the absolute rule of Christ" was the organizational ideal of Barton W. Stone and Alexander Campbell. Stone wrote: "We believe that all are bound to submit to the government and laws of Jesus, the Lord of all."[20] Campbell wrote:

> The last secret of the mystery of Christ, which Peter promulgated on the day of Pentecost, was "Let all the house of Israel know, that God has made that same Jesus, whom you crucified, both LORD and CHRIST." To make him Lord for us, was to invest him with *universal authority*.[21]

That is the basic authority upon which the *Design* draws. The General Assembly has no power over congregations beyond the persuasive power that it has as the largest and most representative deliberative body among those who are bound together in Christian covenant in the Christian Church (Disciples of Christ). The congregations are as "free" as ever.[22]

The rediscovery by the Commission on Brotherhood Restructure of the concept of covenant, which had been eclipsed in the second and subsequent generations of the movement, is represented in the fact that "the idea of covenant was probably the one theological notion which occupied the Commission more than any other and which implicitly permeates the ideology of the *Design*."[23] Before the triumph of the society concept and the rise of "Disciples scholasticism," Alexander Campbell had championed the right of Christians to covenant together.

The process of Restructure was characterized by the supplanting of the society concept as the basis of polity by a *churchly concept*; by *continuity* with the structural evolution that had been occurring among Cooperative Disciples for over a century; by an *increased embodiment of the democratic ideal* in the representative character of the General Assembly; and by the *recovery* of a very Campbell-Stone-like emphasis upon the *lordship of Christ* and the *concept of covenant*.

Restructure was the recognition that an evolutionary process has occurred relative to the basic ideology and structure of the Disciples of Christ. The commitment to restorationism that had dictated a denial of the movement's churchly character was abandoned by the Christian Church (Disciples of Christ). The restoration movement became an ecumenically oriented church. Restructure entailed a full recognition that a second major schism had taken place within the Campbell-Stone movement. This schism was fundamentally between those who would and those who would not embrace the new churchly self-understanding. Those who opposed Restructure, therefore, affirmed restorationism in some form. Restructure extended churchly status to a range of extracongregational organizations that had evolved among Disciples and which exhibited a pattern of continuity before, during, and after Restructure. However, Restructure offered these a new unity of self-understanding as tied together by covenant and as parts of one church.

This study has attempted to analyze the structural and ideological development of the Disciples of Christ in terms of the four basic ideals of unity, restoration, liberty, and mission. Its contention is that Restructure occasioned an articulation of several ideological alternatives in terms of these ideals. To the extent that Restructure was divisive, the division was a reflection of a divergence on these ideals. In other words, the Campbell-Stone movement has not divided over trivial matters, but rather over divergent interpretations of its most cherished ideals. The recognition of this fact is a reminder that persons on both sides of these divisions were striving to be faithful in their responses to God. Restructure did not remove all ideological diversity from the Christian Church (Disciples of Christ). Therefore, one of the challenges that remains for this Disciples polity is to avoid further disintegration as diverse Disciples attempt to be faithful within it.

---

1. DeGroot, *Grounds of Divisions*, 30-31, n. 2.
2. Beazley, "Who Are the Disciples," 27-39; Eikner, "Nature of the Church," 182-220.
3. McAllister and Tucker, *Journey in Faith*, 251-54.
4. Garrett, *Stone-Campbell Movement*, 615-18.
5. Crow, interview.
6. Crow, interview. The date of the Disciples' adoption of that "cumbersome . . . process" suggests that it was occasioned, at least in part, by developments in COCU just prior to that adoption (see Osborn, *Experiment in Liberty*, 101).
7. Osborn, "Theological Issues in Restructure," 306.
8. Crow, interview.
9. Beazley, "Who Are the Disciples," 40.
10. Osborn, *Faith We Affirm*, 65.
11. E.g., Harlan Beach and Burton St. John included the missionary societies of the "Disciples, or Christians" in their directory in *World Statistics of Christian Missions* in the same way that they listed the societies of Baptists, Brethren, Friends, and other denominations.
12. "Provisional Design," 19.

Conclusion 253

13. These were originally the only admissible types of extracongregational bodies and "public ministers."

14. Osborn, *Toward the Christian Church*, 46-47.

15. "Provisional Design," 19, 28.

16. This is especially true in the area of the rights of congregations (see "Provisional Design," 28).

17. "Provisional Design," 18.

18. Osborn, *Faith We Affirm*, 89-90.

19. Teegarden, *We Call Ourselves Disciples*, 58-59.

20. Stone, "Reflections of Old Age," 125-26.

21. Alexander Campbell, *The Christian System* (Bethany, Virginia: By the Author, 1839; reprint ed., Nashville: Gospel Advocate Co., 1964), 36.

22. Osborn, *Faith We Affirm*, 89-90; Osborn, *Experiment in Liberty*, 115.

23. Osborn, "Theological Issues in Restructure," 296.

SELECTED BIBLIOGRAPHY

Books

Ainslie, Peter, ed. *The Equality of All Christians before God: A Record of the New York Conference of the Christian Unity League Held at St. George's Church, New York City*. New York: Macmillan Co., 1930.

Bainton, Roland H. *Christian Unity and Religion in New England*. Boston: Beacon Press, 1964.

Beach, Harlan P., and St. John, Burton, eds. *World Statistics of Christian Missions: Containing a Directory of Missionary Societies, a Classified Summary of Statistics, and an Index of Mission Stations throughout the World*. New York: Committee of Reference and Counsel of the Foreign Missions Conference of North America, 1916.

Beazley, George G., Jr., ed. *The Christian Church (Disciples of Christ): An Interpretative Examination in the Cultural Context*. St. Louis: Bethany Press, 1973.

Blakemore, W. B., gen. ed. *The Renewal of Church: The Panel of Scholars Reports*. 3 vols. St. Louis: Bethany Press, 1963.

_____. *The Discovery of The Church: A History of Disciple Ecclesiology*. The Reed Lectures for 1965. Nashville: Reed & Co., 1966.

_____. ed. *The Challenge of Christian Unity*. The William Henry Hoover Lectures on Christian Unity for 1961. St. Louis: Bethany Press, 1963.

Campbell, Alexander. *A Connected View of the Principles and Rules by which the Living Oracles May Be Intelligibly and Certainly Interpreted; of the Foundation on which All Christians May Form One Communion and of the Capital Positions Sustained in the Attempt to Restore the Original Gospel and Order of Things; Containing the Principal Extras of the "Millennial Harbinger," Revised and Corrected*. Bethany, [West] Virginia: M'Vay & Ewing, 1835.

_____. *The Christian System*. Bethany, [West] Virginia: By the Author, 1839; reprint ed., Nashville: Gospel Advocate Co., 1964.

_____. *Popular Lectures and Addresses*. Philadelphia: James Challen & Son, 1863; reprint ed., Nashville: Harbinger Book Club, n.d.

Cardwell, Brenda M., and Fox, William K., Sr. *Journey Toward Wholeness: A History of Black Disciples of Christ in the Mission of the Christian Church*, vol. 1: *From Convention to Convocation: No Longer 'Objects of' Mission But 'Partners In' the Work (1700-1988)*. National Convocation of the Christian Church, 1990.

Cochran, Bess White, and Cochran, Louis. *Captives of the Word*. Garden City, New Jersey: Doubleday & Co., 1969.

Commission for the Direction of Surveys, Authorized by the International Convention of Disciples of Christ. *Survey of Service: Organizations Represented in International Convention of Disciples of Christ*. St. Louis: Christian Board of Publication, 1928.

Consultation on Church Union (COCU). *The Official Reports of the Four Meetings of the Consultation*. Cincinnati: Forward Movement Publications, 1966.

Corey, Stephen J. *Fifty Years of Attack and Controversy: The Consequences Among Disciples of Christ*. St. Louis: Christian Board of Publication for the Committee on Publication of the Corey Manuscript, 1953.

Crain, James A. *The Development of Social Ideas among the Disciples of Christ*. St Louis: Bethany Press, 1969.

Cummins, Duane. *The Disciples Colleges: A History*. St. Louis: CBP Press, 1987.

Declaration and Address, by Thomas Campbell; Last Will and Testament of the Springfield Presbytery, by Barton W. Stone and Others. Introduction by F. D. Kershner. St. Louis: Bethany Press, 1960.

DeGroot, Alfred T. *The Grounds of Divisions among the Disciples of Christ*. Chicago: By the Author, 1940.

_____. *Church of Christ Number Two*. Birmingham, England: By the Author, 1956.

_____. *The Restoration Principle*. St Louis: Bethany Press, 1960.

_____. *Disciple Thought: A History*. Fort Worth: By the Author, 1965.

_____. *Extra Ecclesiam Nulla Salus (or, Restructure Problems)*. Fort Worth: By the Author, 1968.

DeGroot, Alfred T. and Garrison, Winfred E. *The Disciples of Christ: A History*. 2d ed. St. Louis: Bethany Press, 1958.

England, Stephen J. *The One Baptism*. St. Louis: Bethany Press, 1960.

Fife, Robert O.; Harrell, David Edwin, Jr.; and Osborn, Ronald E. *Disciples and the Church Universal*. The Reed Lectures for 1966. Nashville: Disciples of Christ Historical Society, 1967.

Foster, Charles I. *An Errand of Mercy: The Evangelical United Front: 1790-1837*. Chapel Hill: University of North Carolina Press, 1960.

Garrett, Leroy. *The Stone-Campbell Movement: An Anecdotal History of Three Churches*. Joplin, Missouri: College Press Publishing Co., 1981.

Garrison, J[ames] H[arvey], ed. *The Old Faith Restated: Being a Restatement, by Representative Men, of the Fundamental Truths and Essential Doctrines of Christianity, as Held and Advocated by the Disciples of Christ, in Light of Experience and of Biblical Research*. St. Louis: Christian Publishing Co., 1891.

Garrison, Winfred E. *Religion Follows the Frontier: A History of the Disciples of Christ*. New York: Harper & Bros., 1931.

_____. *An American Religious Movement: A Brief History of the Disciples of Christ*. St. Louis: Bethany Press, 1946.

_____. *A Protestant Manifesto*. New York: Abingdon Press, 1952.

_____. *Christian Unity and Disciples of Christ*. St. Louis: Bethany Press, 1955.

_____. *The Quest and Character of a United Church*. New York: Abingdon Press, 1957.

_____. *Heritage and Destiny: An American Religious Movement Looks Ahead*. St. Louis: Bethany Press, 1961.

_____. *Variations on a Theme: "God Saw that It was Good."* St. Louis: Bethany Press, 1964.

Gerrard, William A., III. *A Biographical Study of Walter Scott: American Frontier Evangelist*. Joplin, MO: College Press, 1992.

Green, F. M. *Christian Missions and Historical Sketches of Missionary Societies among the Disciples of Christ, with Historical and Statistical Tables*. St. Louis: John Burns Publishing Co., 1884.

Hailey, Homer. *Attitudes and Consequences in the Restoration Movement*. N.p., 1945; 2d ed., Rosemead, California: Old Paths Book Club, 1952.

Handy, Robert T. *The American Religious Depression: 1925-1935*. Facet Books Historical Series, ed. Richard C. Wolf, no. 9. Philadelphia: Fortress Press, 1968.

Harrell, David Edwin, Jr., *A Social History of the Disciples of Christ*. Vol. 1: *Quest for a Christian America: The Disciples of Christ and American Society to 1866*. Nashville: Disciples of Christ Historical Society, 1966. Vol. 2: *The Social Sources of Division in the Disciples of Christ, 1865 to 1900*. Atlanta: Publishing Systems, 1973. 2 vols.

Harrison, Ida Withers. *History of the Christian Woman's Board of Missions*. N.p., 1920.

Hatch, Nathan O. *The Democratization of American Christianity*. New Haven: Yale University Press, 1989.

Hughes, Richard T. and Allen, C. Leonard. *Illusions of Innocence: Protestant Primitivism in America, 1630-1875*. Chicago and London: University of Chicago Press, 1988.

Idleman, Finis S. *Peter Ainslie: Ambassador of Good Will*. Chicago: Willett, Clark & Co., 1941.

Jordan, Robert L. *Two Races in One Fellowship*. Detroit: United Christian Church, 1944.

Keith, Noel L. *The Story of D. S. Burnet: Undeserved Obscurity*. St. Louis: Bethany Press, 1954.

Lair, Loran E. *The Christian Churches and Their Work*. St. Louis: Bethany Press, 1963.

_____. *The Christian Church (Disciples of Christ) and Its Future*. St. Louis: Bethany Press, 1971.

Lawrence, Kenneth, ed. *Classic Themes of Disciples Theology: Rethinking the Traditional Affirmations of the Christian Church (Disciples of Christ)*. Fort Worth, TX: TCU Press, 1986.

Lester, Hiram and Lester, Marge. *Inasmuch . . . The Saga of the NBA*. St. Louis: National Benevolent Association, 1987.

Lewis, Grant K. *The American Christian Missionary Society and the Disciples of Christ*. St. Louis: Christian Board of Publication, 1937.

Lindley, D. Ray. *Apostle of Freedom*. St. Louis: Bethany Press, 1957.

Lollis, Lorraine. *The Shape of Adam's Rib: A Lively History of Women's Work in the Christian Church*. St. Louis: Bethany Press, 1970.

McAllister, Lester G. *Thomas Campbell: Man of the Book*. St. Louis: Bethany Press, 1954.

McAllister, Lester G., and Tucker, William E. *Journey in Faith: A History of the Christian Church (Disciples of Christ)*. St. Louis: Bethany Press, 1975.

McLean, Archibald. *The History of the Foreign Christian Missionary Society*. New York: Fleming H. Revell Co., 1919.

Mead, Sidney E. *History and Identity*. American Academy of Religion Studies in Religion, ed. Conrad Cherry, no. 19. Missoula, MT: Scholars Press, 1979.

Montgomery, Riley B. *The Education of Ministers of Disciples of Christ*. St. Louis: Bethany Press, 1931.

Moore, William T. *A Comprehensive History of the Disciples of Christ*. New York: Fleming H. Revell Co., 1909.

Murch, James DeForest. *Cooperation without Compromise: A History of the National Association of Evangelicals*. Grand Rapids, Michigan: Wm. B. Eerdmans Publishing Co., 1956.

_____. *Christians Only: A History of the Restoration Movement*. Cincinnati: Standard Publishing, 1962.

_____. *The Free Church: A Treatise on Church Polity with Special Relevance to Doctrine and Practice in Christian Churches and Churches of Christ*. Washington, D.C.: Restoration Press, 1966.

_____. *B. D. Phillips: Life and Letters*. Louisville: Standard Printing Co., 1969.

_____. *Adventuring for Christ in Changing Times: An Autobiography of James DeForest Murch*. Louisville: Restoration Press, 1973.

Neth, John Watson. *Walter Scott Speaks: A Handbook of Doctrine*. Milligan College, Tennessee: Emmanuel School of Religion, 1967.

Olson, Lani L. J. *Building a Witness: 100 Years of Church Extension*. Indianapolis: Board of Church Extension of the Disciples of Christ, 1983.

Osborn, Ronald E. *Restructure . . . toward the Christian Church (Disciples of Christ): Intention, Essence, Constitution.* St. Louis: Christian Board of Publication, 1964.

_____. *A Church for These Times*. New York: Abingdon Press, 1965.

_____. *In Christ's Place: Christian Ministry in Today's World*. St. Louis: Bethany Press, 1967.

_____. *Experiment in Liberty: The Ideal of Freedom in the Experience of the Disciples of Christ*. The Forrest F. Reed Lectures for 1976. St. Louis: Bethany Press, 1978.

_____. *The Faith We Affirm: Basic Beliefs of Disciples of Christ*. St. Louis: Bethany Press, 1979.

Pugh, Samuel F., ed. *Primer for New Disciples*. St. Louis: Bethany Press, 1963.

Richardson, Robert. *Memoirs of Alexander Campbell*. Vol. 1. St. Louis: John Burns, 1868. Vol. 2. Cincinnati: Standard Publishing, 1890. 2 vols.

Richesin, L. Dale and Bouchard, Larry D., eds. *Interpreting Disciples: Practical Theology in the Disciples of Christ*. Fort Worth: TCU Press, 1987.

Rouse, Ruth, and Neill, Stephen C., eds. *A History of the Ecumenical Movement: 1517-1948*. 2d ed. London: SPCK, 1967.

Scott, Walter. *The Gospel Restored*. Cincinnati: O. H. Donogh, 1836.

_____. *To Themilion: The Union of Christians on Christian Principles*. Cincinnati: C. A. Morgan & Co., 1850.

Seale, James M. *Forward from the Past: The First Fifty Years of the Disciples of Christ Historical Society*. Nashville: Disciples of Christ Historical Society, 1992.

The Second Vatican Council. *The Decree on Ecumenism*. Translated by the Secretariat for Promoting Christian Unity. Glen Rock, New Jersey: Paulist Press, 1965.

Shelton, O. L. *The Church Functioning Effectively*. St. Louis: Christian Board of Publication, 1946.

Smith, William Martin. *For the Support of the Ministry: A History of Ministerial Support, Relief and Pensions among Disciples of Christ*. Indianapolis: Pension Fund of Disciples of Christ, 1956.

Stevenson, Dwight E. *Walter Scott: Voice of the Golden Oracle—A Biography*. St. Louis: Christian Board of Publication, 1946.

Stone, B[arton] W[arren] *Works of Elder B. W. Stone, to which is Added a Few Discourses and Sermons (Original and Selected)*. Compiled by James M. Mathes, 2d ed. Cincinnati: Moore, Wilstach, Keys & Co., Printers, 1859.

_____. "A Short History of the Life of Barton W. Stone." In *The Cane Ridge Meeting House*, 113-204. By James R. Rogers. Cincinnati: Standard Publishing, 1910.

Strong, Josiah. *Our Country: Its Possible Future and Its Present Crisis*. Introduction by Austin Phelps. Rev. ed. New York: Baker & Taylor Co. for the American Home Missionary Society, 1891.

Suggs, James C., ed. *This We Believe*. St. Louis: Bethany Press, 1977.

Teegarden, Kenneth L. *We Call Ourselves Disciples*. St. Louis: Bethany Press, 1975.

Toulouse, Mark G. *Joined in Discipleship: The Maturing of An American Religious Movement*. St Louis: Chalice Press, 1992.

Tucker, William E. *J. H. Garrison and Disciples of Christ*. St Louis: Bethany Press, 1964.

Tyler, Benjamin B. *A History of the Disciples of Christ*. New York: Christian Literature Co., 1894.

Warren, William R. *The Life and Labors of Archibald McLean*. St. Louis: Bethany Press, 1923.

Webb, Henry E. *In Search of Christian Unity: A History of the Restoration Movement*. Cincinnati: Standard Publishing, 1990.

West, Earl I. *The Search for the Ancient Order: A History of the Restoration Movement*, 1849-1906. Vol. 1: *1849-1865*. Nashville: Gospel Advocate Co., 1949. Vol. 2: *1866-1906*. Vol. 3: *1900-1918*. Indianapolis: Religious Book Service, 1950, 1979. 3 vols.

Whitley, Oliver Read. *Trumpet Call of Reformation*. St. Louis: Bethany Press, 1959.

Williams, D. Newell, ed. *A Case Study of Mainstream Protestantism: The Disciples' Relation to American Culture, 1880-1989*. Grand Rapids and St. Louis: William B. Eerdmans Publishing Company and Chalice Press, 1991.

Winter, Gibson. *Religious Identity: A Study of Religious Organization*. Studies in Religion and Society Series. New York: Macmillan Co., 1968.

Wrather, Eva Jean. *Creative Freedom in Action: Alexander Campbell on the Structure of the Church*. St. Louis: Bethany Press, 1968.

Periodicals

Bread and Wine. 1968.

Christian. 1965-66.

Christian Baptist. 1823-27; 1830.

Christian-Evangelist. 1886; 1893; 1903; 1911; 1914; 1917; 1919; 1922; 1935-36; 1941; 1949-50.

Christian Messenger. 1827; 1830-31; 1835; 1843-44.

Christian Standard. 1868-69; 1871; 1875; 1890; 1894; 1897; 1906; 1907; 1909-11; 1916; 1919; 1921-22; 1959; 1961; 1963.

Discipliana. 1977-78; 1980-82; 1986; 1988.

Evangelist. 1832; 1838-39.

Gospel Advocate. 1866-67; 1870-71; 1878; 1882-84; 1889; 1893; 1905.

Gospel Echo. 1870.

Harvard Theological Review. 1984.

Mid-Stream. 1962-65; 1978-80; 1982.

Millennial Harbinger. 1831; 1835-39; 1842-43; 1845; 1847; 1849; 1852; 1855.

Religion and American Culture: A Journal of Interpretation. 1992.

Restructure Report. 1965-66.

World Call. 1962.

Dissertations, Theses, and Manuscript Collections

Atwood, Dee James. "The Impact of World War I on the Agencies of the Disciples of Christ." Ph.D. dissertation, Vanderbilt University, 1978.

Caldwell, Charles Grover III. "Alexander Campbell: Adversary and Advocate of Missionary Organization among Disciples of Christ." M.A. thesis, Middle Tennessee State University, 1970.

Clark, Martin Bailey. "The Missionary Position of the movement of the Disciples of Christ in the Early Years of the Nineteenth Century Reformation." B.D. thesis, Butler University, 1949.

Coffman, Edward. "The Division in the Restoration Movement." M.A. thesis, Vanderbilt University, 1930.

Eikner, Allen Van Dozier. "The Nature of the Church among the Disciples of Christ." Ph.D. dissertation, Vanderbilt University, 1962.

Hamlin, Griffith A. "The Origin and Development of the Board of Higher Education of the Christian Church (Disciples of Christ): 1894-1968." M.S. thesis, Southern Illinois University, 1968.

Major, J. Brooks. "The Role of Periodicals in the Development of the Disciples of Christ, 1850-1910." Ph.D. dissertation, Vanderbilt University, 1966.

Mayes, Gary Wayne. "Restructure in the Light of Structure among the Disciples of Christ, 1832-1964." B.D. thesis, College of the Bible, 1965.

Murrell, Arthur V. "The Effects of Exclusivism in the Separation of the Churches of Christ from the Christian Church." Ph.D. dissertation, Vanderbilt University, 1972.

Paulsell, William O. "The Disciples of Christ and the Great Depression 1929-1936." Ph.D. dissertation, Vanderbilt University, 1965.

Roos, David C. "The Social Thought of Barton Warren Stone and Its Significance Today for the Disciples of Christ in Western Kentucky." D.Div. dissertation, Vanderbilt University, 1973.

Nashville, Tennessee. Disciples of Christ Historical Society. Peter Ainslie Personal Papers File; Atlanta Declaration Group File; Biographical Files; Disciples for Mission and Renewal File; Restructure File; Unified Promotion File; United Christian Missionary Society File.